Food Security and Scarcity

Food Security and Scarcity

WHY ENDING HUNGER IS SO HARD

C. Peter Timmer

CENTER FOR GLOBAL DEVELOPMENT

PENN

UNIVERSITY OF PENNSYLVANIA PRESS

PHILADELPHIA

Published by
University of Pennsylvania Press
Philadelphia, Pennsylvania 19104-4112
www.upenn.edu/pennpress

Printed in the United States of America on acid-free paper
10 9 8 7 6 5 4 3 2 1

Library of Congress Cataloging-in-Publication Data
Timmer, C. Peter.
Food security and scarcity : why ending hunger is so hard / C. Peter
Timmer. — 1st ed.
    p. cm.
Includes bibliographical references and index.
ISBN 978-0-8122-4666-7 (hardcover : alk. paper)
  1. Food security—Developing countries—Economic aspects.   2. Food
security—Government policy—Developing countries.   3. Food supply—
Developing countries—Economic aspects.   4. Food supply—Government
policy—Developing countries.   5. Agriculture and state—Developing
countries—Economic aspects.   6. Agriculture—Developing countries—
Economic aspects.   I. Title.
  HD9018.D44.T55 2015
  363.809172'4—dc23

2014028296

To my students, who always pushed for better answers

CONTENTS

PREFACE

This book draws on well over three decades of thinking about food security and the difficulty in achieving it. Even in the wake of the world food crisis in the mid-1970s, it was obvious that the problem was not the total amount of food produced, but the access of poor households to that food (Timmer 1977). Nevertheless, societies that had rapid increases in domestic food production also had dramatic gains in food security. In some fundamental sense, this is the food security dilemma. More food does not guarantee greater food security, but increases in local food production clearly help.

The dilemma can be resolved by identifying the population that has insecure access to food. It is largely rural households, engaged in agriculture but without enough land to produce enough food for their families. Efforts to raise their productivity (even if not directly in food production or the rural economy) have a dramatic impact on food security. Increased food production on small farms is just one way to raise their overall productivity and provide improved food security.

I have been trying to understand the food security dilemma for some time, and this book draws on much of my research and writing over the past several decades. Inevitably, given my experience, it has an Asian bias and a focus on the world rice economy. That is not all bad: Asia still has most of the world's poor and food-insecure households, and rice has increasingly become the foodstuff of the poor. The lessons on how Asia has coped with these problems are well worth understanding for the light they shine on similar problems in other regions.

Part of the rationale for the long-term perspective of the analysis here is the opportunity to update my earlier writings to reflect transformational changes in the world food economy since the 1970s, in both food production and consumption (and, of course, the two are linked). Another rationale is to point out that "voices in the wilderness" were arguing decades ago that the development profession had misjudged the critical role of agriculture in economic development, and its contribution to enhancing food security and speeding poverty reduction (Timmer 1992). Some of the messages in this book will be new to the development profession because it was hard to get them published when agriculture was so out of favor.

It is sad that it has taken a world food crisis (or more than one) to bring these fairly obvious facts back to the policy agenda, but they are back. Heads of state now worry about food security. They seek guidance on how to achieve it, and there is a cacophony of voices with the answer. But most of the messages from these voices are badly flawed because they fail to understand the critical role of markets in decision-making about food production and consumption. The message here is that markets, for all of their problems and failures, will be at the core of solving the problem of hunger.

In all of the successful escapes from hunger over the past two centuries— from the rich Western countries to the wealthier countries in East and Southeast Asia, markets have done the heavy lifting. Their role in generating signals of resource scarcity and inducing producers and consumers to make decisions that are consonant with those signals has never been carried out successfully by government planners. At the same time, none of the escapes from hunger was driven entirely by market forces. Governments have had to intervene in myriad ways, from stabilizing the economic environment to providing critical public goods such as transportation and communications networks, agricultural research and development, and access to quality health and educational facilities. There is scope for more or less government involvement, depending on institutional capacity, but "none" has never been the right answer. "Too much" has been a common mistake. It is a tricky balance that requires constant analysis, experimentation, and learning.

Ending hunger requires that each society find the right mix of market forces and government interventions to drive a process of economic growth that reaches the poor and ensures that food supplies are readily, and reliably, available and accessible to even the poorest households. Finding this right mix has been a major challenge, and it seems to be getting more difficult as the global economy becomes more integrated and less stable.

A major task of this book is to explain the challenges, but then also to explain how to cope with them. Since coping will be largely a country-specific task, given the heterogeneity of poverty and hunger, the solution will depend on equally country-specific analytical capacities and governance. Countries that want to end hunger can do so, but the decision to do so will require significant interventions into the functioning of their food economies and a political will to empower, and enable, their smallholder farm households. Most of these households need to buy food during much of the year—they are "net deficit" households in the food security jargon. Raising their crop productivity may not be nearly as important as raising their access to productive employment in nearby rural nonfarm enterprises or even in the nearest city. They are vulnerable to spikes in food prices even though they produce some of their own food.

In a narrow sense, then, this book is a reminder that most poor people live on farms, usually quite small. One way to lift them out of poverty and provide sustainable food security is to help them achieve higher yields, gain reliable access to water and to markets that are close enough to allow them to use modern seeds and fertilizer and to get decent prices for their surplus output. Good schools, nearby health clinics, and local financial markets also raise rural living standards, but just raising secure crops and feeding their children is a first priority for these families.

At the same time, not all small farmers can achieve food security on their own small plots. For many of these, escaping poverty will require leaving agriculture—even moving to a city. This process, writ large, is termed the "structural transformation." It occurs as agriculture becomes a smaller share of the economy and the workforce. And it provides a powerful pathway out of poverty. Indeed, if history is any guide, no escape from hunger and poverty has been sustainable without a successful structural transformation. It is no surprise, then, that this book talks as much about structural transformation—successful and unsuccessful—as it does about higher productivity for smallholder farmers. In the end, food security is determined by how much food households consume, not by how much they produce. Without a successful structural transformation, most farmers produce less food than their families need to consume. A retreat further into self-sufficiency will not help these households; they need market opportunities for their labor and entrepreneurial skills to escape from poverty and hunger.

In a broader sense, then, the book argues—to both the development profession and policy makers—that solving the "food problem" is a key step and a powerful catalyst to solving the problem of poverty and finding the path to higher incomes. No country has been able to sustain rapid economic growth until its citizens and investors were confident that food was reliably available in the main urban markets. Rural poverty has always been a later concern. Rural productivity and economic growth provide the ingredients for food security. The two are intimately linked, and the book explains why.

These links mean that government policies to reduce poverty and hunger—to improve food security—are complicated and require an economy-wide perspective on how rural and urban markets are connected. Labor market connections are most important for understanding real wages, labor productivity, and living standards, but input and output markets are also critical. Eventually, integrated financial markets are needed to sustain rapid growth in labor productivity.

That is why ending hunger is so hard—it takes sustained economic growth that systematically includes the poor, along with public actions to stabilize the food economy in which poor households live. It is a historical fact that billions have escaped the scourge of hunger. Those historical lessons inform the way out of hunger for the remaining billion still trapped without enough food to eat day in and day out. It is a tall order. But it can be achieved.

Food Security and Scarcity

CHAPTER 1

Setting the Stage: Food Scarcity and Food Prices

Modern analyses of food security list five essential components: *availability* of food on farms and in markets; *access* to that food by all households; effective *utilization* of the food within the household (a function of food safety, nutritional status, and health); the *sustainability* of the food system that delivers these components; and its *stability* (Timmer 2012a). This definition stresses the elements that *individuals and households* require to be food secure, but food security is also an important objective at the *national* level, where political leaders can be held responsible for failures and successes in maintaining accessible supplies of staple foods at stable prices, especially in major urban markets where many consumers procure their food. Food security is at least as much a political issue as it is an agronomic or economic issue.

At the *global* level, considerable attention is focused on both short-run and long-run balances between food production and food consumption. Rising food prices suggest the production race is being lost to rapid gains in food consumption—in a Malthusian world where population growth and higher incomes cause demand for food to outstrip the resource base for production of food. Falling food prices, on the other hand, suggest that expanded agricultural land, better water control, and improved technologies are generating food surpluses. In this world, Amartya Sen argues that access becomes the limiting factor for household food security, not availability (Sen 1981; Timmer 1977).

In both Malthusian and Senian worlds, food prices are a key signal about what is happening to food security. Two dimensions of food prices are important: their average level and their volatility. Price spikes and collapses can create risks and poverty for consumers and farmers even when average prices are affordable to the poor and create adequate incentives for farmers.

Although highly unstable food prices have serious negative consequences at the micro level for household-level decision makers, food price instability also has a deeper and more insidious impact: it slows down economic growth and the structural transformation that has been the main pathway out of rural poverty (Timmer 1988, 2009a).

The basic perspective developed in this book draws primarily, but not exclusively, on economics: food prices are used as a measure of scarcity to indicate whether food security is improving or deteriorating globally or within individual countries. In a market economy (the only kind of economy with a successful track record of raising labor productivity, and hence living standards, over many generations), markets play three key roles. First, and the one stressed by most analysts proposing solutions to world hunger, markets play an engineering role by moving inputs to farmers and food to consumers. Even socialist, planned economies have to use markets in this role.

Two other roles provide market economies their distinguishing strengths—and often harsh outcomes. First is the role of markets in price discovery: what is a commodity (or service) worth in monetary terms? Markets process billions of pieces of information on a daily basis to generate price signals to all participants. No other form of institutional organization has evolved that is capable of the necessary processing of information required for individuals and firms to see price signals that reflect scarcity and abundance, and thus to make efficient allocation and investment decisions. This is the route to raising long-run productivity. The prices generated in markets dictate such important values as the price of rice or of wages for unskilled labor. Price discovery is about signals of resource scarcity and the distribution of incomes according to who owns what—land, labor, skills, and financial assets.

Finally, markets serve as the arena for allocating society's scarce resources to meet the virtually unlimited needs and desires of consumers. This allocation process, when joined to reasonably efficient price formation, is the reason market economies have outperformed other forms of economic organization over the long haul. Efficiency in resource allocations is essential to raising economic output in a sustainable fashion and thus to reducing poverty and hunger.

Market processes sometimes fail to get this scarcity signal right (at least for long-run decision making), but even when wrong, the market signal is important about underlying factors affecting food scarcity. In nearly all circumstances, food scarcity and high prices for food mean significant food insecurity and hunger. Assuming away (or ignoring) the deep causal reality of this market relationship, as many otherwise sensible and expert guides to ending hunger do, is assuming away the real problem (Conway 2012; Timmer 2012b).

Three major forces drive changes in food security at global and national levels: changing agricultural productivity, especially for staple food grains; changes in the rate of growth and distribution of per capita incomes (thus making population growth an important factor); and changes in the level and volatility of staple food prices. The three are interconnected through both market forces and government interventions. This book explains the nature of these interconnections and the difficulties they present in ending hunger.

Food policy issues have evolved significantly since the early 1980s, and new perspectives have been developed to analyze them. An integration of the "old" and "new" food policy perspectives provides a useful foundation going forward. As part of this foundation, the basics of price formation are helpful, even before the more formal and sophisticated approach developed in Chapter 3. As noted, volatile food prices have both a short-run and long-run impact on food security. Knowing why they are volatile is part of the basic understanding needed to get started on the analysis of poverty and hunger.

Finally, agricultural productivity must keep pace with population growth and the added demand which results from higher incomes if supplies of food are to keep pace with demand for food. The "availability" dimension of food security is the essential starting point for further analysis. An introduction to "getting agriculture moving," to quote the title of an influential book by Art Mosher (1966), raises the fundamental issues of how to raise agricultural productivity on the small farms cultivated by the great majority of households that are poor and hungry.

Framing Food Security and Scarcity: The Audience for This Book

My hope is that the book will speak successfully to several audiences. I want the entire story to be relevant to every reader who picks up the book. Parts will be more important or useful to some readers, of course, but I hope the logic and coherence of the arguments hang together for everyone.

That said, there are a number of messages of special relevance to certain readers. First, and an important motivation for writing the book, is to reach proponents of development strategies that are aimed almost entirely at raising productivity of smallholder farmers, especially in sub-Saharan Africa and South Asia where the Bill and Melinda Gates Foundation has been heavily engaged. I have argued since the mid-1980s that these farmers have been neglected by the development profession broadly and by donors specifically. I have considerable sympathy for this approach. But carried to extremes, as I fear it has been, the strategy risks missing the bigger picture, which is the structural transformation as the historical pathway out of poverty. Some small farmers need to be on that pathway—off of their farms and into urban jobs.

The mirror image of this concern provides a second group of potential readers. Many development economists accept the structural transformation as the basic process of successful economic development, but then they look only at the final outcome—a modern industrial and service economy—and fail to realize the critical role of modernizing agriculture in getting there. No country has succeeded in its industrial revolution without a prior (or at least simultaneous) agricultural revolution. Neglecting agriculture in the early stages of development is neglecting development.

Since the 1980s a new set of actors has become important in the debates over ending poverty and hunger. Nongovernmental organizations (NGOs), issue-oriented think tanks, media-linked lobbying groups, philanthropic foundations, and even concerned and charismatic individuals now conduct analyses of food security issues, shape policy debates, even fund implementation of projects and policies. The attention to the cause is welcome, of course, but many of these voices seem not to understand that sustained progress against poverty and hunger can come only through sustained economic growth that reaches the poor, in a relatively stable food economy. Markets are the arena in which such progress takes place. I hope this book helps these groups come to grips with this critical role of markets so that they can direct their attention to making markets work better—on behalf of the poor.

The book has a special message for trade economists who work on agricultural development and food price formation in world and domestic markets. International trade in goods and services is a powerful force for greater economic efficiency and higher living standards in importing and exporting countries. As climate change causes greater instability in local food production, trade will be even more important in evening out supply and demand on behalf of greater food security. Still, the daily prices for food commodities that are formed in world markets and presented to countries as their opportunity costs—the "border price"—do not necessarily carry reliable or efficient long-run signals about what countries should produce and consume. The book pursues this line of thinking by urging trade economists to think more about increasing the stability of food prices in world markets (and more useful to countries as "real" signals of opportunity costs), and to spend less time calculating the gains in a world of perfectly free trade.

In reality, of course, students are the audience. For more than three decades, since *Food Policy Analysis* (Timmer, Falcon, and Pearson 1983) was published, the book has been required reading for students seeking to learn how to cope with poverty and hunger in a tractable manner. No solutions were on offer, but the book identified the right questions to ask and provided guidelines to the data needed to start the analysis. In retrospect, that has been a winning approach. I hope this volume picks up where *Food Policy Analysis* left off.

The Analytical Perspective: "Old" Food Policy and "New"

Food policy analysis is designed to illuminate welfare trade-offs as producers, traders, and consumers are buffeted by changes in technology, prices, and tastes. These changes can come at the household, sectoral, macro, and global levels. A new food policy paradigm has emerged to help understand these trade-offs and new ones arising from "modernization" of the food system. The original food policy paradigm focused analysis on the links between poverty and food security (Timmer, Falcon, and Pearson 1983). The new food policy stresses the double burden on societies facing substantial degrees of hunger at the same time they face rising levels of nutritional problems of affluence—obesity, heart disease, diabetes, etc. (Maxwell and Slater 2003). With obesity now affecting more people than hunger, this new perspective is timely.

The Food and Health Dimension

At the country level, the concern in the original food policy paradigm for keeping food prices at a level that balanced producer and consumer interests, with price stabilization around this level an important policy objective, gives way in the new food policy paradigm to equally important concerns for the budgetary consequences for governments (at national and local levels) of the health outcomes of dietary choices over entire societies.

At the household level, the traditional focus on access to foods (including intra-household access and distribution) stressed income and price variables, with a very limited role for household education and knowledge (except possibly in the derived demand for micronutrients) (Singh, Squire, and Strauss 1986). Much of the quantitative research in food policy over the past three decades has involved a search for the behavioral regularities that linked households to these market-determined variables (Timmer 1981; Bhargava 2008).

The new concerns are quite different. Health professionals are either pessimistic about the political reality of using economic variables to influence dietary choices or doubtful that economic incentives will actually change dietary behavior where affluence permits a wide array of choices.[1] Consequently, there is a much sharper focus on trying to change lifestyle through improved health knowledge and nutrition education. Supermarkets have become a part of that debate. Early evidence suggests that diets change for the worse when poorer consumers start using supermarkets, with highly processed and high-fat foods replacing less refined and more nutrient-rich foods (Asfaw 2007; Michelson 2013). Still, there is remarkably little hard evidence on the impact of a switch from traditional markets to supermarkets on dietary patterns and nutritional well-being.

The international nutrition community is engaged in a pointed debate over whether approaches to changing lifestyles through education will work. In particular, if the dietary patterns of affluence have a significant genetic component—that is, if humans are "hard-wired" for an environment of food scarcity and have few internal control mechanisms over dietary intake in an environment of permanent affluence and abundance—much more coercive efforts may be needed to change dietary behavior (and activity levels) than is implied by the education approach. On the other hand, such coercion directly contradicts consumer sovereignty and the basic principles of a democratic society. The more prominent attention in the new food policy to health problems arising from modern diets is tending to raise tensions between development economists and nutritional scientists.

The Poverty and Development Dimension

One of the basic food policy messages for developing countries is the link between poverty and food security at both the national and household levels. In turn, poverty has been considered primarily an economic problem that could only be addressed in a sustainable fashion by linking the poor—mostly in rural areas—into the process of economic growth. A dynamic agriculture as a stimulus to forward and backward linkages within the rural economy serves as the prime mover in this process. Through improved agricultural technology, public investments in rural infrastructure, and the end of urban bias that distorted incentives for farmers, policy makers had a simple and clear approach to reducing poverty and improving food security.

With success in the rural economy, migration to urban areas becomes more of a "pull" process rather than a "push," especially if favorable macroeconomic and trade policies stimulate rapid growth in a labor-intensive manufacturing industry (and in construction). In combination, these activities pull up real wages and, when sustained, lead to rapid reductions in poverty (Timmer 2002, 2005b, 2009a). In many ways, this paradigm of successful structural transformation could be described as an inclusion model because of its focus on including the poor in the rural economy, including the rural economy in the national economy, and including the national economy in the global economy. Its greatest success was in East and Southeast Asia since the late 1960s, but the model has been under attack as the benefits of globalization seem not to be as widely shared as earlier hoped.

The failures of globalization provide another theme for the new food policy paradigm around the analytics of "exclusion." At the national level, the question is why so many countries have been "nonglobalizers." The essence of the debate is whether the global economy, in the form of rich countries and transnational corporations, has excluded these countries from participating in trade and technology flows, or whether the countries themselves have been unsuccessful in the process because of domestic shortcomings in policies and governance, including corruption (Resnick and Birner 2006; Acemoglu and Robinson 2012).

The debate has a local focus as well. Within an otherwise well-functioning and growing economy, many groups can be excluded from the benefits of this growth. Unskilled workers unable to graduate to higher technologies and uneducated youth unable to compete in a modern economy are a sizable proportion of the workforce in countries with poor manpower and training policies and resources. Globalization makes it more difficult for these countries to compete for trade and investment flows that would provide the first steps up the ladder of higher productivity (Goldberg and Pavcnik 2007).

Integrating the Two Dimensions

A long-standing criticism of capitalism is that it stimulates a highly unequal process of economic growth. Rich owners of financial capital and privileged workers with higher education and advanced skills are paid high returns in a market-oriented economy. What they possess is scarce, and markets reward scarcity. Individuals with only their unskilled labor to sell are plentiful. Their market wages are low and these individuals are poor. Making growth work for the poor in a market economy requires that these basic and fundamental forces be overcome, either through the sheer rapidity of economic growth or through ancillary measures to ensure that the poor connect to growth.

History is full of experiments on how to make an economy work for the poor, from totalitarian communism to democratic socialism, from central planning to "third way" market economies. These historical experiments have a surprising and powerful lesson: rapid economic growth that connects to the poor has been the *only* sustainable path out of poverty for both countries and individuals (Besley and Cord 2006). The question is how to do it.

Food policy analysis was "invented" to provide a framework for answering such a question. The central analytical vision of food policy, articulated more than a quarter of a century ago, integrated farmer, trader, and consumer decision making into the open-economy, macro framework needed for rapid economic growth (Timmer, Falcon, and Pearson 1983). The explicit goal was a sharp reduction in hunger and poverty, which would be possible if market incentives stimulated productivity and income gains in agriculture while poor consumers were protected by stable food prices and rising real wages. The marketing sector was the key to connecting these two ends of the food system.

The analytical story, policy design, and program implementation were complicated, requiring analysts to integrate models of micro and macro decision making in a domestic economy open to world trade and commodity markets. At its best, the food policy paradigm sharply improved the development profession's understanding of the underlying structure and dynamics of poverty and the role of the food system in reducing it (Eicher and Staatz 1998). As part of this understanding, *food security* came to be seen as involving two separate analytical arenas. The first, at the micro or household level, required analysis of food access and entitlements. The second, at the macro or market level, required analysis of food price stability, market supplies, and inventory behavior.

Food policy analysis provided policy makers a comprehensive but intuitively tractable vision of how to connect these two arenas and improve food security for the consumers in their societies. As an analytical paradigm, this vision was always driven by consumer welfare. Farmers, as food producers, and middlemen in the marketing sector that transformed farm output in time, place, and form, were seen as intermediate actors in the efficient production of consumer welfare. Thus the food policy paradigm fits squarely within the standard framework of neoclassical economic analysis and the long-run structural transformation that underpins modern economic growth.

The Paradigm Shift: From Low to High Food Prices

Although many factors can influence the food security of individual households, the dynamics of food prices help us to understand the short-run forces that affect food security at the societal level. The rate of growth and distribution of per capita incomes are the main forces affecting food security in the longer run, conditional on satisfactory progress in raising agricultural productivity. Especially since the turn of the millennium, food prices have behaved quite differently from those two decades before. There was a gradual increase in prices of basic foods after the price bottom in 2002. Prices rapidly accelerated after mid-2007, reaching very high peaks in the first half of 2008. After mid-2008, they fell sharply, but not to previous levels. The price spiral was repeated in 2011–12 (but rice did not participate in this second price spike). What is driving these price fluctuations, and how do they affect food security?

Two separate dimensions of food prices need to be understood. The first is the *level* of food prices, as compared with incomes of the poor. Chronically high food prices trap poor households in continuing poverty. The second is the *volatility* of those food prices, especially their tendency to spike during shortages (thus severely affecting the ability of food-deficit consumers to access food in markets) or to collapse during surpluses (thus undermining the ability of small farmers to invest in higher crop productivity or even in health and education services for their families).

The causes of the separate dynamics are different. Three general and fundamental factors—all interrelated—combined since 2002 to push up the *level* of food prices at a gradual pace. First, rapid economic growth, especially in China and India, put pressure on a variety of natural resources such as oil, metals, timber, and fertilizers. Demand simply increased faster than supply for these commodities, and their market prices responded appropriately.

Second, a sustained decline in the U.S. dollar added to the upward price pressure on dollar-denominated commodity prices directly, and indirectly fueled a search for speculative hedges against the declining dollar. Increasingly from 2006 forward, these financial hedges were found first in petroleum, then in other widely traded commodities, including wheat, corn, and vegetable oils.

Third, the combination of high prices for fuel and legislative mandates to increase production of biofuels established a price link between fuel prices and ethanol/biodiesel feedstocks—sugar in Brazil, corn in the United States, and vegetable oils in Europe. Because of intercommodity linkages in both supply and demand, food prices now have a floor established by their potential conversion into biofuel. These linkages are not always tight or effective in the short run—rice and corn prices, for example, can be disconnected for some time. But the long-run forces for substitution in both production and consumption are powerful. If high prices for fuel are here to stay, high prices for food are here to stay.

To complicate matters, in the short to medium run, the specifics of individual commodity dynamics can produce divergent price paths. Rice is the clearest example. Large Asian countries acted in their own perceived short-run political interests with little or no regard to consequences for the international market or traditional trading partners, causing sharp volatility in world rice prices. Without significant hope for binding international agreements between rice exporters and importers, this source of unique instability would seem likely to last for some time. A hopeful sign, however, has been the stability of world prices for rice since 2009, despite major spikes in prices for wheat and corn in 2010 and 2012. A quiet understanding seems to have emerged in Asia that beggar-thy-neighbor restrictions on trade in rice undermine confidence in the regional economy and should be used only as a last resort. Renewed confidence in the Asian rice economy since 2009 has made prices for rice much more stable than those for wheat and corn, a reversal of historical patterns of price instability.

Contributing to the price spikes were low stocks for most grain. It is virtually impossible to have a sharp run-up in grain prices when stocks are ample. Still, understanding the reasons stocks were low is part of the puzzle (Timmer 2009d). As the supply-of-storage model explains (see Chapter 3), the level of stocks and market prices are endogenously determined—they each influence the other. Levels of both production and consumption were part of the story, but stocks-to-use ratios for wheat and corn were near or at historic lows.

Even though prices on world markets for these grains are well off their peaks, the vulnerability to even a modest supply shock is clear. It would take several years of sustained high prices to stimulate production (and dampen demand), rebuild stocks, and reduce the vulnerability of the world's poor to yet another sharp shock in food prices. With significantly higher costs of production across the board, driven especially by continuing high prices for energy, it seems unlikely that world prices for food will return to the declining trends seen between the mid-1970s and the early 2000s.

The Changing Intellectual Approach

The international context for domestic food policy decision making with respect to food security has changed substantially since the mid-twentieth century. Several basic trends stand out, especially with respect to expectations in the early 1980s, after the full impact of the world food crisis in 1973–74 was felt. From the 1950s through the 1970s, scholars had been developing an understanding of how to do agricultural development and why success in doing so was so important for the rest of the economic development process. The focus was primarily on identifying the constraints on raising farm productivity, because it seemed that so obviously needed to be done. But early voices also pointed out the critical role this higher productivity could play in stimulating the rest of the economy (Lewis 1954; Johnston and Mellor 1961; Eicher and Staatz 1984).

Hayami and Ruttan (1971) introduced the first comprehensive approach to agricultural development. Their induced innovation model generalized such divergent development pathways as in Japan, which could not bring more land under agricultural production. Biological and chemical innovations were needed to raise output per hectare. In the United States, Canada, and Australia/New Zealand, the constraint was labor availability, and increasing labor's productivity through mechanization was essential. Their seminal book heavily influenced the drafting of *Food Policy Analysis* (Timmer, Falcon, and Pearson 1983). The focus of the book expanded to the role of markets and government interventions into both the macro economy and the marketing system to improve access of the poor to food. Although the book was influential within the food policy community, the broader economics profession responded with quiet indifference. By the mid-1980s, agricultural development and food security were already slipping out of favor in the donor community and government policy. Market processes had solved the problem and would keep it solved! By the end of the first decade of the new millennium, however, the global context changed and, gradually, professional thinking changed as well (World Bank 2007). The debate about markets, government intervention, and the role of trade has resurfaced. Agricultural development specialists, at least the few who remain, are back in demand but are astonished by the radical changes in the world food system since the early 1980s, when *Food Policy Analysis* was published.

The Changing Global Context

First, surprisingly rapid economic growth occurred, especially in Asia, with hundreds of millions of people pulled out of poverty. The strong connection between inclusive economic growth, especially in rural areas, and rapid reduction of poverty was simply not apparent in the empirical record in the early 1980s. *The East Asian Miracle* (World Bank 1993) did not appear for another decade. This rapid growth validated the central theme of the food policy perspective—poverty cannot be reduced without greater economic productivity of unskilled, especially rural, labor. That theme remains powerfully relevant even as the sources of such productivity increases are more and more elusive.

Second, a communications revolution at both household and international levels radically reduced transactions costs and increased access to knowledge.

Again, the centrality of markets and price formation in the food policy perspective—and in understanding food policy design and implementation— was boosted because marketing margins narrowed under improved and more informed competition. Consumers and farmers both benefited from more competitive local food markets. The supermarket revolution has merely accelerated these changes. The current challenge is to keep small farmers in modern supply chains (Timmer 2009b; Reardon and Timmer 2012).

Third, global financial markets became interested in emerging economies. The early 1980s were an era of fixed exchange rates, tight controls on the flow of foreign capital, and virtually no financial intermediation beyond state banks. At first, the influx of foreign capital in the 1990s was welcomed as a sign of confidence, but except for foreign direct investment in real assets, such as factories and real estate, the global financial interest in emerging economies was a two-edged sword. A rapid influx of foreign capital could cause currency appreciation and a loss of competitiveness; its rapid exit when the economy started to decline or foreign investors saw better opportunities elsewhere caused a crisis in local financial markets. Global financial integration came with very poorly understood risks, and the global financial crisis in 2009 demonstrated them clearly. The growth of foreign investments in land to produce food and/or biofuels for export—so-called landgrabs—is controversial, but at least the capital cannot leave the country quickly. The injection of new capital into agriculture in poor countries may not be all bad. Much will depend on who benefits from the new production—foreigners or local farmers.

Fourth, biofuels are now a significant source of demand for basic food commodities such as corn, sugar, and palm oil. Very senior and experienced commodity analysts dispute the share of biofuels' contribution to high grain prices—various estimates range from 25 percent to over 75 percent. An empirical model—that is, one not based on analytically derived behavioral relationships—from the New England Complex Systems Institute (NECSI) suggests that nearly all of the trend increase in food prices since 1990 has come from biofuel demand, whereas spikes along the trend are entirely due to financial speculation (Lagi et al. 2011).

Whether the demand comes from legislative mandates or from high prices for fuel, establishing a direct link between prices for energy and prices for food is a powerful new force in global commodity markets. The outlook for continued high prices for crude oil thus has direct implications for the outlook for prices of staple foods. Most knowledgeable analysts of the U.S. biofuel industry feel that corn-based ethanol will remain economically competitive in the absence of specific taxes on the conversion of food grains into ethanol. In the absence of such taxes, high-priced petroleum means high-priced corn (de Gorter and Drabik 2012). Because of its multiple end uses in consumption and land competition with soybeans (and to a lesser extent, with wheat) in the United States, high-priced corn (specifically) means high-priced food (generally), including, in the long run, even rice.

Finally, climate change is now widely recognized as a reality, although its likely impact is still highly controversial. There seems to be agreement about the increased probability of extreme weather events in general. The impact on global and localized food security outcomes is less clear. Innovative empirical studies by David Lobell and his colleagues show that warmer temperatures have already reduced agricultural yields in Europe since 1990 by as much as 10 percent, controlling for other factors (Lobell, Schlenker, and Costa-Roberts 2011). Peaks in summer nighttime temperatures can reduce rice yields by a third in only a day or two. Although the search is on for genetic material that resists the severe impact of high temperatures on grain yields, it will take decades for significant results, if they are even possible, to be seen in average yields.

Despite the changing climate, it is important to remember that ecosystem services provided by the climate are essential for all agricultural production—photosynthesis remains the most efficient way to capture solar energy for human use. The most important effects of climate change on agriculture are likely to include a net global loss of agricultural land, changing crop suitability in particular regions, and an increase in the frequency of natural disasters. It will also have negative effects on other areas of agriculture broadly interpreted. Climate change will reduce the carrying capacity of many rangelands and pose threats to fisheries and aquaculture production systems. In-country "climate-smart agriculture" adaptation projects and programs now form part of the food policy agenda. The challenge is to design, analyze, and implement these projects and programs, a complex task because they need to be country-specific.

What Have We Learned About Food Price Formation?

The rapid emergence in the 1990s of China and India as global growth engines meant a gradual shift in the drivers of demand for commodities and natural resources. Advanced economies had increased their knowledge and became less dependent on energy, metals, and other basic commodities—including food commodities—to fuel their economic growth. The price depression for nearly all commodities in the 1980s and 1990s reinforced the view that the future depended on value added from skills and knowledge, not from exploitation of natural resources. But industrialization, especially as practiced by China and India, is a very intensive user of natural resources (and producer of greenhouse gases). By the turn of the millennium, it was increasingly clear that the growth path of developing countries was the primary impetus to higher commodity prices, starting with energy prices but quickly extending to food prices. The Malthusian challenge was back, but with two decades of neglected investments in raising agricultural productivity (because of low agricultural prices), the challenge is turning out to be hard to meet.

World Grain Prices: Levels and Volatility

Are food grain prices high? It depends on the commodity and the time horizon of comparison and whether the prices are in nominal or real terms. Even from the perspective of just two decades, deflated prices—corrected for inflation—are not exceptionally high. A longer-run view, from 1950 to the present, is even more surprising. The price trends over more than half a century reveal that even the highest price levels experienced in 2007 and 2008 are substantially below the peaks in the previous world food crisis in 1973–74. Indeed, real prices in mid-2013 for maize, wheat, and rice remain well below what was considered normal until the full impact of the green revolution was felt after 1980 (Figure 1).

Still, food prices are significantly higher than they were at the lows experienced in the early 2000s. The new price environment has now existed long enough to have generated a flow of analyses and policy perspectives. There have been urgent appeals to ramp up food aid funding and support for agricultural research (IFPRI 2008). Falling grain stocks since 2000 gradually changed world commodity markets from surplus to deficit and provided the supply/demand fundamentals for sharply higher prices (Abbot, Hurt, and Tyner 2008, with update).

These changing fundamentals can be seen in an especially compelling way when comparing rates of population growth in Asia with rates of

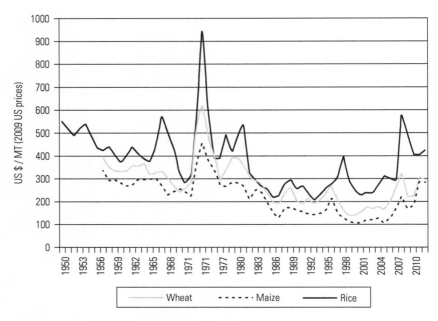

Figure 1. Long-Run Movements in World Grain Prices Since 1950
Note: The world prices of maize, rice, and wheat are based on U.S. No. 2 Yellow, FOB Gulf of Mexico; Thailand 5% broken milled white rice; and No. 1 Hard Red Winter, ordinary protein, FOB Gulf of Mexico, respectively.
Source: International Monetary Fund, available http://www.imf.org.

growth in rice yields (Figure 2). The Green Revolution produced a surge in rice production, and rice surpluses, between 1980 and 1990, but a widening gap in the two trends opened up after 1990. Interestingly, this productivity gap has started to close again, partly under the stimulus from high rice prices in 2007–8. Agricultural productivity growth tends to be depressed when output prices are low in relation to the costs of production; high prices induce both more intensive production techniques and the search for new, more productive technologies.

A major policy issue emerged due to the suddenness of the price spikes in 2007–8: the extent to which outside financial speculation—by pension and hedge funds, or newly created commodity index funds available to small investors—has been driving up prices for key staple foods (and petroleum). India, for example, has banned futures trading in important food

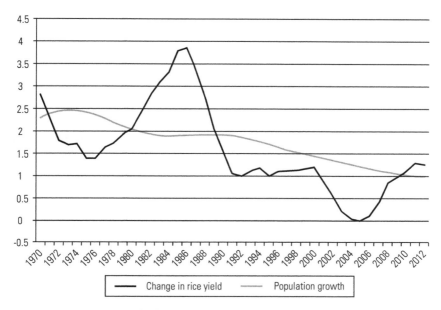

Figure 2. Five-Year Period Change in Rice Yield and Population Growth in Rice-Producing Asian Economies Percentage per year
Note: The annual average percentage change in rice yields and population are computed as the change between successive rolling five-year period data in sixteen rice-producing Asian economies (Bangladesh, Cambodia, People's Republic of China, India, Indonesia, Japan, Malaysia, Myanmar, Nepal, Pakistan, Philippines, Republic of Korea, Sri Lanka, Thailand, and Vietnam). For example, the data for 1969 are the change between 1965–69 and 1960–64.
Source: Adapted from Dawe (2008) and updated with FAO data.

staples. Nearly all economists and market analysts agree that financial speculation cannot drive up prices in the long run—over a decade or longer. Only the fundamentals of supply and demand can do that.

But there is much more controversy over the role of new speculative activity on price formation in the short run, and especially the potential for such speculation to create spikes in prices, or bubbles, that disconnect the market price from underlying fundamentals (OECD 2008; Munier 2012; Galtier 2009, 2013a). It is very difficult to explain the creation of such bubbles or price spikes across a wide range of commodities without a significant role for financial speculation based on expectations of higher prices (Tadesse et al. 2013).

The key lessons from the 2007–8 food price spikes can be summarized as follows. First, the distinction between short-run responses of supply and demand to price changes and longer-run responses is crucial. This is a result familiar to agricultural economists, who have used Nerlovian-type distributed lag models of farmer and consumer behavior for half a century (Nerlove 1958). The simple model developed in Chapter 3 to explain food price formation captures this distinction and suggests that much of the *gradual* increase in the prices of food commodities—from 2002 to 2007—was a direct result of sharply declining prices a decade before. We are paying a high price, literally, for the destocking of grains since the mid-1990s, a process which pushed down prices and contributed to the lack of investment in agricultural development.

Simultaneously, this destocking was a rational response to falling grain prices. The simultaneity between stock levels and price expectations—emphasized in the theory of the supply of storage (Brennan 1958; Williams and Wright 1991)—is another neglected aspect of most analyses of current high food prices. Considerable insight comes from remedying that neglect simply by recognizing that in market economies stock changes do not happen exogenously from price formation.

Second, the pervasive impact of exchange rates on commodity prices is confirmed even in the very short run. It is important to remember that exchange rates are financial variables conditioned by their macroeconomic and trade context. Almost inherently, then, commodity prices will be linked to financial markets, even in the long run (Frankel 2006). Price formation in organized commodity markets depends on financial factors as well as real supply and demand factors.

Finally, the short-run price linkages among exchange rates, oil prices, and the prices of important food commodities can be tested with modern statistical techniques—Granger Causality analysis (see Timmer 2008a, 2010c). These linkages are almost certainly driven by the intermediation of financial markets, that is, speculators engaged in commodity futures (and other derivatives) markets who have no physical connection to the commodity businesses themselves. These results provide tantalizing evidence of the role of financial speculation in short-run price behavior, but the role is not nearly as uniform and pervasive as most critics seem to think. Speculative pressures come and go, for reasons not apparent from the data. Short-run speculators really do operate in the short run—hours and days.

Layers of Causation in the Formation of Commodity Prices

When compared with the long-run decline in most commodity prices visible in Figure 1, the run-up in prices since the turn of the millennium appears to be a reversal of history. The timing of the rise varies by commodity, so some commodity-specific stories will be needed to explain the patterns. But there seem to be common elements to the rise as well. The general patterns since 2000 are clear enough in Figure 1. From 2000 to 2004 all the tracked commodities moved more or less in tandem, and by relatively small amounts. Soybean prices spurted in 2004 after production problems in the United States but returned to normal levels in 2005. From then until early 2007, prices of wheat, corn, and soybeans remained flat, but rice prices had already started a steady rise from their historic low in 2001. Crude oil prices (and metals, which make up a large share of the International Monetary Fund commodity price index) had also started a steady rise by 2004. Clearly, by mid-decade, commodity prices were beginning to show signs of life not seen for a decade. Something had changed.

The change is most apparent in crude oil and the metals-heavy IMF index. Food staples, excepting rice, remained stable until 2007. Such a pattern is best explained by the accelerating demands for industrial raw materials and energy as the economies of China and India consolidated their momentum of very rapid growth after the turn of the millennium. China and India are typically not large factors in global grain markets, however. Their rapid economic growth did not spill over directly to higher prices for wheat, corn, and rice. The rising prices for rice need a special explanation, as detailed in Chapter 6. By 2006, however, it was clear that rapid growth in the developing world, especially China and India, could move global commodity markets. This realization set the stage for new expectations among commodity traders in particular and the broader investment community in general. By 2006, expectations of higher commodity prices were well established. The paradigm shift was under way.

It is useful to think about the factors causing high food prices in terms of cumulative layers of causation (Timmer 2008a). Several basic drivers seem to be stimulating rapid growth in demand for food commodities. Rising living standards in China, India, and other rapidly growing developing countries lead to increased demand for improved diets, especially greater consumption of vegetable oils and livestock products (and the feedstuffs to produce them). China is a major importer of soybeans for both the meal and oil and India is a significant importer of vegetable oils. It is important to realize, however, that consumption of wheat and rice in India and China is not rising significantly, and both countries are largely self-sufficient in both commodities.

The rapid depreciation of the U.S. dollar against the euro and a number of other important currencies drove up the price of commodities priced in U.S. dollars for both supply and demand reasons. The depreciation of the U.S. dollar also causes investors "long" in dollars (i.e., most U.S.-based investors, but holders of U.S. dollars globally as well) to seek hedges against this loss of value. Commodities were one attractive option, especially when investments through financial derivatives into commodity index funds (and other options) were available.

Mandates for corn-based ethanol in the United States (and biodiesel fuels from vegetable oils in Europe) cause ripple effects beyond the corn economy, which are stimulated by intercommodity linkages (Naylor et al. 2007; Timmer, Falcon, and Pearson 1983). There is active debate about whether legislative mandates or high prices for oil are driving investments in biofuel capacity (Naylor 2012) but no doubt about the quantities of corn and vegetable oil being utilized as biofuel feedstocks (Elliott 2008).

Massive speculation from new financial players searching for better returns than in stocks or real estate has flooded into commodity markets. The economics and finance communities are unable to say with any confidence what the price impact of this speculation has been, but virtually all of it has been a bet on higher prices.

On the supply side, significant fluctuations in weather patterns in major grain-producing regions—the U.S. Midwest, Russia and Ukraine, and Australia, for example—have resulted in major production shortfalls for wheat and corn. Whether these fluctuations are now more frequent and severe because of climate change is a subject of intense scientific debate. But for the longer run, climate change seems certain to alter basic crop production potential. It is expected to have highly variable effects on different regions. Tropical and equatorial regions will bear the heaviest burdens, with sub-Saharan Africa probably facing the greatest challenges, and with some gains in yields and land availability in temperate regions. Since rural poverty is concen-

Food price

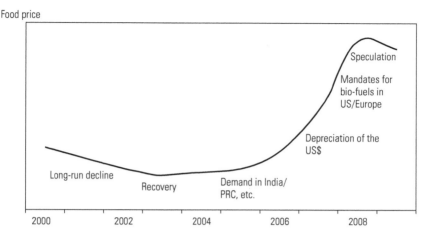

Figure 3. Food Prices

trated in tropical and, in South and Southeast Asia, coastal areas, climate change is expected to have a disproportionate effect on the already vulnerable. The growing urbanization of poverty, the result of dysfunctional structural transformations (especially in Africa and India), may change the geographic incidence of the impact of climate change on the poor, but probably not the overall level (Ravallion, Chen, and Sangraula 2007; Badiane 2011; Binswanger-Mkhize 2012).

Underneath all of these drivers is the high price of petroleum and other fossil fuels. Figure 3 shows an impressionistic attribution of the four non-oil demand factors causing the recent run-up in food commodity prices. The figure also shows the recent component of the "normal" long-run decline in food prices that has been experienced since 1980 and a modest recovery from the lows reached in the early 2000s, a recovery that was partly stimulated by the long-run response to earlier price declines (i.e., slower growth in supply and faster growth in demand as a response to these low prices eventually led to rising prices—see the detailed model in Chapter 3). However, the surge in food prices that has attracted so much attention did not start until late 2006 or so, depending on the commodity. Substantial speculative investments in food commodities seem to have started only in mid-2007 and were clearly winding down by mid-2013.

Each of the four demand-driven causes is a little different for each basic commodity, but the structural forces—rapid demand growth in developing

Table 1. External Drivers of Supply and Demand

	Supply	Demand
Low variance		
	Seed technology	Population growth
	Irrigation	Income growth
	Total harvested area	Dietary changes/tastes
	Climate change	Meat/livestock economy
	Knowledge and management skills	
High variance		
	Weather	Exchange rates
	Diseases	Speculation
	Crop-specific harvested area	Biofuels (predictable from mandates; not predictable from oil prices)
	Fuel costs	
	Fertilizer costs	Panic/hoarding
		Government trade and inventory policies

countries and depreciation of the U.S. dollar—are similar for all the commodities of interest here (again, with rising oil prices as a foundation). These factors have been in play for years and have been fairly predictable, driven as they are by macroeconomic fundamentals. The two top layers, however, have come on the scene much more recently and have the potential to change the price formation equation rapidly and unexpectedly. Table 1 summarizes this perspective for supply and demand drivers according to their predictability, that is, whether the drivers are low variance (and easy to predict) or high variance and very difficult to predict.

Understandably, the low-variance drivers of both supply and demand have lengthy time horizons in terms of policy influence, whereas the high-variance drivers demand a much more flexible short-run horizon.

The Biofuel Debate

Biofuels are enormously controversial, and this chapter is not the place to review the debate over their full economic and environmental impact (see Elliott 2008; Collins 2008; Runge and Johnson 2008; and Naylor 2012 for useful, if sobering, reviews). The problem is that none of the formal models used to evaluate the impact of biofuels on commodity prices (and hunger) fully capture the cross-commodity supply and demand linkages between corn—the primary grain used to make ethanol—and other commodities such as soybeans, wheat, and other feed grains. As a simple example, increased planting of corn led to reductions in soybean acreage in 2007 in the United States. The reduced output of soybeans meant that soy oil production was also lower, which caused increased demand for palm oil in Asia and a spike in prices. Although China is not a significant importer of corn, it is a massive importer of soybeans to crush for both soybean meal and soy oil. With reduced supplies of soybeans available (a ripple effect of the increased acreage devoted to corn), China turned to Asian-produced palm oil to meet its growing demand for vegetable oils (Naylor et al. 2007). India is also a substantial importer of vegetable oils and of palm oil in particular.

Corn is the quintessential multi-end-use commodity, and the economics of which end use is driving market prices depends on the supply and demand structure of all the alternative commodities, as well as on macroeconomic conditions and trade policies in importing and exporting countries. Modeling this is difficult. In the precise language of Chen, Rogoff, and Rossi (2008), the multiple end uses lead to "parameter instability" in the relationship between supply, demand, and price. It is entirely possible that in one month, demand for corn to make ethanol is driving up the price of corn, soybeans, and palm oil, whereas in another month, price formation across these commodities can be completely delinked, depending simply on each commodity's own supply and demand situation (or on other forces). Thus not only would the parameters of a multi-end-use commodity price model vary from period to period, so also would the entire structure of the model. Perhaps it is not surprising that different analysts and different models produce very different estimates of what is causing high food prices. Parameter instability is the fundamental reason that careful analysts such as Abbott, Hurt, and Tyner (2008) argue that it is impossible to place quantitative weights on the causes of higher food prices, at least weights that would have continuing validity over time and across commodities.

It is possible to see this parameter instability and changing structure if price data are available with sufficiently high frequency. Using daily price data from December 31, 1999, to July 2, 2008, Timmer (2010c) tests the structure of price interaction across exchange rates and commodities, and the structure clearly changes frequently—often several times a year.

As noted, not all of the action is on the demand side. For some food commodities, especially wheat, there have also been significant supply shocks from drought and disease. Normally these would cause only modest increases in price, with supplies from stocks and a pattern of year-round production in the Northern and Southern Hemispheres dampening upward movements. But wheat stocks were at historic lows even before the bad crops rippled around the world in 2007. The spike in wheat prices started early in 2007 and was quite dramatic. The recovery of Australia's wheat crop in 2008 caused a significant decline in wheat prices after early April 2008. The drought in Ukraine and Russia in 2010 caused another round of price spikes for wheat, as did the drought in the American Midwest for corn in 2012.

The decline in stock-to-use ratios for corn since the late 1990s is the main rationale offered by analysts who see corn-based ethanol demand as the major driver of higher prices for staple food grains. Because corn has multiple end uses that are economically efficient at normal prices, a shift in demand from one of the end uses (e.g., biofuels) can create ripple effects throughout many other commodity markets. Corn is a primary feedstuff for livestock but competes in this end use with wheat. Wheat and rice are consumption substitutes in parts of Asia. In another direction, corn oil competes with soy oil and palm oil. Rapid growth in demand for vegetable oil in Asia can indirectly stimulate corn production in the United States.

Competition and substitution can also take place on the supply side. Corn and soybeans compete directly for acreage in much of the United States. Increased demand for corn for biofuel production can reduce soybean acreage, causing soybean meal and soy oil prices to rise. Thus there are many mechanisms by which higher demand for corn to convert into ethanol might impact a wide range of food commodity prices around the world. With stock-to-use levels for corn so low in the mid-2000s, it was these mechanisms that led analysts such as Mitchell (2008) and Collins (2008) to single out rising demand for ethanol in the United States as the trigger for higher food prices across the board.

The Response to High Food Prices

The main explanatory factors behind the gradual run-up in food prices from the early 2000s to mid-2007 were spillover from the broad resource demands generated by rapid demand growth, the declining U.S. dollar, and the lagged effect of earlier declines in real food prices and their (endogenous) impact on stock-to-use ratios. But these factors do not explain the sharp run-up in many staple food prices from mid-2007 to mid-2008. The explanation for these price spikes varies by commodity and time period, but in addition to the broad factors affecting all commodity markets just noted—especially high oil prices and the declining U.S. dollar—new end uses for food grains and vegetable oils as biofuels, bad weather, diseases, and political decisions by food exporters to insulate their consumers from world prices led to the sharp increases in food prices. Panicked hoarding on the part of countries and individuals clearly played a role in the spike in rice prices (see Chapter 6), and financial speculation may have contributed to spikes in other commodities, especially oil, wheat, corn, and vegetable oils.

The longer-run question is whether supply dynamics will begin to match the rapid growth in demand. In past episodes of high food prices and fears of Malthusian crises, supply responses have been vigorous, albeit with a lag, returning world food prices to their long-run downward trend. This time, arguments are increasingly being heard that there is little supply response left in the system, for three basic reasons.

- There is little high-quality agricultural land to be opened.
- The yield potential of existing agricultural technologies has been static for decades (reflecting a serious lack of investment in agricultural research since the mid-1980s). Closing the gap between this yield ceiling and yields obtained by actual farmer practices is the only source of increased output until new agricultural technologies come on stream by 2020 or later. This yield gap has been closing rapidly everywhere except Africa.
- The costs of inputs needed to achieve higher yields are high and rising, especially for fuel, fertilizer, and water. Continued high prices for grain may also cause land rents and rural labor costs to rise.

A dampened response in agricultural productivity growth will be a direct threat to continued reductions in poverty and hunger. The appropriate policy response to high food prices, then, is to find ways to stimulate growth in the agricultural sector, especially in investments to raise productivity of basic food crops. High prices for food now provide plenty of incentives to make those investments, but many of those investments—especially in research and extension—would have paid off at the prices of 1990 or 2000 if donors and governments had recognized the full social value of raising agricultural productivity (Timmer 1995a, 2009a). These are political decisions that are driven only indirectly by market realities. Perhaps it is good news that the market is sending very clear signals to politicians on what to do.

Raising Agricultural Productivity

> Agriculture is characterized by much stronger constraints of land
> on production than most other sectors of the economy. Agricultural
> growth may be viewed as a process of easing the constraints on
> production imposed by inelastic supplies of land and labor.
>
> (Hayami and Ruttan 1985: 4)

Despite over half a century of trying, no broad theory of agrarian change has been robust enough to withstand the enormous variance of agro-ecological conditions, starting conditions in terms of land distribution, tenure rights, organization of the household, and human capital formation; and market conditions and policy environments.[2] Still, the need for a clear and intuitive framework for understanding and speeding the process of agrarian change has not gone away. Insights from Art Mosher's writings in the 1960s continue to be relevant and are used here to focus attention on *binding constraints* that prevent higher crop yields or greater farm incomes. Understanding the nature (and sequencing) of these constraints then informs an agricultural development strategy. In this sense, a theory of agrarian change needs to be built on removing constraints, and policies to improve food security need to understand what those constraints are.

The Mosher Perspective

To increase the agricultural production of a country is a complex task. It is frequently a baffling task as well. It is complex because so many different conditions have to be created or modified, by different persons and groups of people. It is baffling because the *spirit* of a people is involved also. Techniques are not enough. They have to be combined and used with intelligence, imagination, experimentation, and continuing hard work. Agricultural development is as dependent on how effectively people work together as it is on the natural resources with which they begin.

Yet agricultural development does occur. Farmers experiment with new crops, frequently with no other encouragement than seeing these crops grow in neighbors' fields. Research workers develop new strains of crops and discover improved practices in the use of fertilizers and in the management of soil moisture. Engineers, and sometimes individual farmers, produce improved implements. Merchants develop better methods of handling farm products brought to the market and better and cheaper ways of transporting them. Governments adopt new patterns of land holding, taxation policies and price policies that make the adoption of better farming methods more profitable. These and many other steps to increase agricultural production have their effect. (Mosher 1966: 9)

Policy analysts can use Mosher's perspective to determine the nature of constraints facing the agricultural sector. It is easiest to identify crop-specific constraints—identifying issues for campaigns to raise the output of wheat or rice, for instance, is easier than dealing with the complexity of multicommodity farming systems. At the early stages of agricultural development this commodity focus is not a serious shortcoming because major productivity gains from new technology tend to be commodity-specific, and most agricultural development plans are organized around particular commodities. At later stages in development, however, efforts to raise agricultural productivity usually encounter complicated trade-offs among commodities as well as competition for farm labor from wage labor markets. Then more sophisticated analytical techniques will be necessary, particularly the use of multiple farming system tableaux organized so that formal activity analysis is possible using mathematical programming techniques.[3] Going forward, it is clear that climate change will pose increasingly challenging constraints to farmers, agricultural scientists, and policy makers alike.

Removing Constraints to Stimulate Agricultural Productivity

There are *no* theoretical propositions that can provide operational guides to economic policy in the absence of empirical knowledge regarding the magnitudes of variables and parameters in the *specific* economy for which the policy choices are relevant. Let me draw an analogy from biology. Knowledge of the principles of plant nutrition does not permit the extension worker or farmer to recommend accurately the appropriate application of nitrogen to rice on a *specific* field; it can only guide him in designing an efficient trial or test in the farmer's field to provide the relevant empirical information. Similarly, the role of growth models or theories is not to provide direct insight regarding policy choices; rather, it is to serve as a *guide* for the empirical research needed to project the quantitative effects of the manipulation of alternative instrumental variables. (Ruttan 1969: 358)

Gordon Conway, the most knowledgeable and distinguished agro-ecologist of his generation, takes on directly this problem of breaking constraints to raise agricultural productivity (Conway 2012). Hunger *can* be solved, he argues, if we decide it *should* be solved. The problem is that food is produced in order to make a profit. Food is marketed and sold in order to make a profit. Households without the economic means to participate in that for-profit system of food production and consumption go hungry. More than a billion people fall into that trap.

Raising agricultural productivity in a sustainable fashion is the primary way out of this trap. To bring this about, Conway has little role for the market processes of efficient resource allocation in his twenty-four steps of what is needed to solve hunger through a "doubly green revolution." The Conway approach is basically that of a planner who knows what needs to be done and thus can tell a competent government what to do.

I am not so naïve as to believe that simply "getting prices right" will solve the problem of hunger, although I wrote a book by that title long ago (Timmer 1986). But I also do not believe we can plan our way out of hunger by making markets do our will. Even well-intentioned governments cannot end hunger by themselves. Markets, working alone, leave many in poverty. Government policy and markets have to work together to bring poor households into a growing economy that is based on a productive, sustainable, and stable food system. This theme runs throughout the book. It is the key to ending hunger and keeping it ended.

Conclusions: Whither Food Prices?

In view of the difficulties in raising agricultural productivity, it seems unlikely that basic food prices will return to their real long-run downward trend. Instead, a return to the real average prices seen in 2007 would be considered a major accomplishment. That is, when the panic subsides and the financial speculators move on to greener pastures, the new equilibrium price for rice, for example, is likely to be in the $400 to $500 range, not in the $300 to $400 range (in 2013 prices). Other basic food commodities are likely to exhibit similar patterns. It is a sign of hope that prices for low-quality rice in most world markets have indeed fallen back to about $400 per ton (in mid-2014).

Should policy makers try to do anything about this apparent new equilibrium level of food prices? Clearly, it was appropriate to do everything possible to prick the speculative price bubbles in 2008, especially for rice. *Reversing the dynamic of rising price expectations and the private hoarding that exacerbated them brought dramatic price relief in just a few months.* It is unfortunate that the world does not have any internationally mandated mechanism for stabilizing grain prices or for keeping large countries from destabilizing them. But that is the world we live in. Domestic policies will trump international cooperation whenever politicians see a short-run advantage to closing borders or subsidizing trade. Equally it was appropriate for the international community to rally resources on behalf of increased food aid to the most affected populations. Safety nets for poor consumers are essential in a world of highly unstable food prices. But no one should be fooled into thinking that such safety nets are a solution to poverty, or even high food prices, in more than a transitory way. *The only sustainable solution for these households is inclusive, or pro-poor, economic growth that provides reliable real incomes and stable access to food from home production or in local markets.*

Beyond that, it would be foolish for a book, with its lengthy writing and production processes, to make specific price predictions for either the short run or the long run. The major argument in this chapter has emphasized the difficulties agricultural policy makers face in coping with food price volatility in the short run while investing to raise agricultural productivity in the long run. Facing these difficulties successfully is the only way to end hunger in a sustainable fashion. The basic steps for understanding what to do and how to do it are the topics of the rest of the book.

CHAPTER 2

Learning to Manage Food Security:
A Policy Perspective

From a policy perspective, food security as a global issue presents an enormous paradox. At one level, steady progress has been made since the middle of the twentieth century in bringing hundreds of millions of people out of poverty and hunger. Measured by the key determinants of food security—improved availability, access, utilization, and stability—food security has been improving. Large pockets of food-insecure populations remain, especially in sub-Saharan Africa and South Asia, but because of rapid economic growth, aggressive efforts to stabilize food prices, and/or safety net programs that deliver food to the poor, the rest of Asia and Latin America are coping reasonably well with challenges to their food security.

At the same time, food security strategies and policies are in almost total disarray. A fundamental disconnect exists between what most countries say their food security strategies are and what policies they are actually pursuing. The disconnect is most manifest with rice policy in Asia, where high prices for rice farmers are implemented to "reduce poverty," when in fact most of the poor and hungry in the region are net buyers of rice and thus suffer more hunger and poverty from high prices for rice. But many countries, not just in Asia, do not have coherent strategies to improve their food security. An important reason for this disconnect is a basic misunderstanding in the political arena of the interconnected role of markets and government policies in providing sustainable food security. Food policy analysis aims to overcome this misunderstanding while being sensitive to the legitimate political concerns of leaders who fear the wrath of their citizens if food disappears from local markets or prices spike suddenly, leaving poor consumers to face increased hunger.

The Food Policy Perspective

Analytical and policy flexibility is needed to cope with market instability and the problems of poverty (Timmer, Falcon, and Pearson 1983). Such flexibility is not a natural feature of domestic policy making, in the food sector or elsewhere; providing the analytical tools for understanding how to create flexible responses both to high- and low-price environments is a genuine challenge. The starting point is usually to understand the food marketing system, which transforms commodities in a farmer's field in time, place and form, into food on the table. It is impossible to understand the challenges facing efforts to eliminate hunger without understanding the role of markets and operation of the food marketing system. This food policy perspective has been very helpful to many countries as they plan investments and policy initiatives to reduce poverty and improve food security.

The food policy agenda focuses on rapid and sustained reduction of poverty. There are four basic food policy objectives, and all four are important:

- faster economic growth (the efficiency objective),
- more equal distribution of income from that growth (the welfare objective),
- a guaranteed nutritional floor for the poor (the safety net objective), and
- secure availability and stable prices in food markets (the food security objective).

There are many trade-offs (and significant overlap) among these objectives, and substantial analysis of a country's food system is necessary to understand, if even roughly, the quantitative details of the trade-offs. The central organizing theme of the analysis is the food price dilemma—an explicit recognition that a single market-clearing food price cannot satisfy all four objectives simultaneously. A pure market solution does not work. Additional policy instruments are needed, but they all need to operate compatibly with market prices. The most important lesson is the centrality of food prices and the signals they send to farmers, traders, consumers, and finance ministers. The behavior of these decision makers dictates market outcomes but also responds to those market outcomes. The food system that food policy analysts need to understand encompasses micro behavior on the farm and in the household, market-level behavior by traders, processors, and retailers, and macroeconomic responses by policy makers.

The Role of Markets

As emphasized in Chapter 1, in a market economy markets play three key roles: an engineering role by moving inputs to farmers and food to consumers, storing and processing it along the way; a role in price discovery—determining what a commodity (or service) is worth in monetary terms; and a role as the arena for allocating society's scarce resources to meet the virtually unlimited needs and desires of consumers.

The dilemma, as noted earlier, is that markets often fail at tasks that society regards as important, such as reducing poverty, achieving nutritional well-being, or maintaining stable food prices. We now understand that these failures are not just for technical reasons—externalities, spillovers, monopoly power, or asymmetric information, for example. They also have deep behavioral roots based in loss aversion, widespread norms of fairness, and the regularity of "other-regarding preferences" (see Chapter 6). Policies designed to correct these market failures must factor into their design both the technical and behavioral dimensions.

Simply "getting prices right" in markets will not solve the problem of hunger. The efficient price for unskilled and abundant labor could be too low for a worker to afford a nutritious diet. It is also not possible to plan our way out of hunger by making markets deliver food to the poor. Government policy and markets need to work together to bring poor households into a growing economy that is based on a productive, sustainable, and stable food system. Only a few countries have managed this process successfully. Most of them are in East and Southeast Asia, although the state of Kerala in South India and Costa Rica in Central America offer interesting lessons as well. Many of the examples in this book draw from these success stories, although a constant effort is made to understand how generalizable these stories, and

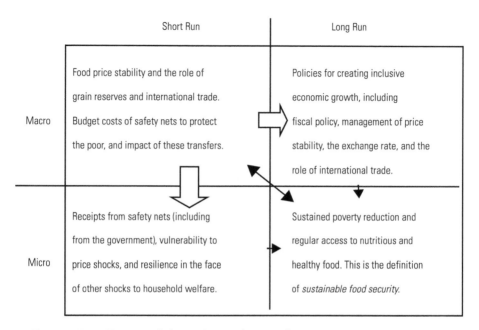

Figure 4. Basic Framework for Understanding Food Security Issues

their policy implications, might be to other regions—sub-Saharan Africa and South Asia, in particular.

Pathways to Food Security: From Short Run to Long Run and from Macro to Micro

To see how political (and populist) misunderstanding arises and why it persists, consider a very simple model of food security that focuses on the short run versus the long run and on the macro level (of policy makers) versus the micro level (of household decision makers) (Figure 4). The policy objective in this simple model is for all households to have reliable and sustainable access to nutritious and healthy food. Thus food security is achieved by ending up in the bottom right box of the matrix. The starting point, however, is the upper left box of the matrix, where policy makers deal primarily with macro-level issues in the short run. To the extent they are concerned about the welfare of poor households, the best they can do in the short run is stabilize food prices and send transfer payments—via safety net mechanisms—to those households most affected during a food crisis when prices rise sharply.

When the global economy is reasonably stable, and when food prices are well behaved, policy makers at the national level can concentrate their political and financial capital on the process of long-run, inclusive growth. Keeping the poor from falling into irreversible poverty traps is easier and less costly in a world of stable food prices. The poor are then able to use their own resources and entrepreneurial abilities to connect to long-run, sustainable food security for themselves.

In an ideal world, policy makers could use economic mechanisms under their control to shift households directly to the long-run objective (the lower right box of Figure 4), in which sustainable food security is achieved. In return, policy makers would receive political support for this achievement, hence the two-way diagonal arrow connecting the upper left and lower right boxes. The diagonal arrow reflects a technocratic view of the world in which policy makers take informed actions on behalf of public objectives and are rewarded when they succeed.

In fact, market economies, and politics, do not work that way. Policy makers at the macro level must implement long-run measures to stimulate inclusive, pro-poor economic growth and sustain that growth for decades in order to have a measurable impact on poverty (via the small vertical arrow connecting the upper right box to the lower right box). These long-run measures are reflected in the broad arrow from the upper left to the upper right, but it is hard to concentrate the political and financial resources needed to make this arrow an effective mechanism to stimulate economic growth if most policy attention, and fiscal resources, are being devoted to short-run crises.

Simultaneously, and creating tensions for the policies favoring long-run growth, policy makers must also find enough resources, and efficient transfer mechanisms, to ensure that the poor do not fall into irreversible poverty traps during times of economic crisis, including food crises. These transfers can impose substantial fiscal costs and hence challenge the necessary investments for long-run growth. Design and implementation of these transfers involve human and political capital that also adds real opportunity costs to the growth process. Thus a focus on the broad downward arrow is necessary to ensure the continued viability and participation of poor households, but these activities have opportunity costs in terms of economic growth.

However, with success in achieving the objectives in the upper right and lower left boxes, market forces gradually—over decades—bring the poor above a threshold of vulnerability and into sustained food security (connecting macro to micro and short-run to long run). The country has then managed the escape from hunger that Robert Fogel documented for Europe and America in the late eighteenth and early nineteenth centuries and which a number of Asian countries have managed in the twentieth century (Fogel 1991, 1994; Timmer 2004a, 2005a).

By contrast, a world of heightened instability—in global finance and the world food economy—forces policy makers to concentrate their resources in the upper left box, where they are trying to stabilize domestic food prices and keep the poor from slipping deeply and irreversibly into poverty. During food crises, vulnerable households often deplete their human and financial capital just to stay alive. This is the world of poverty traps and enduring food insecurity. We are also trapped in short-run crisis management, both macro and humanitarian. Donors such as the U.S. Agency for International Development (USAID) and the World Bank, as well as governments, can be trapped in crisis mode and end up spending their human and financial resources on emergency relief rather than longer-run development strategies and investments.

Important as crisis management is, it comes directly at the expense of significant progress out of the short-run box on the upper left, both to the right and from top to bottom. From this perspective, instability is a serious impediment to achieving long-run food security. In a world of greater instability induced by climate change, by new financial arrangements, even by the pressures from new political voices, food security is likely to suffer.

The Macro Dimensions of Food Security

At the macro level, famine and food security are at opposite ends of a spectrum.[1] It is only in modern times that entire societies, as opposed to privileged members of those societies, have been able to escape from chronic hunger and the constant threat of famine (Fogel 1991, 1994). Many countries in the developing world, especially in Africa and South Asia, have not managed this escape. In these countries, understanding the factors that cause widespread hunger and vulnerability to famines and the mechanisms available to alleviate their impact remain important intellectual challenges (Ravallion 1987, 1998; Sen 1981; Drèze and Sen 1989; Barrett 2013).

There is a different way to pose the question, however. Rather than asking how to cope with hunger and famine, the question might be how to escape from their threat altogether. As Fogel has emphasized, this is a modern question that is only partly answered by the institutional and technological innovations that are at the heart of modern economic growth (Kuznets 1966). Without these innovations, to be sure, the modern escape from hunger to food security would not have been possible. But the record of economic growth for developing countries since the 1950s shows that even in countries with relatively low levels of per capita income, government interventions to enhance food security can lift the threat of hunger and famine. The countries most successful at this task are in East and Southeast Asia, although the experience in South Asia has been instructive as well. A long-standing debate has been under way for decades on the relevance of these Asian experiences to sub-Saharan Africa (Timmer 1991a; Rozelle 2013).

Food Security and the Escape from Hunger

That rich countries have little to fear from hunger is a simple consequence of Engel's law (the share of a household's budget spent on food declines as its income increases); consumers have a substantial buffer of nonfood expenditures to rely on, even if food prices rise sharply. In a market economy, the rich do not starve. Wars, riots, hurricanes, and floods, for example, can disrupt the smooth functioning of markets, and all in their wake can perish. But rich societies usually have the means to prevent or alleviate such catastrophes, social or natural. Food security in such societies is simply part of a broader net of social securities.

Without the buffer of Engel's law, consumers in poor countries are exposed to routine hunger and are vulnerable to shocks that set off famines (Anderson and Roumasset 1996). And yet, several poor countries have used public action to improve their food security.[2] The typical approach reduces the numbers of the population facing daily hunger by raising the incomes of the poor, while simultaneously managing the food economy in ways that minimize the shocks that might trigger a famine. These countries, some of them quite poor, have managed the same escape from hunger that Fogel documents for Western European countries during the nineteenth century.

History makes it very clear that an early escape from hunger is not primarily the result of private decisions in response to free-market forces. Improved food security stems directly from a set of government policies that integrate the food economy into a development strategy that seeks rapid economic growth with improved income distribution. With such policies, countries in East and Southeast Asia offer evidence that poor countries can escape from hunger in two decades or less—that is, in the space of a single generation. Although two decades may seem an eternity to the hungry and those vulnerable to famine, it is roughly the same as the time between the first World Food Summit in 1974 and the second one in 1996. Despite much well-meaning rhetoric at the earlier summit, including Henry Kissinger's pledge that no child would go to bed hungry by 1985, the failure to place food security in a framework of rural-oriented economic growth, in combination with policies to stabilize domestic food economics, meant that two decades were wasted in many countries. Amazingly, another decade was lost after 1996 before serious attention began to be paid to the role of agricultural development in reducing poverty and increasing food security (World Bank 2007).

Food Security and Economic Analysis

When food security is an objective of national policy, the emphasis is at the macro level. At that level, policy makers have an opportunity to create the aggregate conditions in which households at the micro level can gain access to food on a reliable basis through self-motivated interactions with local markets and home resources. The perspective taken is thus primarily an economic one.

Surprisingly, however, literature on food systems and economic development since the 1980s makes such an economic assessment of food security a difficult task. Three bodies of literature are potentially relevant to analyzing the escape from hunger and provision of food security, and yet none addresses the topic directly.

First, there is a substantial literature on the achievement of rapid economic growth (World Bank 1993; Lucas 1988; Barro and Sala-i-Martin 1994). Export orientation and openness to trade tend to be the dominant policy issues in this literature. In none of this literature is food security even mentioned, and agriculture receives only passing notice. Both omissions are surprising in view of the historical links between agriculture and economic growth and the fact that no country has sustained rapid economic growth without first achieving food security at the macro level (Timmer 2005a).

Second, agriculture is treated in the literature on rapid alleviation of poverty through rural-oriented economic growth (Timmer 1991a, 1995a, 2004a;

Birdsall, Ross, and Sabot 1995; Ravallion and Datt 1996; Lipton 1977; Mellor 1976; World Bank 2007). But even though the agricultural sector and the rural economy are the focus of this literature, no connections are made to price stability or other dimensions of food security. Trade issues are largely ignored.

Third, there is a growing literature on stabilization of domestic food economics and the contribution of stability to economic growth (Bigman 1985; Chisholm 1982; Sarris 1982; Newbery and Stiglitz 1981; Morduch 1995; Timmer 1989, 1996; Dawe 1996; Ramey and Ramey 1995). But the stabilization literature is badly bifurcated into micro-based analyses of decision maker response to risk (both consumers and producers) and macro-based assessments of the impact of instability, usually measured by rates of inflation, on economic growth. Virtually no analysis has been done to connect these two topics, which is surprising in view of the macroeconomic significance of the food sector in most developing countries. A further connection links food security to political stability, which is increasingly important as a factor influencing investment, including foreign direct investments and portfolio investments in these countries.

The Asian Approach to Food Security

Not surprisingly, food security strategies in Asia have been little influenced by this economic literature. The lack of influence stems from at least two factors. First, the dominance of rice in the diets of most Asians, coupled to the extreme price instability in the world market for rice, forced all Asian countries to buffer their domestic rice price from the world price. This clear violation of the border price paradigm and the accompanying restrictions on openness to trade seem to have escaped many advocates of the East Asian miracle, who saw the region's rapid growth as evidence in support of free trade (World Bank 1993).

Second, most Asian governments have paid little attention to formal efforts to define food security as a prelude to government interventions that would be seen as their approach to food security. Instead, the food security strategies of most countries in East and Southeast Asia have had two basic components, neither of which is specifically linked to any of the standard definitions of food security used by international agencies. They have based their strategies on two elements of their domestic food system over which they have some degree of policy control: the sectoral composition of growth in incomes per capita, and prices of food.

The rate and distribution of economic growth are primarily matters of macroeconomic and trade policy (once asset distributions are given as an initial condition). Although there is now widespread controversy over what role Asian governments played in stimulating growth and channeling its distribution, there is no disagreement that high rates of savings and investment, coupled with high and sustained levels of capital productivity, in combination with massive investments in human capital, explain most of the rapid growth that occurred up to 1997 (World Bank 1993; van Donge, Henley, and Lewis 2010). Growth that reached the poor was one component of the food security strategy (Timmer 2004a).

In the second element of the strategy, Asian governments sought to stabilize food prices, in general, and rice prices, in particular. Engel's law ensures that success in generating rapid economic growth that includes the poor is the long-run solution to food security. In the language of Drèze and Sen (1989), such economic growth provides "growth-mediated security." In the meantime, stabilization of food prices in Asia ensured that short-run fluctuations and shocks did not make the poor even more vulnerable to inadequate food intake than their low incomes required.

Most economists are highly dubious that such stability is economically feasible or even desirable. Stabilizing the price of food is not a key element of the "support-led security" measures outlined by Drèze and Sen (1989). In a review of food security and the stochastic aspects of poverty, Anderson and Roumasset (1996) essentially dismiss efforts to stabilize food prices using government interventions:

> Given the high costs of national price stabilization schemes (Newbery and Stiglitz 1979, 1981; Behrman 1984; Williams and Wright 1991) and their effectiveness in stabilizing prices in rural areas, alternative policies decreasing local price instability need to be considered. The most cost-effective method for increasing price stability probably is to remove destabilizing government distortions. Government efforts to nationalize grain markets and to regulate prices across both space and time have the effect of eliminating the private marketing and storage sector. Rather than replacing private marketing, government efforts should be aimed at enhancing private markets through improving transportation, enforcing standards and measures in grain transactions, and implementing small-scale storage technology. (Anderson and Roumasset 1996: 62)

Although this condemnation of national price stabilization schemes might well be appropriate for much of the developing world, it badly misinterprets both the design and implementation of interventions to stabilize rice prices in East and Southeast Asia (Timmer 1993, 1996; Rashid, Gulati, and Cummings 2008; HLPE 2011; Galtier 2009, 2013a).

For food security in this region, the stabilization of domestic rice prices was in fact feasible in the context of an expanding role for an efficient private marketing sector. The resulting stability was not an impediment but was probably conducive to economic growth. In addition, the stabilization scheme and economic growth had to work in tandem to achieve food security as quickly as possible.

Both elements of the Asian strategic approach to food security—rapid economic growth and food price stability—address the macro dimensions of food security, not the micro dimensions found at and within the household. Governments can do many things to improve food security at the household and individual levels, and most countries in East and Southeast Asia have programs to do so. Rural education accessible to females and the poor, family planning and child-care clinics in rural areas, nutrition education, and extension specialists helping to improve home gardens are just a few of the possibilities. Most of the literature on food security deals with approaches at this level, but problems of definition, measurement, project design, and management vastly complicate strategies that rely on household-level interventions (Maxwell 1996).

The complications, in turn, sharply limit the number of households that can be reached with a micro approach. Without dismissing the potential effectiveness of these approaches to enhance food security in particular circumstances, it is still important to realize the scale of the problem. Hundreds of millions of people still do not have food security in Asia, and programs directed at households will not bring it. Only food security at the macro level can provide the appropriate facilitative environment for households to ensure their own food security (Timmer 2005a).

Lessons from Asia

To achieve and sustain food security through rapid economic growth, the Asian experience suggests that the agricultural sector must be linked to food security through three elements: poverty alleviation, stability of the food economy, and growth itself. The effectiveness of these links depends critically on the initial conditions at the start of the process of rapid growth. In particular, agriculture can contribute little to equity if it is based on a "bimodal" distribution of production or to stability if it is concentrated on a single export crop subject to substantial price fluctuations. Even in these circumstances, however, agriculture can be a significant contributor to economic growth (Timmer 1988).

Because of the dominance of rice in Asian diets, the prevalence of smallholder cultivators, the large size of many Asian countries, and the instability of the world rice market, the most successful countries in achieving food security developed effective programs and policies to raise the productivity of their own rice farmers. Many of these programs were explicitly motivated by the objective of self-sufficiency in rice, especially after the world food crisis in 1974, when the world rice market in Bangkok disappeared for nearly half a year. When long-run costs of production are less than the costs of importing, such programs make economic sense, and the self-sufficiency slogan can be used effectively to mobilize political and bureaucratic support.

But self-sufficiency campaigns can do much mischief. Many countries have a deep aversion to international trade, an aversion seen since well before the Corn Laws debate in England in the early nineteenth century. Lindert (1991) has documented an "anti-trade bias" in agricultural pricing and trade policy that has deep historical roots. In the face of this clear political preference for self-sufficiency, Asian countries have had a difficult time distinguishing legitimate concerns for food security from a simple desire not to import anything that could be produced domestically, whatever the costs.

Even in Indonesia—which had an admirable record on stabilization of rice prices until the Asian financial crisis in 1998, higher productivity of rice farmers, and food security for nearly the entire population—self-sufficiency for a broad array of staple foods became a policy objective (Timmer 1994). An assessment of the steps needed to reach this objective concluded as follows:

> If economic considerations should play a significant (but not complete) role in determining appropriate policy for rice and its contribution to Indonesia's food security, the economic arguments are even stronger for all non-rice commodities. There is simply no nutritional, political, or logistical rationale to override the long run signals from the world market on which foods Indonesia should produce domestically and which it will be more economic to import, because

these economic signals are the surest indicators of where to allocate resources for increased productivity and incomes. (Timmer 1994: 39)

Such openness to short-run price signals from world markets for all but the most important staple food, and for all commodities in the long run, will require more open and stable markets in the future than have existed in the past. One major attraction to developing countries of the Uruguay Round of the General Agreement on Tariffs and Trade (GATT) negotiations, which became operational in 1995, was the promise that liberalized agricultural trade would result in more stable prices on world grain markets. However, this promise was obviously premature (Greenfield, de Nigris, and Konandreas 1996; Islam 1996; Dawe 2010a).

The shortages that caused high prices for grain in world markets in 1995 and 1996 served to renew anxieties about future food supplies. Policy-induced reductions in grain stocks caused greater, not less, instability in grain prices. Grain prices stopped declining in 2002 and started to rise gradually until late 2007, when a combination of forces impinged to cause another sharp spike in grain prices (Abbott, Hurt, and Tyner 2008). Asia, with nearly half the world's population to feed, was understandably concerned about how much to respond with new investments in domestic production and how much to rely on privately held stocks available in international markets for supplies of basic grains.

However the balance is struck on domestic versus imported supplies, the striking improvement in food security in Asia since the mid-1960s, especially in East and Southeast Asia, is not likely to be threatened. That is the advantage of "growth-mediated" food security. From this perspective, the lesson from East and Southeast Asia for achieving and maintaining food security can be summed up in this way: a growth process stimulated by a dynamic rural economy leads to rapid poverty alleviation, which, in the context of public action to stabilize food prices, ensures food security.

This approach might not work in other settings—for example, where the staple food grain is traded in more stable world markets, or where landholdings are highly skewed, or where technologies are not available to raise agricultural productivity. At least part of Africa's failure to achieve widespread food security for its population can be attributed to these factors, but part must also be attributed to differential treatment of agriculture by prevailing development strategies in Africa.

Two dimensions are important. First, because government policy makers maintained a macroeconomic environment that supported exports, Southeast Asia invested heavily in building a comparative advantage in a wide range of agricultural exports. The contrast with Africa is striking.

> Much can be learned from Asia's experience of changing its long-term comparative advantage in export commodities through investments in research, training and market development over the past three decades. For example, Thailand, Pakistan and Vietnam are routinely selling rice throughout Africa by outcompeting African farmers even after international and internal transport charges are taken into account. Moreover, Nigeria, Kenya and many other countries are importing palm oil from Malaysia to meet their growing demand for cooking oil. This is especially humbling to Nigeria because at independence in 1960, it was the world's leading producer and exporter of palm oil. Today, Malaysia's production of palm oil is about ten times larger than that of Nigeria. (Eicher 1992: 80)

Second, governments in Southeast Asia actively sought to provide food security to domestic consumers, both urban and rural. Their ability to do so had both economic and political roots. Because populations were large in relation to agricultural resources, and because domestic rice consumption was large in relation to supplies available in world markets, countries in Southeast Asia were forced to develop successful rice intensification programs to ensure domestic food security (Djurfeldt et al. 2005; van Donge, Henley, and Lewis 2010).

As noted earlier, this food security was implemented in the short run through policies that stabilized rice prices. But these policies would have been impossible to sustain without raising productivity in the domestic rice economy. One broader theme of this volume—that food price stabilization is a major determinant of investment rates and subsequent economic growth—is also, in the context of Southeast Asia, an argument for substantial investment to raise productivity in the cultivation of food staples.

However, the multistaple food economies of Africa differ markedly from the irrigated rice economies of Southeast Asia. Stabilization of rice prices in Asia stimulated economic growth. It is not known whether similar linkages can be established in the agricultural environment of Africa. If the rice economy of Asia is sufficiently different from food systems of Africa, which are based on maize, millet, sorghum, cassava, and yams, substantial doubt will be cast on the relevance to Africa of the models of food security and economic growth that propelled Southeast Asia. Unless new growth models can be discovered specifically for the African context—and, in several decades of trying, the search is still on—such doubts are very troubling. We may be in the awkward position of knowing that agricultural development and stabilization of the domestic food economy are necessary for rapid economic growth but not knowing how to do it in Africa (Badiane 2011).

How Governments Learn About Food Security: Asia and Africa

The very nature of irrigated rice cultivation means that farmers are not able to raise their rice yields successfully unless the government provides key ingredients in the intensification process. At the same time, governments cannot intensify rice cultivation directly. Farmers are needed to make all the key managerial decisions that translate productive potential into high yields. An important symbiosis exists in the relationship between farmers and governments, even if the political system does not support a democratic voice for the rural population. Each party is dependent on the other to provide a crucial element of success.

Modernizing Asian Agriculture

Asian rice cultivation uses a small-farmer technology that offers high rewards to farmer knowledge and skilled management. These rewards depend on availability of high-yielding varieties, productive inputs, and incentives for their use, all of which can be delivered efficiently only through a system of competitive rural markets. Governments have had to build rural marketing systems that were able to connect farmers with local buying agents, thus transmitting market information and permitting exchange to take place, which generated gains in efficiency from trade. The marketing system serves to transform agricultural commodities at the farm gate into foods at the time, place, and form desired by consumers. An efficient marketing system has to solve the problem of price discovery, at least at the local level and seasonally, even if government price policy sets a band in which such price discovery must take place.[3]

Asian governments have also had to make large-scale investments in rural infrastructure. Managing these investments generated important opportunities for "learning by doing" on the part of government bureaucrats and policy makers. Part of this rural infrastructure supported the marketing system—roads, communications systems, market centers, and so on. But large investments were also needed in irrigation systems so that rice cultivation could be intensified successfully. Such systems have been the responsibility of governments nearly everywhere. The coordination and planning skills required to design, build, and maintain large-scale irrigation systems imposed serious obligations on those governments that undertook the tasks successfully. On the other hand, governments that acquired these skills by learning how to manage irrigation-based agriculture also acquired a confidence in governance that was quickly applied to other dimensions of managing economic growth.

The key steps in the argument are now in place. Food security became the principal task of Asian governments in countries with large populations in relation to their arable land resources. Policies to stabilize rice prices were the key interventions used to provide food security at the national level. Heavy reliance on rice imports was not feasible unless the country was small—for example, Singapore, Hong Kong, and to some extent Malaysia. But the larger countries of Southeast Asia had to grow nearly all of their own rice. Inducing farmers to produce rice for their own needs as well as surpluses for urban consumers required governments to pursue an agricultural development strategy that focused on small farmers, reached them via markets, and raised the productivity potential of rice cultivation through large investments in rural infrastructure, irrigation, and research on high-yielding rice varieties.

In a comparative context there are two important questions. Does the analytical support for policies that stabilize food prices hold only for rice economies? Is the implementation of such policies inherently more difficult and expensive in multistaple food economies? If the benefits are smaller and the costs are larger in African food systems, stabilizing food prices might not be necessary or desirable. But if food prices are not stabilized, how can the investment climate be stabilized for farmers and urban industrialists? How can consumers be assured of food security? What would stimulate the dynamic linkages between agriculture and industry that were the basis of rapid economic growth in East and Southeast Asia?

Both tasks undertaken by Asian governments—reaching small farmers via markets and raising agricultural productivity—created positive externalities for the overall process of economic growth in addition to the direct contribution from higher output of the staple food grain and the consequent lowering of the real wage bill.[4] First, making rural markets work is a direct lesson in the efficacy of a market-oriented economy. Building an efficient rural marketing system requires careful intervention and support from the government, but not too much if the private sector is to grow, learn how to take risks, and compete effectively. Governments must learn how to play their role in a market economy just as traders, banks, shipping companies, and supporting institutions must learn theirs. Solving the problem of food security in Asia forced governments to learn the importance of a market-oriented economy and the means to make it work.

Simultaneously, however, the need to invest in public infrastructure, irrigation, research, and extension systems and to ensure the price stability that enabled the market economy to grow quickly and efficiently also forced Asian governments to develop a high degree of governmental competence in economic management. Without both components—a market economy and a competent government investing in agriculture—Asian countries could not have developed the high degree of food security that they have achieved at the national level. Not all countries have been equally successful in translating this aggregate degree of food security into equitable access to food on the part of all households. That success would require a government devoted to alleviating poverty as well as stimulating growth while maintaining political stability. Among the countries of Southeast Asia, Malaysia, Vietnam, and Indonesia have good records of achieving all three objectives of growth, stability, and improved welfare.

If this argument for a market economy and competent management on the part of government is correct, the rapid economic growth in Southeast Asia since the 1960s can be traced to a considerable extent to the development of a new rice technology that greatly increased yield potential when the surrounding environment—economic, ecological, and political—was conducive to rapid adoption by farmers. The elements of this environment are well known for irrigated rice systems, but they have never been assembled successfully for the staple foods of sub-Saharan Africa.

Impediments to Modernizing African Agriculture

The staple food economies of sub-Saharan Africa are not easily described with the simplicity possible for rice cultivation in Asia. Two standard references on African food systems, Johnston (1958) and Grigg (1974), stress the heterogeneity and complexity of production systems even within small localities. The point can be made in a vivid fashion by comparing the area around Karawang in West Java, Indonesia, one of the country's major rice bowls, and the Machakos region of Kenya, home to many of the country's most progressive small farmers. A drive across Karawang reveals that irrigated rice is grown as far as the eye can see. Small home gardens surround the many villages, but farming is almost completely a matter of managing a homogeneous ecological environment to grow one crop. The relative simplicity of developing a high-yielding technology for this environment and of learning to optimize its management accounts for the nearly universal adoption of International Rice Research Institute (IRRI) varieties and the high and stable yields produced by them.[5]

The contrast with Kenya and the rest of sub-Saharan Africa is striking. Wherever it is possible to drive through regions of intensive food production—and the poor state of the road networks often makes driving difficult—an unbroken stretch of a single food crop is uncommon. Small patches of land with multiple crops and intercropping are the norm, and the pattern shifts radically as one crosses areas with changed altitude, soil type, or rainfall. Maize, sorghum, millet, cassava, yams, groundnuts, cowpeas, and many others are intercropped in complex combinations, which reflect the farmer's knowledge of local growing conditions, available technologies, market prices, and the family need for food.

Productivity Gains in Multistaple Food Systems

Raising the productivity of such complicated, multistaple food systems requires more of agricultural scientists than improving the average yield of a single crop when grown under ideal conditions in a pure stand. As with upland regions in Asia, the farming systems research has not been extensive enough to identify the constraints facing farmers in these heterogeneous environments.[6] The economic as well as the ecological interactions among various crops need to be analyzed and incorporated into the research strategy. When successful results have been achieved at the research center, they must then be transmitted back to farmers through messages that contain the same range of complexity that stimulated the development of new crop varieties and farming systems in the first place.

The point here is not that rice intensification is easy—that would misrepresent the hard-won achievements in Asia since the mid-1960s and the continuing challenge facing Asian researchers, farmers, and policy makers—but it is obviously harder to achieve similar results in Africa. The farming systems that produce the great bulk of Africa's food staples are much more complicated and less understood by researchers and operate under environmental stresses that vary more widely, especially moisture stress, than in the rice-based systems of Asia. A major difference between Africa and Southeast Asia is the role of women in household decision making and management of food crop production, which complicates the design of institutions that provide modern inputs, new technology, and credit to farmers. None of these difficulties is insurmountable with appropriate investments in research, infrastructure, and incentives. It remains to be seen how much more expensive these investments will be in Africa than they were in Asia.[7] A serious test has yet to be made.

A multistaple food system is more complicated to modernize not only at the farm level but also at the level of marketing inputs and output. Marketing a wide variety of different commodities with varying degrees of substitutability requires greater knowledge on the part of traders, higher storage and transactions costs because of smaller average lots handled, and far more sophisticated policy designs if governments attempt to stabilize prices for the three or four important food staples (Jayne 2009). But is this degree of intervention in pricing necessary? In the specific context of Ghana, Alderman (1992) asked whether cross-commodity substitution in consumption, production, and storage is adequate to link prices of maize with prices of sorghum and millet. The answer is a qualified yes, with price integration requiring three months on average. Such integration offers the potential for government policy to stabilize the price of maize only, if that is desirable, while allowing market forces to transmit these stable prices to other staple foods that are close substitutes.[8]

Reliance on Imported Food

The food economy of Africa has one other feature that distinguishes it from the rice economy of Southeast Asia: its heavy reliance on imported wheat to provision urban areas. Although wheat is an increasingly popular food in urban Asia, in none of the Southeast Asian countries does it account for as much as 10 percent of caloric intake. By contrast, in the cities of sub-Saharan

Africa, where roughly 30 percent of the population lives, an average of 50 kilograms per capita of imported grain, most of it wheat, provides nearly 500 calories per day, or nearly 25 percent of daily energy intake. To a substantial extent, sub-Saharan Africa is dependent on world grain markets to provision its urban (and vocal) population.

But the world market for wheat (and yellow maize) is not nearly as unstable as the world rice market (at least historically—experience since 2009 has been reversed). Total volumes traded are much higher—on the order of 100 million tons per year each for wheat and maize, compared with only 30 million tons for rice. The shares of production are similarly larger. Rice trade is just 5 to 7 percent of world production, whereas wheat and maize are 20 and 15 percent, respectively. The thinness of the world rice market has made it notoriously unstable, thus forcing policy makers in rice-consuming countries to insulate their domestic rice economies from the world market. Such insulation is not nearly so important for economies whose staple food is wheat or yellow maize. Many African cities depend heavily on imported wheat for their staple food supply, and several suffered food riots during the price spikes in 2008 and again in 2010.[9]

Compared with a rice-based, domestically supplied economy, a wheat-based, import-supplied food economy does not have the same imperative to develop its domestic food production. When the domestic staples produced are root crops or specialized coarse grains not available in world markets, governments are even less inclined to invest in domestic food production. If a political economy with a powerful urban bias is superimposed on this bifurcated food economy, the historical neglect of African food producers is easily understandable.[10] It is not easy to see how to end this neglect, either politically or economically. In particular, if price stabilization of staple foods is important to both consumers and producers, the nontradable status of root crops rules out the trade-oriented approach used in Southeast Asia. Price fluctuations in world markets for white maize and local varieties of sorghum and millet are similar to those for rice, and high costs for transportation mean extraordinarily wide margins between CIF import and FOB export prices.[11]

Price Stability, Agricultural Productivity, and Economic Growth

Switching the role of food imports from the mainstay of food security to a vehicle for stabilizing the domestic food economy at levels that provide ample incentives to farmers to increase productivity is an enormous challenge for African governments. Cereal imports are increasing steadily, and many of them are provided as food aid. Most urban food systems are not well linked to domestic supplies but rely heavily on imports (but see Chapter 5 for early signs that African supply chains are beginning to connect domestic producers with urban consumers). Redressing this bias requires more than simply improving price incentives to farmers, although this step is necessary. A marketing system that is "pointing in the wrong direction" requires substantial changes in ways of doing business, infrastructure, institutions, and credit facilities before food supplies grown domestically can be the foundation of a stable and secure food system.

Without these changes, it is difficult to see how stability in food prices and genuine food security can be achieved in Africa. Reliance on food aid and cheap grain imports undermines the political will needed to invest in domestic agriculture through a form of "Dutch disease"—the bias in a domestic economy that occurs when foreign exchange is available very cheaply, from petroleum or mineral exports, for example—that undervalues local food production. Such reliance is not sustainable in the long run, especially if world grain prices remain high by recent historical standards. Even worse, it may not be stable in the short run. Africa relies heavily on exports of primary commodities to earn the foreign exchange needed to finance a food import strategy. The prices of these commodities in world markets are highly unstable. The result is that earnings of foreign exchange are also highly unstable, thus destabilizing the entire macro economy. Research by Dawe (1996) has demonstrated that this destabilization takes a significant toll in terms of economic growth. Because it is harder to stabilize export earnings than to stabilize food prices, a switch in priority away from export crops toward domestic production of food crops is likely to improve food security as well as stimulate economic growth.

Nothing said so far suggests that such a switch will be easy. A new priority will have to be placed on rural infrastructure and research on raising productivity of farming systems. Governments will have to intervene to restructure incentives in favor of food production, and these incentives will involve both stability and price levels for inputs and output. Such priorities were not so difficult to establish in the Asian context, where populations are large relative to land resources and where the density of economic activity justifies an extensive network of roads and traders who use them. Population pressures and favorable ecological settings also justified massive investment in irrigation systems that have stabilized Asian agricultural output while raising crop yields. It is easy to see how the emphasis on increasing domestic rice production evolved in the Asian context as a mechanism for stabilizing rice prices. This focus on production was the key to food security at the national level. It is difficult to see how a similar orientation can evolve in Africa.

Mastering the Political Economy of Development

The failure of African countries to look to domestic agriculture as the basic mechanism for providing food security comes at a high cost in a final arena: learning how to manage the ingredients of rapid economic growth. By solving their food problems through agricultural development, Asian governments arguably learned both the appropriate role of the government in this process and the careful management of the economic environment required to bring it about. "Asian governments realized, in the words of Lee Kuan Yew, that they 'must create an agricultural surplus to get their industrial sector going.' Rich and industrious rice-farmers have been the foundation of Asia's industrialization" (*Economist* 1991: 18). There is an obvious economic rationale to the strategy articulated by Lee Kuan Yew, even if, as prime minister of Singapore, he did not have to follow it for his own country. The high level of governmental competence in Asia in managing the process of economic growth can be explained as resulting from the learning that took place from the necessity and complexity of solving Asian countries' domestic food problems. The low level of competence at similar tasks in Africa—demonstrated from the 1960s until quite recently—can be traced to development strategies that met growing urban food needs from imports. That is, much of the differential competence can be traced directly to how governments treated and learned from their agricultural sectors. The underlying political economy of the different approaches has already been explained, but the full consequences of the difference are just now being recognized.

CHAPTER 3

Understanding Food Security Dynamics: Models and Numbers

From a macro perspective, the two main drivers of food security in a country (and globally) are household incomes and food prices. To understand the dynamics of food security, it is necessary to understand the dynamics of these two drivers. That, of course, is no small task. Still, the development profession has learned a lot about the causes and determinants of rapid economic growth that reaches the poor (pro-poor growth) and the reasons for high and volatile prices for food. The agricultural economy, it turns out, is central to both.

Achieving food security through a macro strategic approach involves active development of the agricultural and rural economy to link and stimulate rapid economic growth, poverty alleviation, and stability (Figure 5). In turn, each of these three elements is a primary input into food security at both the macro and micro levels.

The mechanisms behind this strategic approach to food security are not well understood analytically or quantified empirically, and they obviously vary from country to country. The basic arguments, however, are straightforward and have been made for some time. Improvements in agricultural productivity that are stimulated by government investment in rural infrastructure, agricultural research and extension, irrigation, and appropriate price incentives contribute directly to economic growth, poverty alleviation, and stability (Johnston and Mellor 1961; Mellor 1976; Timmer 1992, 1995b, 2009a; World Bank 2007).

For the large countries of Asia, investments to raise the productivity of domestic rice producers brought greater stability to the rice economy at the macro level, mostly because reliance on the world market was destabilizing

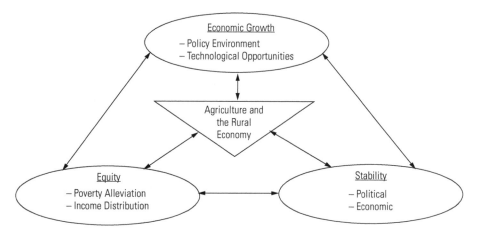

Figure 5. The Development Trilogy and the Role of Agriculture
Source: Timmer (2000).

in relation to domestic production. Expanded rice production and greater purchasing power in rural areas, stimulated by the profitable rice economy, improved the stability of food intake of rural households.

The dynamic rural economy helped to reduce poverty quickly by inducing higher real wages. The combination of government investment, stable prices at incentive levels, and higher wages helped reduce the substantial degree of urban bias found in most development strategies (Lipton 1977, 1993). Equity is nearly always enhanced when urban and rural areas compete equally for policy attention and resources.

Once the process of rapid growth is under way, political tensions are inevitably induced by a structural transformation that takes place too rapidly for resources to move smoothly from the rural to the urban sector (Anderson and Hayami 1986; Anderson, Rausser, and Swinnen 2013; Timmer 1993, 2009a). The agricultural sector is less prone to these tensions if the gap between rural and urban incomes does not widen too much. All successfully growing countries have had to find ways to keep this gap from widening so much that it destabilizes the political economy and jeopardizes continued investment.

Growth in agricultural productivity connects to more rapid economic growth in the rest of the economy. An entire body of literature exists that analyzes the role of agriculture in economic growth (Johnston and Mellor 1961; Eicher and Staatz 1998 Timmer 1988, 1992, 1995b). Specific linkages that have been identified in this literature work through the capital and labor markets, as analyzed by Lewis (1954); through product markets, as specified by Johnston and Mellor (1961); and through a variety of nonmarket connections that involve market failures and require nonequilibrium growth models to understand (Timmer 1995a).

In turn, economic growth, poverty alleviation, and stability are linked to each other through the "virtuous circles" reviewed by Birdsall, Ross, and Sabot (1995). Greater stability of the food economy contributes to faster economic growth by reducing signal extraction problems, lengthening the investment horizon, and reducing political instability (Ramey and Ramey 1995; Dawe 1996; Dawe and Timmer 2012). In the other direction, stability contributes to equity and poverty alleviation by reducing the vulnerability of the poor to sudden shocks in food prices or availability (Galtier 2009, 2013a). Greater equity also stimulates investment in human capital, especially in rural areas (Williamson 1993; Birdsall, Ross, and Sabot 1995), thus speeding up economic growth.

One important outcome of this strategic approach is the achievement of food security. This occurs when economic growth has raised the poor above a meaningful poverty line and when stabilization of the food economy prevents exogenous shocks from threatening their food intake. In this approach, food security is sustained by the productivity of the poor themselves, but this security continues to depend on public action to maintain a stable macro environment, including the food economy, as the precursor to that productivity.

The Analytics of What Causes Food Price Spikes

Understanding causation implies an empirically refutable model of mechanisms of action. For food prices, this means an analytical model based on supply and demand mechanisms with equilibrium prices derived from basic competitive forces. There are many such models in existence but none that address the specific issues discussed here (Munier 2008; Trostle 2008).

We want to understand the contribution from a wide range of basic causes to high prices of important food commodities—for example, rice, wheat, corn, and palm oil. Some of these causes may be exogenous—for example, weather shocks or legislated mandates for biofuel usage. But many will be endogenous—for example, responses of producers and consumers to prices

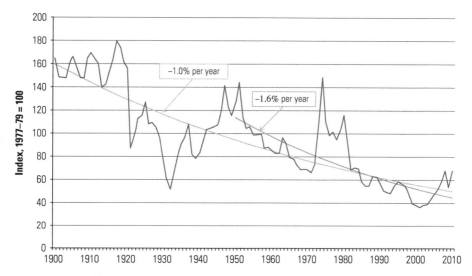

Figure 6. Grillis and Yang Global Agricultural Price Index (updated)
Note: Adjusted for inflation by the U.S. GDP price deflator.

themselves, perhaps even policy responses of governments to prices. Export bans for rice or wheat as a way to prevent domestic food price inflation are an obvious example (Brahmbhatt and Christiaensen 2008).

The model of price formation presented here is designed to build intuition about what causes run-ups in world market prices. The price spike in 2007–8 provides the empirical background to the model's logic and development (Figure 6).

A Simple Model of Price Formation to Use as a Heuristic Device

Consider the most basic model of commodity price formation that is capable of illuminating our problem.[1]

$$D_t = f(a_{t,} P_t, sr_d, P_{t-n}, lr_d) = a_t P_t^{sr_d} P_{t-n}^{lr_d}.$$
$$S_t = g(b_{t,} P_t, sr_s, P_{t-n}, lr_s) = b_t P_t^{sr_s} P_{t-n}^{lr_s}$$

where D_t = demand for the commodity during time t; S_t = supply of the commodity during time t; f and g = functional forms for demand and supply functions, respectively; a_t = time-dependent shifters of the demand curve;

b_t = time-dependent shifters of the supply curve; P_t = equilibrium market price during time t; P_{t-n} = market price during some previous time period $t-n$; and, sr_d, sr_s, lr_d, and lr_s = indicators that demand and supply responses will vary depending on whether they are in the short run sr or long run lr. In the specification below, these will be short-run and long-run supply and demand elasticities.

In short-run equilibrium, $D_t = S_t$. For simplicity (and the ability to work directly with supply and demand elasticities), assume the demand and supply functions are Cobb-Douglas. Then

$$\log a_t + sr_d \log P_t + lr_d \log P_{t-n} = \log b_t + sr_s \log P_t + lr_s \log P_{t-n}$$

Solving for the equilibrium price P,

$$\log P_t = [\log b_t - \log a_t] / [sr_d - sr_s] + \log P_{t-n} [lr_s - lr_d] / [sr_d - sr_s]$$

Taking first differences to see the factors that explain a change in price from $t-1$ to t reveals a somewhat complicated result:

$$d \log P_t = \{[\log b_t - \log b_{t-1}] - [\log a_t - \log a_{t-1}]\} / [sr_d - sr_s]$$
$$+ [\log P_{t-n} - \log P_{t-(n+1)}][lr_s - lr_d] / [sr_d - sr_s],$$

where $d \log P_t$ = the percentage change in price from time period $t-1$ to time period t (for relatively small changes). This is what we are trying to explain. What "causes" changes in $d \log P_t$? Why are food prices high or low?

To answer these questions, it helps to simplify the equation. Let SR = the net short-run supply and demand response $sr_d - sr_s$, which is always negative because $sr_d < 0$ and $sr_s > 0$. Let LR = the net long-run supply and demand response $lr_s - lr_d$, which is always positive, for similar reasons (note that the demand coefficient is subtracted from the supply coefficient in this case, the opposite from the short-run coefficients above). Let $d \log b_t = \log b_t - \log b_{t-1}$, which for small changes is the percentage change in the supply shifters. Let $d \log a_t = \log a_t - \log a_{t-1}$, which for small changes is the percentage change in the demand shifters. Finally, let $d \log P_{t-n} = \log P_{t-n} - \log P_{t-(n+1)}$, which for small changes is the percentage change in the commodity price for some specified number of time periods in the past, for example, five or ten years (after which the long-run producer and consumer responses to price have been realized).

Combining all of these new definitions, we have a simpler equation explaining percentage changes in commodity prices:

Percent change in P_t = [percent change in b_t – percent change in a_t]/SR
+ [percent change in P_{t-n}] LR/SR

The surprising result is how simple the answer appears to be. There are four key drivers:

- the relative size of changes in a_t to b_t—that is, factors shifting the demand curve relative to factors shifting the supply curve;
- the relative size of short-run supply and demand elasticities (sr_s and sr_d);
- the relative size of long-run supply and demand elasticities (lr_s and lr_d); and
- how large the price change was in earlier time periods.

Why the Analytics Matter

A simple numerical example, with plausible parameters, shows the power of this explanatory equation. Assume the following numerical parameters for purposes of illustration:

$sr_d = -0.10$
$sr_s = +0.05$
$lr_d = -0.30$
$lr_s = +0.50$

These values imply that $SR = -0.15$ and $LR = 0.80$.

The short-run elasticities assumed here are quite low but realistic for annual responses. Demand responds 1 percent for a 10 percent change in price; supply only responds by half a percent to a similar 10 percent price change (the signs, of course, are negative for demand and positive for supply responses).

The long-run elasticities are also on the low side of econometric estimates but again seem realistic for a world facing increasing resource constraints. Although some estimates of long-run supply response are quite high—approaching unity or higher—these were estimated for time periods when acreage expansion was significant and fertilizer usage was just becoming widespread (Peterson 1979).

Assume, as seems to be the case since the early 2000s, that demand drivers have been larger than supply drivers, with demand shifting out by 3.0 percent per year and supply shifting out just 1.5 percent per year. Finally, assume that prices in the past have been low. The change in P_{t-n} is -10.0 percent. What do all these parameters mean for current price change?

Plugging these values into the price change equation yields the following result:

$$Percent\ change\ in\ P_t = [1.5\% - 3.0\%]/-0.15 + [-10.0\%]0.80/-0.15$$
$$= [10.0\%] + [53.3\%]$$
$$= 63.3\%\ higher.$$

This is a very dramatic result. The imbalance between current supply and demand drivers causes the price to rise by 10 percent, but the historically low prices (and only a 10 percent decline in the earlier period) cause current prices to be 53 percent higher, as the long-term, lagged response from producers and consumers to these earlier low prices has a very large quantitative impact. Much of the slow run-up in food prices from 2003 to 2007 would seem to be caused by producers and consumers gradually responding (i.e., reflecting their "long-run" responses) to earlier episodes of low prices, especially from the late 1990s until about 2003. For example, between 1996 and 2001, the real price of rice declined by 14.7 percent per year in world markets!

Over long periods of time, the first driver is obviously the most important—how fast is the demand curve shifting relative to the supply curve? At the level of generality specified in this model, the actual underlying causes of these shifts do not matter. All that matters is the net result. If the demand curve is shifting outward by 3 percent per year, and the supply curve is shifting out by just 1.5 percent per year, the difference of 1.5 percent per year will push prices higher by an amount determined by net short-run supply and demand elasticities with respect to price. The simple fact is that changes in commodity prices are driven by the net of *aggregate* trends in supply and demand, not their composition.

The analytical model of price formation makes a sharp and important distinction between factors that shift the demand and supply curves (the a_t and b_t coefficients) and the responsiveness of farmers and consumers to changes in the market price (the sr_s and sr_d coefficients), which show up as movements along the supply and demand curve. Analytically, the distinction is very clear, but empirically, it is often hard to tell the difference. If farmers use more fertilizer in response to higher prices for grain, should this count as part of the supply response or as a supply shifter? If governments and donor agencies restrict their funding of agricultural research because of low prices for grain, is the resulting lower productivity potential a smaller supply shifter a decade later or a long-run response to prices? Whatever the labels, it is important to understand the causes.

The Composition of Changing Demand and Supply Trends

This ambiguity can be a serious problem, because it is the composition of changing demand and supply trends that we are seeking to understand, even quantify, as a way to understand the causes of food price spikes. The list of possible factors is long. For demand, it includes (in order of predictability):

1) Population (driven by demographic transition, fertility, mortality, famine)
2) Income growth (driven by economic policy, trade, technology, governance)
   a) Direct consumption
   b) Indirect consumption through livestock feeding or industrial utilization
3) Income distribution (driven by globalization, food prices, agricultural growth, structural transformation, technological change, and tax policy)
4) Biofuel demands (driven by political mandates and the price of petroleum)
   a) Direct demand for corn and vegetable oils
   b) Ripple effects on other commodities
5) U.S. dollar depreciation (most commodities on world markets are priced in dollars)
6) Food prices (endogenous, driven by supply/demand balance and technical change; impact felt through the demand elasticities)
7) Private stockholding
   a) Commercial (driven by price expectations and supply of storage)
   b) Household (driven by price panics and hoarding)

8) Public stockholding (driven by buffer stock policy)
    a) Trade policy
    b) Procurement policy
9) Financial speculation
    a) Futures/options markets and sophisticated speculators
    b) Role of commodity index funds available to general investors

For supply, the list is not as long, but the factors may be even more difficult to understand and quantify:

1) Area expansion
    a) Irrigation and cost of water
    b) Deforestation and environmental costs
    c) "Benign" area expansion in Africa and Latin America?
2) Yield growth
    a) Availability and costs of inputs
      i) Costs of fertilizer
      ii) Costs of energy
      iii) Sustainability issues
    b) Seed technology and the GMO debate
    c) Management improvements/farmer knowledge
3) Variability
    a) Weather
    b) Climate change

It would be nice to put quantitative weights on each of the supply and demand factors in terms of their role in causing the current high levels of food prices for key commodities: rice, wheat, corn, and palm oil. The main debates have been over how much biofuels and financial speculation have caused the run-up in food and oil prices. A paper by Don Mitchell, senior commodity economist at the World Bank, for example, caused a furor when it was "leaked" to the press in July 2008. Mitchell found that perhaps three-quarters of the run-up in grain prices was caused by U.S. policy toward ethanol production from corn (Mitchell 2008). At the same time, the U.S. secretary of agriculture was arguing publicly at the FAO Food Summit in June 2008 that biofuel production played only a minor role in high food prices—2 to 3 percent. Somebody was wrong.

The point is that these are contentious issues and have no clearly accepted methodology for resolving them, a point also stressed by Abbot, Hurt, and Tyner (2008: 8, emphasis added): "The factors driving current food price increases are complex. We make no attempt to calculate what percentage of price changes are attributable to the many disparate causes, and, indeed, *think it is impossible to do so.*" The simple model here reveals why. If, for example, population growth is adding 1.5 percent per year to demand for a staple food grain, income growth is adding 0.5 percent per year to direct demand for that grain, and indirect demand via livestock feeding is adding 1.0 percent per year, demand is growing by 3 percent per year. If, at the same time, supply is growing by 1.5 percent per year (0.5 percent from area expansion and 1.0 percent from annual yield growth, for example), the net result is that aggregate demand growth exceeds aggregate supply growth by 1.5 percent per year, and this deficiency will put upward pressure on the equilibrium price of this food grain. Even if lagged prices had been in long-run equilibrium until demand shifters started to outstrip supply shifters, just this imbalance of 1.5 percent per year leads to price increases of 10 percent per year, with the assumed short-run supply and demand elasticities.

There is no meaningful way to identify the element of demand that is growing too fast as long as each of the components of growth in demand is growing relatively steadily. Indeed, the blame for the rising price for grain can equally be laid at supply growth that is too slow. Market-clearing prices are driven by the aggregate of supply and demand in that market at a point in time. Prices themselves cannot reveal the underlying composition of those supplies and demands (the origin of the classical identification problem).

This perspective on formation of market prices presents a conundrum. The slow and steady shifters of both supply and demand can explain gradual increases in prices, such as those seen from the mid-2000s until late 2007. The lagged response to earlier periods of low prices can explain some acceleration in these prices, especially for rice and wheat. But the explosion in food prices late in 2007 and in the first half of 2008 clearly requires additional explanation involving factors not incorporated in the simple model of price formation just outlined. Much of the additional analytical explanation of short-run price movements will be provided from the supply-of-storage model, with its focus on links between inventory movements and price expectations in futures markets.

None of these general models of price formation is directly relevant to any particular country's specific experience at a point in time. Prices in world markets are usually transmitted into domestic economies fairly completely over long periods of time. From year to year, however, transmission of prices is often restricted by import and export controls at the border. These controls—the essence of domestic price stabilization policies—are the subject of Chapter 6.

The Supply-of-Storage Model and Short-Run Price Behavior

The link between the supply of grain held in storage and prices in both spot and futures markets has long been the subject of analytical attention (Working 1933, 1948, 1949; Keynes 1936; Kaldor 1939; Telser 1958; Brennen 1958; Cootner 1960, 1961; Weymar 1968; Williams and Wright 1991). The basic supply-of-storage model that has emerged from this theoretical and empirical work is the foundation for understanding short-run price behavior for storable commodities (Houthakker 1987). It stresses the interrelated behavior of speculators and hedgers as they judge inventory levels in relation to use. The formation of price expectations is the key to this behavior.

The basic supply-of-storage model is a simple extension of the supply/demand model already used here. The formulation here follows Weymar's presentation, with three behavioral equations and one identity (error terms are omitted for simplicity), where C = consumption, P = price, P^L = lagged price, H = production (harvest), I = inventory, and P^* = price expected at some point in the future:

$$C_t = f_c(P_t, P_t^L) \tag{1}$$
$$H_t = f_h(P_t, P_t^L) \tag{2}$$
$$(P_t^* - P_t) = f_p(I_t) \tag{3}$$
$$I_t = I_{t-1} + H_t - C_t, \tag{4}$$

The first two equations, indicating the dependency of consumption and production on current and/or lagged price, reflect traditional micro economic theory. While other variables may appear in these relationships (e.g. consumer income, government support levels), their exclusion here will not affect the discussion that follows. [The third equation] represents the "supply of storage" curve . . . and reflects the notion that the amount of a commodity that people are willing to carry in inventory depends on their expectations as to future price behavior. If they feel that the price will increase substantially, they will be willing to carry heavier inventories (supply more storage) than would otherwise be the case. Because the inventory level is in fact determined by the identity expressed in [the fourth equation], the supply of storage function can be used to explain the gap between the current price and price expectations in terms of the current inventory level. (Weymar 1968: 28)

Thus the relationship between current inventories and current price helps explain price expectations, and vice versa. These price expectations can then be expressed in prices on futures markets. The actual working out of this theory empirically requires a close understanding of the behavior of market participants—farmers, traders, processors, and end users (consumers)—in their role as hedgers or speculators. The current controversy over the role of "outside" speculators—investors who are not active participants in the commodity system—has many precursors in the history and analysis of commodity price formation on futures markets (see, for example, the Telser-Kaldor debate reviewed by Cootner [1960]).

The empirical difficulty in using the supply-of-storage model to understand short-run price behavior is having current information on inventory levels. This is not such a severe problem when virtually all the commodity storage is in commercial hands, as with cocoa or wheat, and stock levels for such commodities can be estimated fairly accurately. For a commodity such as rice, however, which is mostly grown by smallholders, marketed by a dense network of small traders and processors, and purchased by consumers in a readily storable form (milled rice), stock levels can change at any or all levels of the supply chain, and there are virtually no data available on these inventory levels. To make matters worse, a number of countries (especially China) regard the size of publicly held stocks of grain as a state secret. It is thought that China holds as much rice in storage as the rest of the world combined.

For the purposes here, then, the main advantage of the supply-of-storage model is its ability to build conceptual links between long-run supply and demand trends, where basic models of producers and consumers provide operational guidelines to decision making and price formation, and very short-run movements in prices that often seem totally divorced from supply and demand fundamentals. Because long-run trends are gradually built up from short-run observations, these links are essential for understanding price behavior even in the long run.

The key, then, to making the supply-of-storage model operational in the short run is to use it to gain insight on formation of price expectations. In the very short run, from day to day or week to week, these expectations seem to be driven by a combination of price behavior for commodities broadly and the specifics of individual commodities. Broad commodity price trends are captured by the IMF commodity price index, the *Economist* price index, or the Goldman-Sachs commodity price index, for example. Thus, traders operating in any one specific commodity market, such as oil, corn, or wheat, will be following closely the broader price movements for all commodities (Sanders and Irwin 2008; Irwin, Sanders, and Merrin 2009). These broad price movements seem to be driven by basic macroeconomic forces such as rates of economic growth, the value of international currencies, especially the U.S. dollar, and relative rates of inflation.

But traders are also following closely the specifics of the commodity as well. Here inventories (especially relative to actual use for consumption) are the key to price formation, once the harvest/supply situation for the crop is established. At this point, the analytics of price behavior for oil or metals begin to look quite different from the analytics of food commodities at this stage, as seasonal production and the inherent need to store the commodity for daily use throughout the year drive inventory behavior via the supply of storage (Wright 2012).

Typically, commodities for which inventory data are reasonably reliable tend to have their prices driven by unexpected supply behavior. Commodities with poor data on inventories, especially where significant inventories can be in the hands of millions of small agents—farmers, traders, or consumers—tend to have their extremes in price behavior generated by rapidly changing price expectations themselves, and consequent hoarding or dishoarding. The short-run price dynamics for rice thus look significantly different from those for wheat or corn, partly because of the different industrial organization of the respective commodity systems. There are surprisingly few studies of individual commodity systems that are set within this broader macroeconomic and organizational framework (see Timmer

[1987] for an exception). The world food crisis in 2008 provides ample rationale for major new studies within this framework for all of the major food commodities.

Modeling the Strategic Approach

The strategic approach to food security that stresses pro-poor growth and stable food prices can be understood more clearly if it is developed into a simple model of economic development. A framework borrowed from Reutlinger and Selowsky (1976) is used here to organize the discussion (Figure 7). A calorie-income relationship, illustrated in panel A, is used to identify a "poverty line" and a "famine line" (World Bank 1986, Annex A). The standard Engel relationship in panel A portrays a representative consumer or household whose income (Y) determines calorie intake (C) according to a semilogarithmic function, conditional on food prices (P). When food prices are held at their "average" level (P_A), the relationship shows that individual i will be below the poverty line C^* when Y_i is below Y^*. A further reduction in income to Y^F would make the individual vulnerable to severe hunger. Famine would be widespread if individual i is representative of a broad class of individuals.[2]

Panel A illustrates what happens to individual i when there are exogenous shocks to the food system, shown as equally likely "good" shocks, when food prices are low (P^L), and "bad" shocks, when food prices are high (P^H). When prices are high, more income is required to stay above the poverty line or the famine line. Obviously, factors other than food prices might affect similar vulnerabilities in particular households: illness, death of a wage earner, an additional child, and so on. The framework here abstracts from such idiosyncratic shocks to focus on individual income (or household income, where unitary decision making makes that a sensible approach) or economy-wide shocks.

From Individual Behavior to National Aggregates

The translation from individual behavior to national indicators of poverty or vulnerability to famine is shown in panel B of Figure 7, which displays the distribution of income for the society. The starting point for the discussion

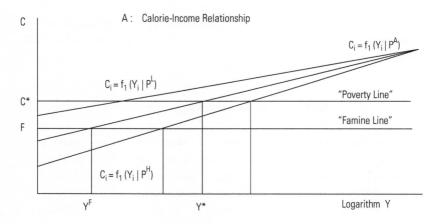

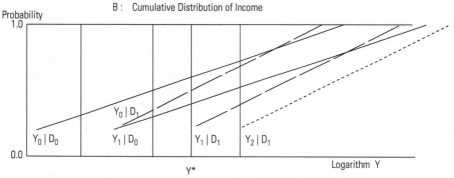

$Y_0 | D_0$ = Starting point (widespread poverty and prone to famine)

$Y_0 | D_1$ = "Revolution" (static redistribution of income)

$Y_1 | D_0$ = "Trickle-down Growth" (no redistribution of income)

$Y_1 | D_1$ = "Redistribution with Growth"

$Y_2 | D_1$ = "Redistribution with Rapid Growth"

Source: See Table 2

Figure 7. Poverty, Famine, and Food Security

is $Y_0|D_0$, where average per capita income Y^A is distributed in a log-linear fashion, with each income quintile having double the per capita income of the quintile below (see Table 2 for illustrative data). Such a distribution means the top quintile has a per capita income that is 16 times higher than the bottom quintile, a "poor" but not "bad" distribution of income. For comparison, Indonesia started its modern growth process in the late 1960s with a top 20/

bottom 20 ratio of 7.5:1, whereas, in the 1970s, it was 15:1 in the Philippines and more than 30:1 in Brazil.

Table 2 offers a concrete idea of income levels that might be appropriate for this discussion. To start, the society has an average income per capita of US$310 per year (about the level of India in the mid-1990s), distributed in such a way that the lowest quintile has an income per capita of US$50 and the top quintile US$800. The poverty line is drawn such that $Y^* = $ US$200 and C^* would be on the order of 2,100 kilocalories per capita per day.[3] Panels A and B can be read in combination to indicate the national degree of poverty and vulnerability to famine. To start, 60 percent of the population has incomes at or below the poverty line, and 30 percent is vulnerable to famine.

Table 2. Illustrative Data Showing Relationships Among Poverty, Famine, Income Levels, Income Distribution, and Food Prices

Income Quintile	Per Capita Income, US $				
	$Y_0\vert D_0$	$Y_0\vert D_1$	$Y_1\vert D_0$	$Y_1\vert D_1$	$Y_2\vert D_1$
Lowest	$50	$100	$100	$200	$320
Second	100	160	200	319	494
Third	200	254	400	508	787
Fourth	400	398	800	797	1235
Highest	800	638	1600	1276	1978
Average	$310	$310	$620	$620	$961
Ratio: Top 20% to Bottom 20%	16:1	6.4:1	16:1	6.4:1	6.4:1

Proportion of Population Below the Poverty Line, C^* (POV) or Prone to Famine, $C < F$ (FAM), at Various Food Prices

$P = P^A$	Average price level, or stabilized prices				
POV	0.6	0.5	0.4	0.2	0
FAM	0.3	0	0	0	0
$P = P^H$	High "price shock"				
POV	0.72	0.68	0.52	0.38	0
FAM	0.5	0.35	0.3	0	0
$P = P^L$	Low "price shock"				
POV	0.37	0	0	0	0
FAM	0	0	0	0	0

Source: Author calculations

This is a very poor, famine-prone society. The question is, how does such a society achieve food security?

For the purposes of this analytical exercise, define food security as an environment in which the lowest income quintile has a near-zero probability of being vulnerable to famine. The "escape from hunger" has a more challenging definition; it requires a similar near-zero probability of falling below the poverty line (defined strictly in calorie terms). Within the framework presented here, the escape from hunger and famine can be accomplished through one or a combination of three approaches. First, incomes can grow with no change in income distribution. Second, income distribution can improve with no change in average incomes per capita. Third, the domestic food economy can be stabilized to eliminate shocks that result in P^H as the prevailing price environment. The argument here, following Figure 7, is that the East and Southeast Asian approach of growth with redistribution, relying heavily on stimulation of the rural economy, in combination with a policy to stabilize domestic food prices, is the fastest approach to managing this escape (Chenery et al. 1974; Timmer, Falcon, and Pearson 1983; Dasgupta 1993; Timmer 1995b, 2004a; Birdsall, Ross, and Sabot 1995).

What Is Feasible?

Both theory and the empirical record of economic growth since the 1950s argue that only certain combinations of growth, redistribution, and price policy are feasible as long-run strategies. In particular, two appealing strategies for overcoming hunger in the short run must be ruled out. The first, a strategy of keeping food prices low (P^L) through direct subsidies and macroeconomic distortions such as overvalued domestic currencies eliminates all probability of famine in our illustrative society (see the bottom line in Table 2), and it ends poverty with either doubled incomes per capita (Y_1) or a sharp redistribution of income (D_1). The problem with this strategy, unfortunately, is one of incentive compatibility. The strategy is not sustainable because it fails to provide incentives to the rural sector and, consequently, it is unable to maintain levels of agricultural productivity (Timmer, Falcon, and Pearson 1983; Nerlove 1958; Taylor 1998). Without this productivity, the entire growth process is threatened.

The second strategy that fails is an immediate redistribution of income from D_0 to D_1. In Figure 7 and Table 2, this redistribution is shown as a change in the top 20/bottom 20 ratio 16:1 to 6.4:1. These particular numbers result from doubling the income per capita of the bottom quintile, holding average income per capita at the initial level, and then maintaining a log-linear distribution for the remaining income quintiles. This doubling accomplishes immediately what economic growth takes years to accomplish—the elimination of vulnerability to famines in an environment of price stability. Unfortunately, such revolutionary redistributions of income have carried powerful, negative consequences for economic growth because they disrupt property rights and incentives for investment. Without such investment, economic output cannot be maintained (Barrett 1995; Levine and Renelt 1992; Barro and Sala-i-Martin 1994; Taylor 1998).[4]

Trickle-Down Growth

Two other strategies offer more hope. The first is economic growth with unchanging income distribution $(Y_1 | D_0)$. On the face of it, this strategy would seem to require a very long time to eliminate vulnerability to famine and hunger (World Bank 1986). In the event of an adverse price shock, for example, even a doubling of income per capita in the lowest quintile leaves 30 percent of the population vulnerable to famine and more than half the population below the poverty line. In addition, with such an adverse income distribution and price instability, doubling of incomes per capita is likely to be slow, requiring twenty to thirty years (growth rates of income per capita of 2.4 to 3.6 percent per year) (Williamson 1993; Birdsall, Ross, and Sabot 1995). It is not surprising that such trickle-down growth strategies have a poor reputation among most development specialists.

However, if the probability of P^H is reduced to near zero through public action to stabilize the food economy, even such a modest growth performance benefits the poor quite quickly by eliminating their vulnerability to famine. Many remain below the poverty line, 40 percent in the illustration, but they are protected from falling to the famine line because adverse price shocks are eliminated by the stabilization policy. This approach, in conjunction with urban food distributions to holders of ration cards, is a rough characterization of the Indian experience with food security (Gaiha, Jha, and Kulkarni 2013).

The Indian experience is particularly interesting because the country started with a relatively egalitarian distribution of income. Because the country was so poor, however, absolute poverty was widespread, thus presenting a difficult dilemma. If substantial resources were used to subsidize food intake of the poor, sufficient funds would be diverted from productive investments to slow the rate of economic growth. Thus the strategic choice in much of South Asia—to opt for food security through distribution mechanisms that were built during British colonial rule to alleviate famines— may have sacrificed some of the potential for economic growth in order to provide "support-led" poverty alleviation (Drèze and Sen 1989).

Growth with Redistribution

An alternative strategy of bringing the poor more directly into the process of economic growth offers considerably greater hope than trickle-down policies, even with effective stabilization of food prices. The alternative is, however, much more complicated to implement. Here, redistribution with growth is attempted, in order to shift from $Y_0|D_1$ to $Y_1|D_1$ in a relatively short period of time. In this strategy, incomes per capita double on average, as before, but redistribution of the increased output doubles the incomes of the poorest quintile yet again. Such a strategy, if it is possible, eliminates all vulnerability to famine, even in the face of a price shock, and nearly eliminates poverty when the growth strategy is implemented in conjunction with a policy of price stabilization. This was the Indonesian approach (Timmer 1995b, 2004a).

What are the barriers to such a strategy? It is obviously difficult to find a way to structure the growth process so that the poor gain in relation to the rich. Historically, the only way to do that has been a rural-oriented development strategy that raises productivity and incomes of the broad population of small farmers and other rural workers (Mellor 1976; Tomich, Kilby, and Johnston 1995; Timmer, Falcon, and Pearson 1983).

Such a strategy, however, requires significant price incentives to create the rural purchasing power that in turn stimulates the rural growth needed to make the strategy consistent with overall macroeconomic performance. This consistency is essential to maintaining internal economic balance (World Bank 1993; Timmer 1995a). Thus a growth strategy that aims at $Y_1|D_1$ is probably not feasible without a price policy that approaches P^H as an average rather than as an extreme shock. This food price dilemma, in which poor consumers have their food intake threatened in the short run in order to fuel a long-run growth process that removes them from poverty, has been emphasized before (Ravallion 1989; Timmer, Falcon, and Pearson 1983; Sah and Stiglitz 1992). But experience in East and Southeast Asia since the 1970s shows that such a strategy, when implemented in the context of large-scale investments in rural infrastructure, human capital, and agricultural research, can lead to economic growth and an increase in average incomes per capita of 5 percent per year or more, with the rate of growth in the bottom two quintiles faster than that in the top (World Bank 1993; Huppi and Ravallion 1991; Ravallion and Huppi 1991; Timmer 1995b, 2004a).

With doubling times of ten to fifteen years for incomes per capita and redistribution in favor of the poor, the rural-oriented, price-led strategy has the potential to reach outcome $Y_1|D_2$, illustrated in Figure 7. With this strategy, the escape from hunger and famine is as complete as in the United States, Western Europe, and Japan. At the rates of growth experienced by Malaysia, Thailand, and Indonesia since the mid-1960s, the escape has been managed in less than three decades.[5]

Empirical Results

The FAO's flagship publication, *State of Food Insecurity in the World 2012*, provides a sophisticated new methodology for estimating the prevalence of undernutrition.[6] It uses the new methodology and the latest data to present the best indicators available on the state and dynamics of food security at the country level between 1990–92 and 2010–12 (FAO, WFP, and IFAD 2012). Table 3 summarizes the key data for the world, Latin America, sub-Saharan Africa, and subregions of Asia, for comparative purposes. For each region, data are shown for 1990–92, 2000–2002 and 2010–12. Changes are calculated between decades.

Four different indicators of food security are shown for each region. First is the prevalence of undernutrition, the headline indicator used to measure progress on the Millennium Development Goals (goal 1, target 1.9). The traditional FAO measure of hunger, the prevalence of undernutrition, is the proportion of the population at risk of caloric inadequacy.

Second is a new measure of average dietary energy supply adequacy. This indicator expresses each country's or region's average supply of food calories that are available for consumption (including imports), as a percentage of requirements for dietary energy on average for the population, as calculated by FAO.

Third is a measure of the depth of the food deficit facing the undernour-ished, also as calculated by FAO. It indicates how many calories would be needed to lift the undernourished from their status, normalized by total pop-ulation, everything else held constant. The measure shown in Table 3 uses the depth of the food deficit in kcal per capita per day as a percent of the minimum dietary energy requirement (MDER). It is on a similar scale as the food supply measure.

Finally, a food security gap is calculated for this chapter to indicate the rough balance between food supplies available and the depth and extent of hunger. This gap is simply the "surplus" food supply available (food supply − 100) minus the food deficit, as calculated and reported in Table 3. A nega-tive gap means the food deficit is larger than the food surplus, with the inevi-table consequence that people will be hungry even with equitable distribution. Sharply positive levels of the gap mean there is plenty of food for all.[7] Sub-stantial hunger (high prevalence) in these environments suggests a highly unequal distribution of economic resources. This measure of the food secu-rity gap is a particularly sensitive indicator of progress (or lack thereof) in reducing undernourishment, and whether availability or access is the limit-ing factor.

As the data in Table 3 show, substantial progress has been made in reduc-ing food insecurity since 1990. Prevalence of undernutrition at the global level has fallen from 18.6 percent in 1990–92 to 12.5 percent in 2010–12, a decline of 6.1 percentage points (almost a third).

Both Southeast Asia and developing East Asia (mainly China) have made enormous progress in lowering food insecurity since 1990, with prevalence dropping by 18.7 percentage points and 9.3 points, respectively. Most remark-ably, both regions moved from negative food security gaps to sharply positive ones. In Southeast Asia, a very large negative gap of −12.3 percent was trans-formed into a very large positive gap of 15.7 points in just twenty years. Im-proved supplies (up 20 percent) and dramatically lowered food deficits (down 8 percent) both contributed to this amazing performance. The strategic ap-proach to food security that emphasized pro-poor growth and a stable food economy, outlined above, paid high dividends.

Significant challenges remain, of course. The prevalence of undernutrition in sub-Saharan Africa remains very high, 26.8 percent, although the trend is for modest improvements. In South Asia the rate has fallen by 9 percentage points since 1990, although it remains relatively high at 17.6 percent under-nourished in 2010–12.

Table 3. Food Security Indicators

Region/Indicator	Time period (and change from previous time period)				
	1990–92	2000–2002	(change)	2010–12	(change)
World					
Prevalence[a]	18.6	14.9	(−3.7)	12.5	(−2.4)
Food supply[b]	114.0	117.0	(+3.0)	121.0	(+4.0)
Food deficit[c]	7.2	5.8	(−1.4)	5.1	(−0.7)
Food security gap[d]	6.8	11.2	(+4.4)	15.9	(+4.7)
Sub-Saharan Africa					
Prevalence	32.8	29.7	(−3.1)	26.8	(−2.9)
Food supply	100.0	104.0	(+4.0)	109.0	(+5.0)
Food deficit	13.7	12.7	(−1.0)	11.8	(−0.9)
Food security gap	−13.7	−8.7	(+5.0)	−2.8	(+5.9)
Latin America					
Prevalence	14.6	11.2	(−3.2)	8.3	(−2.9)
Food supply	117.0	121.0	(+4.0)	125.0	(+4.0)
Food deficit	5.4	4.1	(−1.3)	3.2	(−0.9)
Food security gap	11.6	16.9	(+5.3)	21.8	(+4.9)
South Asia					
Prevalence	26.8	21.3	(−5.3)	17.6	(−3.7)
Food supply	106.0	104.0	(−2.0)	107.0	(+3.0)
Food deficit	10.2	8.6	(−1.6)	7.1	(−1.5)
Food security gap	−4.2	−4.6	(−0.4)	−0.1	(+4.5)
Southeast Asia					
Prevalence	29.6	19.2	(−10.4)	10.9	(−8.3)
Food supply	100.0	107.0	(+7)	120.0	(+13.0)
Food deficit	12.3	7.4	(−4.9)	4.3	(−3.1)
Food security gap	−12.3	−0.4	(+11.9)	15.7	(+16.1)
Developing East Asia (mainly China)					
Prevalence	20.8	14.3	(−6.5)	11.5	(−2.8)
Food supply	107.0	117.0	(+10.0)	124.0	(+7.0)
Food deficit	8.2	5.2	(−3.0)	4.0	(−1.2)
Food security gap	−1.2	11.8	(+13.0)	20.0	(+8.2)

[a] Prevalence of undernourishment.
[b] Average adequacy of dietary energy supply.
[c] Food deficit is the depth of the food deficit in kcal per capita per day as a percentage of MDER (minimum dietary energy requirement).
[d] Food security gap = (Supply − 100) − Food deficit = FSgap. When FSgap = 0, there is exactly enough "surplus" food supply to offset the entire food energy deficit.

The most sensitive indicator of changes in the status of food security is the gap measure. Only sub-Saharan Africa and South Asia continue to have negative gaps. These indicate an overall shortage of food available in the countries in each region. Even these negative gaps have narrowed significantly. At one level, the relationship between an improving food security gap and reductions in prevalence of malnutrition is obvious. More food and smaller deficits translate into less hunger.

This relationship changes gradually as countries become richer and solve their food problems. Statistical analysis shows that the relationship is not linear—there are diminishing returns to improving the food security gap in terms of lowering the prevalence of undernutrition.[8] As societies succeed in reducing the incidence of poverty and hunger in their populations, food insecurity becomes less a problem of overall food availability and mass poverty, and more a structural problem of people "left behind." Even in rich countries, hunger remains among the elderly, disabled, and populations living in remote areas or regions with poor resources.

CHAPTER 4

Structural Transformation as the Pathway to Food Security

All successful developing countries undergo a structural transformation, which involves four main features:

- a falling share of agriculture in economic output and employment,
- a rising share of urban economic activity in industry and modern services,
- migration of rural workers to urban settings, and
- a demographic transition in birth and death rates that always leads to a spurt in population growth before a new equilibrium is reached.

These four dimensions of structural transformation are seen by all developing economies experiencing rising living standards; diversity appears in the various approaches governments have tried in order to cope with the political pressures generated along that pathway. Finding efficient policy mechanisms that will keep the poor from falling off the pathway altogether has occupied the development profession for decades. There are three key lessons.

First, the structural transformation has been the main pathway out of poverty for all societies, and it depends on rising productivity in both the agricultural and nonagricultural sectors (and the two are connected). The stress on productivity growth in both sectors is important, as agricultural labor can be pushed off of farms into even lower-productivity informal service sector jobs, a perverse form of structural transformation that has generated large pockets of urban poverty, especially in sub-Saharan Africa and India.[1] It is no accident that these are the two regions of the world where food insecurity remains severe.

Second, in the early stages, the process of structural transformation widens the gap between labor productivity in the agricultural and nonagricultural sectors—a process seen in Figure 8. This widening gap puts enormous pressure on rural societies to adjust and modernize. These pressures are then translated into visible and significant policy responses that alter agricultural prices. The agricultural surpluses generated in rich countries because of artificially high prices then cause artificially low prices in world markets and a consequent undervaluation of agriculture in poor countries. This undervaluation of agriculture since the mid-1980s, and its attendant reduction in agricultural investments, was a significant factor explaining the world food crisis in 2007–8 and continuing high food prices.

Third, despite the decline in the relative importance of the agricultural sector, leading to a "world without agriculture" in rich societies, the process of economic growth and structural transformation requires major investments in the agricultural sector itself (Timmer 2009a). This seeming paradox has complicated (and obfuscated) planning in developing countries as well as for donor agencies seeking to speed economic growth and connect the poor to it. Because of active policy concerns about providing food security to their citizens, countries in East and Southeast Asia have largely escaped much of this paradox, but sub-Saharan Africa has not.

For poverty-reducing initiatives to be sustainable over long periods of time, the indispensable necessity is a growing economy that successfully integrates factor markets in the rural sector with those in urban sectors and stimulates higher productivity in both. That is, the long-run success of poverty reduction, and with it, improvements in food security, hinge directly on a successful structural transformation. The historical record is very clear on this path.

The structural transformation involves declining shares of agriculture in gross domestic product (GDP) and employment, almost always accompanied by serious problems closing the gap in labor productivity between agriculture and nonagriculture. The basic cause and effect of the structural transformation is rising productivity of agricultural labor. Figure 8 presents an especially graphic illustration of the structural transformation in eighty-six countries between 1961 and 2000. Each circle represents the share of agriculture in total employment for a particular country and year. Similarly, each triangle represents the share of agriculture in economic output, or GDP, for the same country and year. Finally, each square is the difference between these two shares, measured so that the value—which is simply

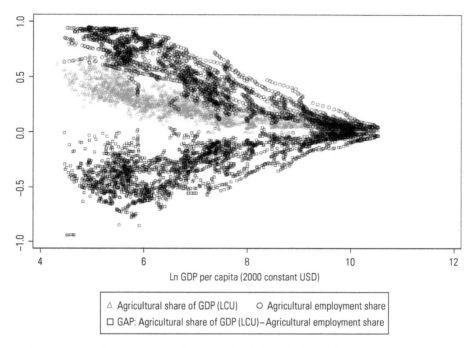

Figure 8. The Structural Transformation in Eighty-Six Countries from 1965 to 2000
Source: Timmer and Akkus (2008).

the gap in labor productivity between agriculture and nonagriculture—is negative.

Managing the ingredients of rapid transformation and coping with its distributional consequences have turned out to be major challenges for policy makers. "Getting agriculture moving" in poor countries is a complicated, long-run process that requires close, but changing, relationships between the public and private sectors. Donor agencies are not good at this. More problematic, the process of agricultural development requires good economic governance in the countries themselves if it is to work rapidly and efficiently. Aid donors cannot hope to contribute good governance and may well impede it.

The strong historical tendency toward a widening of income differences between rural and urban economies during the initial stages of the structural transformation is now extending much further into the development process. Consequently, with little prospect of reaching quickly the turning point where farm and nonfarm productivity and incomes begin to converge, many poor countries are turning to agricultural protection and farm subsidies sooner rather than later in their development process. The tendency of these actions to hurt the poor is then compounded, because there are so many more rural poor suffering food deficits in these early stages.

The Structural Transformation and Economic Development

No country has been able to sustain a rapid transition out of poverty without raising productivity in its agricultural sector (if it had one to start—Singapore and Hong Kong are exceptions). The process involves a successful structural transformation where agriculture, through higher productivity, provides food, labor, and even savings to the processes of urbanization and industrialization. A dynamic agriculture raises labor productivity in the rural economy, pulls up wages, and gradually eliminates the worst dimensions of absolute poverty. Somewhat paradoxically, the process also leads to a decline in the relative importance of agriculture to the overall economy, as the industrial and service sectors grow even more rapidly, partly through stimulus from a modernizing agriculture and migration of rural workers to urban jobs.

Despite this historical role of agriculture in economic development, both the academic and donor communities lost interest in the sector, starting in the mid-1980s, mostly because of low prices in world markets for basic agricultural commodities. Low prices, while a boon to poor consumers and a major reason why agricultural growth specifically, and economic growth more generally, was so pro-poor for the general population, made it hard to justify policy support for the agricultural sector or new funding for agricultural research or commodity-oriented projects (World Bank 2004). Historical lessons are a frail reed in the face of market realities and general equilibrium models that show a sharply declining role for agriculture in economic growth. The current realities of the structural transformation—low farm prices and extensive rural poverty—stare policy makers in the face rather than its underlying mechanisms that actually require rising productivity in agriculture.

Still, historical lessons have a way of returning to haunt those who ignore them. This is especially true when the lessons are robust, have been observed for very long periods of time, and fit within mainstream models of how farmers, consumers (and politicians) behave. The lessons from the structural transformation fit these conditions. We can translate those historical lessons into an understanding of the connections between the sectoral composition of economic growth and reductions in poverty. With this understanding come new insights into how to manage agricultural development to enhance both efficiency and equity and thus its impact on food security.

The Historical Perspective

The structural transformation is the defining characteristic of the development process, both cause and effect of economic growth. The final outcome of the structural transformation, already visible on the horizon in rich countries, is an economy and society where agriculture as an economic activity has no characteristics distinguishing it from other sectors, at least in terms of the productivity of labor and capital, or the location of poverty. This stage also shows up in Figure 8, as the gap in labor productivity between agricultural and nonagricultural workers approaches zero when incomes are high enough.[2]

All societies want to raise the productivity of their economies. That is the only way to achieve higher standards of living and sustain reductions in poverty. The mechanisms for doing this are well known in principle if difficult to implement in practice. They include the utilization of improved technologies, investment in higher educational and skill levels for the labor force, lower transactions costs to connect and integrate economic activities, and more efficient allocation of resources. The process of actually implementing these mechanisms over time is the process of economic development. When successful and sustained for decades, it leads to the structural transformation of the economy.

The structural transformation complicates the division of the economy into sectors—rural versus urban, agriculture versus industry and services—for the purpose of understanding how to raise productivity levels. In the long run, the way to raise rural productivity is to raise urban productivity, or as Chairman Mao famously but crudely put it, "The only way out for agriculture is industry." Unless the nonagricultural economy is growing, there is little long-run hope for agriculture. At the same time, the historical record is very clear on the important role that agriculture itself plays in stimulating growth in the nonagricultural economy (Timmer 2002, 2005b, 2008b).

In the early stages of the structural transformation in all countries there is a substantial gap between the share of the labor force employed in agriculture and the share of GDP generated by that work force. Figure 8 shows that this gap narrows with higher incomes. This convergence is also part of the structural transformation, reflecting better integrated labor and financial markets.

However, in many countries this structural gap actually widens during periods of rapid growth, a tendency seen in even the earliest developers. When overall GDP is growing rapidly, the share of agriculture in GDP falls much faster than the share of agricultural labor in the overall labor force. The turning point in the gap generated by these differential processes, after which labor productivity in the two sectors begins to converge, has also been moving to the right over time.[3]

This lag inevitably presents political problems as farm incomes visibly fall behind incomes being earned in the rest of the economy. The long-run answer, of course, is faster integration of farm labor into the nonfarm economy (including the rural nonfarm economy), but the historical record shows that such integration takes a long time. It was not fully achieved in the United States until the 1980s (Gardner 2002), and evidence shows the productivity gap is increasingly difficult to bridge through economic growth alone (Timmer 2009a).

This lag in real earnings from agriculture is the fundamental cause of the deep political tensions generated by the structural transformation, and it is getting worse. Historically, the completely uniform response to these political tensions has been to protect the agricultural sector from international competition and ultimately to provide direct income subsidies to farmers (Lindert 1991; Anderson, Rausser, and Swinnen 2013). Neither policy response tends to help the poor, even those remaining in rural areas.

The Structural Transformation as a General Equilibrium Process

The economic and political difficulties encountered during a rapid structural transformation are illustrated schematically in Figure 9, which shows a representative structural transformation, and numerically in Table 4, which presents the simple mathematics of structural change over a twenty-year period of economic growth and transformation. Although Figure 9 shows the share of agricultural labor in the total labor force and the contribution of agriculture to overall GDP, with both declining smoothly until parity is reached when a country is "rich," the actual relationship between the two shares depends critically on the pace of change outside of agriculture and on the labor-intensity of those activities.

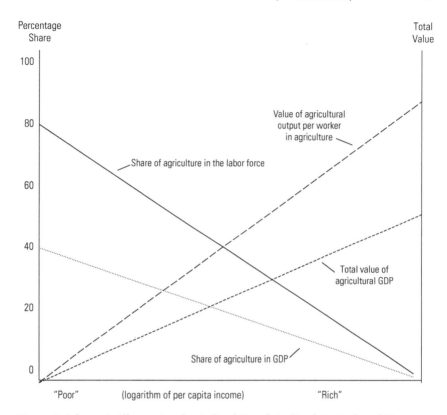

Figure 9. Schematic Illustrating the Stylized Trends in Total Agricultural Output, Output per Agricultural Worker, Agriculture as a Share of the Labor Force and in GDP, During the Course of the Structural Transformation (from Poor to Rich)

Figure 9 also shows a basic fact that is often overlooked in political discussions about the failure of agriculture to grow as fast as the rest of the economy and thus its decline as a share of GDP and in the labor force: despite the structural transformation, agricultural output continues to rise in absolute value. Even as the number of farmers falls toward zero, total farm output sets new records. That is what rising productivity is all about. The sustainability of the production practices that generate such high levels of labor productivity in modern agriculture is the subject of intense debate (Naylor et al. 2007).

Table 4 quantifies the impact of three alternative paths for a country's structural transformation. At the starting point, industry, services, and agriculture contribute 20, 30, and 50 percent to GDP, respectively, and the share of workers in each sector is 9.7, 20.8, and 69.5 percent, respectively, which is fairly typical for a country in the very early stages of development. Labor productivity in each sector is 3, 2, and 1, respectively; so overall labor productivity for the entire economy is the weighted average, or 1.4 (units of output per worker per year).

The economy then grows for twenty years. Industry grows 7.5 percent per year, services 5.0 percent per year, and agriculture 3.0 percent per year. The overall rate of growth at the start is 4.5 percent per year. These rates of growth result from technological change that is sector-specific on the supply side, and on differential patterns of demand that reflect Engel's law. The trade implications of these differential growth rates, which are representative of long-run rates seen in successful developing countries, are not shown in Table 4, but the economy must be relatively open to trade to sustain such rates.

The simple mathematics of the structural transformation shows what happens to the economy and to labor productivity through twenty years of reasonably rapid growth. At an aggregate level, total GDP grows from 100 to 255, an annual growth rate of 4.8 percent per year. Notice the acceleration in the growth rate despite the assumption that each sector grows at a constant rate for twenty years, a result of changing sectoral weights. Indeed, GDP growth in the last year of the exercise is 5.2 percent, compared with just 4.5 percent per year at the start, despite the fact that each sector continues to grow at a constant rate. If the labor force grows by 2.0 percent per year during this exercise, labor productivity in aggregate will grow to 2.4 (from 1.4 in the base year), a healthy growth rate of 2.7 percent per year.

But the important story is at the sectoral level, where the structural transformation becomes visible. Table 4 shows three possible growth paths that encompass modern development experience. Path A, following the basic logic of the Lewis model, holds labor productivity constant in the industrial and service sectors, as they absorb labor from the agricultural sector at the same rates as each sector itself expands. This labor-intensive path of industrial and service growth leads to the fastest structural transformation of the three scenarios. It is so successful in pulling "surplus" labor out of agriculture that labor productivity in agriculture is actually higher at the end than in the service sector, and only 23 percent less than that in the industrial sector. No country has actually managed a growth path with quite that much labor intensity, although the East Asian experience comes closest. The structural transformation is extremely rapid with this path, and the absolute number

Table 4. The Simple (but Implacable) Mathematics of the Structural Transformation

Start (year 0)	Industry	Services	Agriculture	GDP
Output (in domestic currency units)	20	30	50	100
Share of GDP, in percent	20	30	50	100
Number of workers[a]	7	15	50	72 (total)
Labor productivity (output/worker)	3	2	1	1.4
Share of workers in total	9.7	20.8	69.5	100
Sectoral growth rates (percent/year)	7.5	5.0	3.0	4.5
Contribution to growth in year 1	1.5	1.5	1.5	4.5
End (year 20)				
Output	85	80	90	255
Share of GDP	33.3	31.4	35.3	100
Number of workers[b]				
Path A	28	40	39	107
Path B	14	24	69	107
Path C	7	15	85	107
Labor productivity				
Path A	3.0	2.0	2.32	2.4
Path B	6.3	3.3	1.31	2.4
Path C	12.7	5.3	1.06	2.4
Share of workers in total				
Path A	26.2	37.4	36.4	100
Path B	13.1	22.4	64.5	100
Path C	6.5	14.0	79.5	100
Contribution to growth in year 20	2.5	1.6	1.1	5.2

Ratio of labor productivity (wages or income) in the top quintile of workers relative to the bottom quintile

Start	2.55
Path A	1.50
Path B	4.02
Path C	7.27

[a] The active labor force will grow by 2.0 percent per year.
[b] Path A assumes that labor productivity in industry and services remains constant as the two sectors absorb new laborers at the same rate as output expansion (the classic Lewis assumption). Agricultural employment remains the residual, with changes there consistent with general equilibrium. In Path B, labor productivity in industry and services increases at half the rate of output. In Path C, labor productivity in the industrial and services sectors increases at the same rate as sectoral output. No new labor is hired. Note that Paths A and C are extremes that are somewhat outside historical experience.

of workers in agriculture is already declining after twenty years of rapid growth.

Path C looks at the opposite extreme, where labor productivity in the industrial and service sectors grows at the same rate as the sectors themselves. Thus neither sector absorbs any new workers at all. The entire increase in the labor force remains in agriculture. Because agricultural GDP is still rising faster than the labor force, labor productivity in the sector does rise slightly, but at only 0.3 percent per year. This pattern is closer to the African experience, although Indonesia in the 1950s and early 1960s looked similar. Not only is the absolute number of workers in agriculture still rising on this path, so too is the share of agricultural labor in the total labor force.

Path B is halfway between these two extremes, with labor productivity in the industrial and service sectors growing at half the rate of increase in sectoral output. The result is similar to the Indonesian experience since 1970. The agricultural labor force continues to rise (to 69, from 50 at the beginning) but is clearly near its peak—ten more years of such growth would see the agricultural labor force in absolute decline. Labor productivity in agriculture increases by 1.4 percent per year over the entire period, somewhat less than the rate found by Fuglie (2004) for Indonesia from 1961 to 2000, the years of both rapid and slow growth in productivity.

But even this successful pattern of structural transformation leaves a serious problem for policy makers. As Table 4 also shows, income distribution deteriorates under this scenario, at least as measured by the ratio of labor productivity (wages) in the top quintile of laborers to the bottom quintile. From a starting ratio of 2.55, even Path B yields a ratio of 4.02. Of course, things could be worse. If output expansion in industry and services does not employ new workers (Path C), the ratio deteriorates to 7.27! Only a pure Lewis-style pattern of growth leads to an improvement in the distribution of labor income (Path A).

The point of this exercise is to emphasize the power, the inevitability, and the paradoxical nature of the structural transformation. Even a narrow focus on agricultural productivity per se must be set within this transformation. The important point is that the faster the structural transformation, the faster is the decline in the share of agriculture in both the economy and the overall labor force. And the paradox is that, the faster the structural transformation, the faster rural productivity—proxied by rural labor productivity—rises (as in Path A). This is true even though the rate of growth of agricultural GDP is the same in all three scenarios. Consequently, a broader focus on rural productivity and pathways out of rural poverty will inevitably incorporate the structural transformation as the basic framework for macro consistency and general equilibrium. Achieving and sustaining widespread food security depends on rising rural productivity and reduced poverty, and hence structural transformation and food security are inextricably linked.

Agricultural Transformation

Although the structural transformation is a general equilibrium process that is not easily visible from inside the agricultural sector, the changing patterns of demand and productivity induce significant change within the sector itself (Timmer 1988). Domestic demand, opportunities for international trade, commercialization of decision making, and technical change contribute to this agricultural transformation. Technical change can be specific to a commodity, as in Green Revolution varieties of wheat and rice. Or it can be sector-wide, involving better inputs, improved knowledge, communications, infrastructure, and financial intermediation. In certain circumstances, nonstaple commodities, such as palm oil, and such nonfood commodities as coffee and rubber, play larger roles.

Measuring the Agricultural Transformation

No single measure of the pace and extent of agricultural transformation captures the complexity and heterogeneity of the process. Much is country-specific and time-specific. The most graphic and general representation of the process of agricultural transformation is the "Ruttan-a-gram," which measures productivity per hectare on the vertical axis and productivity per worker on the horizontal axis (Figure 10). This two-dimensional perspective on agricultural development in individual countries or regions of the world was developed by Hayami and Ruttan (1971). It was a powerful tool to demonstrate the multiple paths to a successful agricultural transformation.

The Asian path relied heavily on new biological and chemical technologies to raise yields in land-scarce, labor-surplus environments, whereas mechanical technologies were used to raise labor productivity in land-abundant, labor-scarce environments. Japan characterized the former approach to raising agricultural productivity; the United States, Canada, and Australia/New

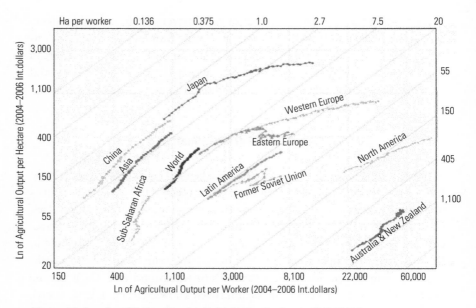

Figure 10. Land and Labor Productivity in Agriculture, 1961–2010
Source: Pardey (2011).

Zealand characterized the latter. Western Europe was, appropriately, between these two more extreme approaches.

Two things are striking. First, the gain in productivity in most regions
was very rapid. The extent of productivity gain is indicated by the overall
length of the line for each country or region, because both axes are measured
in logarithms. Japan and China have both seen major gains in labor and land
productivity, especially since about 1980.

Western Europe has seen gains in labor productivity via larger farm size
and higher yields. Eastern Europe and the former Soviet Union suffered severe reversals after the fall of communism and are only now regaining former levels of productivity. The global food economy has a substantial stake
in the recovery because Russia and Ukraine are important exporters of wheat.

Latin America has shown steady progress in both land and labor productivity. For much of the period between 1961 and 2010, average farm size
in Latin America hovered at about twenty hectares per worker (the diagonal
lines in Figure 10 show constant levels of land per worker). Since 2000, however, farm size in Latin America has started to creep upward, reflecting the

growing importance of very large farms in Brazil. The global food economy has a substantial stake in Brazil's performance as well. Brazil is now China's leading supplier of soybeans and is increasingly important in exports of corn.

An unmistakable feature of Figure 10, however, is the stagnation of growth of labor productivity in sub-Saharan Africa. Although yields per hectare were increasing slowly, there has been virtually no gain in labor productivity in agriculture since 1961.

A second striking feature of Figure 10 is that land consolidation had barely begun at a global level by 2010. Indeed, farm size continues to get smaller on average, driven by the gradually shrinking farms in Asia and the more quickly falling farm size in Africa. As noted, farm size had been virtually constant in Latin America until about 2000. Uncertain land ownership and tenancy laws in Asia and sub-Saharan Africa might account for some of this "stickiness" in reported farm size—it is difficult for entrepreneurial farmers to expand their farms because it is difficult for smallholder farmers who wish to exit agriculture to sell their land. Outmoded statistical definitions might also be a factor. Workers might be counted in the agricultural labor force even if most of their income is derived from off-farm sources.

The Changing Role of Rice in Asia

The composition of agricultural output also can change significantly during the transformation process. The changes tend to be geographically specific, and one of the most dramatic changes in terms of global influence on food security has been the changing role of rice in production and consumption, especially in Asia, where rice has been the staple food grain for millennia— the touchstone of food security. Most Asian policy makers still think it is, or at least they think that keeping rice accessible at stable prices remains the operational definition of food security. At one level, this attitude is correct, as the poor in Asia depend heavily on rice for their daily consumption needs. But in a broader sense, rice is simply no longer all that important to most farmers, consumers, or to the macro economy. Things have changed.

It is hard to imagine a more compelling picture of the changing role of rice in the global and Asian economies than the simple black-and-white data presented in Table 5. The objective of the table is simple: to show how the structural transformation has altered the role of rice in the agricultural and overall economies of Asia and the rest of the world. The calculations, however, turn out to be complex. It is no wonder that these results will strike most readers as new and perhaps surprising.

Still, the approach is straightforward. The first step is to determine the share of cereal production in total agricultural production, something that is now possible with the new FAO production index that reports these values in 1991 international dollars, by country and for regional aggregates (Table 5, sections 1–3). At a global level, the share of cereals has not changed much from 1961 to 2011, rising slightly from 1961 (20.8 percent) to 1980 (23.5 percent), reflecting the productivity impact of the new technologies for rice and wheat. By 2011, however, the share of cereals had declined to 19.8 percent of total agricultural production, virtually unchanged from the 1961 value.

There is substantial regional variation in this pattern. The share of cereals in East Asia's total agricultural production rose from 37.2 percent in 1961 to 39.6 percent in 1980, before falling sharply to 18.4 percent in 2011. A rapid agricultural transformation was going on in East Asia after 1980, both cause and effect of the rapid economic growth in the region and its accompanying structural transformation. South Asia saw similar, but more modest changes, as did Southeast Asia, from a higher base. Africa, of course, relies much less heavily on cereals in its agricultural production, and there is little change in that pattern from 1961 to 2011.

The next step is to determine the role of rice in cereal production, something not possible directly from the FAO production index. An alternative approach is straightforward, however. Sections 4 to 7 in Table 5 use physical production of total cereals and of rice to calculate the share of rice in the total. In these calculations, the amount of paddy rice is used in the comparison, despite the milling losses needed to produce an edible product. Although this approach tends to overstate the role of rice, an offsetting factor is that rice tends to be more valuable as a foodstuff per unit of weight. The end result is about right. Further, whatever biases are introduced by this approach will not change much over time, and it is primarily the temporal patterns that are of interest.

Again, at a global level, the share of rice in total cereal production does not change a lot between 1961 and 2011, starting at 24.6 percent and rising gradually to 27.9 percent. But the regional patterns of change are quite dramatic. First, it is obvious that Asia relies far more heavily on rice than the rest of the world, as East Asia's share of rice fell steadily from 56.2 percent in 1961 to 40.6 percent in 2011. A similar, but slower decline from a higher base

Table 5. Rice and the Structural Transformation, 1961–2011

	Annual Totals			Average Annual % Change		
	1961	1980	2011	1961–80	1980–2011	1961–2011
1. Total agricultural production, value (in billions of 2004–6 international $)						
World	746.4	1,180.2	2,405.0	2.44%	2.32%	2.37%
East Asia	83.9	168.8	591.1	3.75%	4.13%	3.98%
South Asia	83.7	126.0	347.9	2.18%	3.33%	2.89%
Southeast Asia	32.7	63.0	187.4	3.51%	3.58%	3.55%
Africa	50.8	77.8	201.6	2.27%	3.12%	2.80%
2. Total cereal production, value						
World	155.3	277.8	475.8	3.11%	1.75%	2.26%
East Asia	31.2	66.9	108.9	4.10%	1.58%	2.53%
South Asia	27.9	44.7	93.1	2.51%	2.40%	2.44%
Southeast Asia	13.6	25.2	62.1	3.30%	2.95%	3.08%
Africa	7.8	12.2	28.4	2.38%	2.76%	2.62%
3. Cereal production as % of total agricultural production [2/1]						
World	20.8%	23.5%	19.8%	0.65%	−0.56%	−0.10%
East Asia	37.2%	39.6%	18.4%	0.34%	−2.44%	−1.39%
South Asia	33.3%	35.5%	26.8%	0.33%	−0.91%	−0.44%
Southeast Asia	41.6%	40.0%	33.1%	−0.20%	−0.61%	−0.45%
Africa	15.4%	15.7%	14.1%	0.11%	−0.35%	−0.17%

(continued)

Table 5. (continued)

	Annual Totals			Average Annual % Change		
	1961	1980	2011	1961–80	1980–2011	1961–2011
4. Cereal production, MMT						
World	876.9	1,549.9	2,589.1	3.04%	1.67%	2.19%
East Asia	140.3	306.2	542.2	4.19%	1.86%	2.74%
South Asia	120.8	198.0	417.3	2.63%	2.43%	2.51%
Southeast Asia	50.8	95.8	241.6	3.40%	3.03%	3.17%
Africa	46.3	72.6	163.9	2.40%	2.66%	2.56%
5. Rice (paddy) production, MMT						
World	215.6	396.9	722.6	3.26%	1.95%	2.45%
East Asia	78.9	163.0	219.9	3.89%	0.97%	2.07%
South Asia	73.6	112.2	229.1	2.24%	2.33%	2.30%
Southeast Asia	46.0	84.5	203.0	3.25%	2.87%	3.01%
Africa	4.31	8.61	26.1	3.71%	3.64%	3.67%
6. Rice as % of cereal production [5/4]						
World	24.6%	25.6%	27.9%	0.21%	0.28%	0.25%
East Asia	56.2%	53.2%	40.6%	−0.29%	−0.87%	−0.65%
South Asia	60.9%	56.7%	54.9%	−0.38%	−0.10%	−0.21%
Southeast Asia	90.6%	88.2%	84.0%	−0.14%	−0.16%	−0.15%
Africa	9.3%	11.9%	15.9%	1.28%	0.96%	1.08%
7. Rice as a % of agriculture [3×6]						
World	5.1%	6.0%	5.5%	0.87%	−0.28%	0.15%
East Asia	20.9%	21.1%	7.5%	0.05%	−3.29%	−2.04%
South Asia	20.3%	20.1%	14.7%	−0.05%	−1.01%	−0.65%

Southeast Asia	37.7%	35.3%	27.8%	−0.34%	−0.76%	−0.60%
Africa	1.4%	1.9%	2.2%	1.40%	0.61%	0.91%
8. Agricultural value added as % of GDP [from World Bank]						
World	10.5%	7.3%	3.1%	−1.89%	−2.69%	−2.38%
East Asia	16.9%	7.5%	5.8%	−4.19%	−0.83%	−2.12%
South Asia	41.9%	34.5%	18.1%	−1.02%	−2.06%	−1.67%
Southeast Asia	30.8%[a]	21.8%	12.5%	−1.80%	−1.78%	−1.79%
Africa	22.0%	18.2%	11.9%	−1.00%	−1.37%	−1.23%
9. Rice as % of GDP [7×8]						
World	0.5%	0.4%	0.2%	−1.04%	−2.96%	−2.23%
East Asia	3.5%	1.6%	0.4%	−4.14%	−4.09%	−4.11%
South Asia	8.5%	6.9%	2.7%	−1.07%	−3.05%	−2.30%
Southeast Asia	11.6%	7.7%	3.5%	−2.14%	−2.53%	−2.38%
Africa	0.3%	0.3%	0.3%	0.39%	−0.77%	−0.33%

[a] 1970 estimate

Source: Based on Timmer 2010b, with updates.

is seen in South Asia. Southeast Asia is heavily dependent on rice. It accounted for 90.6 percent of cereal production in 1961, and rice still accounted for 84.0 percent of cereal production in 2011.

Perhaps surprisingly, Africa has steadily increased its production of rice since 1961 (by 3.7 percent per year), and the role of rice in overall cereal production. In 1961, rice was 9.3 percent of total cereal production in Africa, and this share has risen steadily to become 15.9 percent in 2011. Rice has become a significant cereal crop in Africa.

The final three sections of Table 5 show the calculations needed to understand the changing role of rice in overall agricultural production and for the entire economy. In Section 7, rice as a share of total agriculture is calculated by multiplying the values in Section 3 times the values in Section 6. The results are just arithmetic but are interesting nonetheless. Rice has been about 5 to 6 percent of agricultural production since 1961, but the share varies enormously by region. In East Asia, rice's share has dropped from about a fifth of agricultural output to less than a tenth. Rice remains more significant in South Asia, contributing 14.7 percent in 2011. In Southeast Asia, rice contributed 37.7 percent of agricultural output in 1961, a figure that has dropped steadily, but slowly, since then. In 2011, rice still contributed 27.8 percent of agricultural output in Southeast Asia.

The share of rice in Africa's agriculture is small, just 1.4 percent in 1961. But unlike the patterns in Asia, the share of rice in Africa is rising; it was 2.2 percent in 2011. Although still a small factor in Africa's overall agricultural production, it is a commodity with a promising future.

Section 8 of the table reports the share of agricultural value added in overall GDP, a value reported regularly in all countries' national income accounts and available from the World Development Indicators (WDI) published by the World Bank. In its crudest form, this is the structural transformation. For the entire world, agriculture contributed a bit over 10 percent of economic output in 1961 and just 3.1 percent in 2011. These low numbers are the result of the economic dominance of rich countries in global GDP and the very small contribution of agriculture in these economies.

Asia is much more dependent on agriculture, although the rapid structural transformation in East and Southeast Asia means that dependence has fallen rapidly. For East Asia, the share of agricultural value added in overall GDP declined from 16.9 percent in 1961 to 5.8 percent in 2011. In Southeast

Asia, the agricultural share of GDP declined from 30.8 percent in 1970 (the World Bank does not report these data back to 1961) to 12.5 percent in 2011. The share of agriculture in South Asia's economy is higher, starting at 41.9 percent in 1961 and declining to 18.1 percent in 2011. The share of agriculture in Africa's economy is surprisingly low, and it has declined significantly because of the increased role of mineral and energy exports, from 22 percent in 1961 to 11.9 percent in 2011.

The contrast between Asia and the rest of the world is sharp: in 1961, agriculture was 2.8 times as important to Asian economies as to the world as a whole (taking the population-weighted average of East, Southeast, and South Asia). This ratio had climbed to 3.9 times as important in 2011. Despite the rapid transformation of Asian economies, agriculture remains very important (which is mostly because Asian economies remain, on average, quite poor).

Finally, Section 9 provides the bottom line to our question: how has the role of rice changed? At a world level, rice accounted for just over one half of one percent of GDP in 1961. Over the next half century, the share of rice in GDP for the entire world fell to just 0.2 percent of GDP. In terms of overall economic output on a global scale, rice is a very small factor.[4]

In Asia, rice is far more important, although its share in national economies is not as large as many observers think. Even in 1961, rice accounted for just 3.5 percent of GDP in East Asia, 8.5 percent in South Asia, and 11.6 percent in Southeast Asia. Naturally, because of the structural transformation and the declining role of agriculture in successfully growing economies, and the agricultural transformation whereby farmers diversify out of production of low-value rice, the share of rice in Asian economies (share of GDP) has declined very rapidly. In 2011, it was just 0.4 percent in East Asia, 2.7 percent in South Asia, and 3.5 percent in Southeast Asia. So, even in Asia, rice is less important economically than livestock, construction, or transportation, even banking. Total employment in the rice economy might still rival these other sectors, but that is because the economic returns to working in the rice sector are so low—a failure of the structural transformation to absorb rural workers fast enough.

The implications for food security of this rapid change in the role of rice in the agricultural economies of Asia need to be understood from two perspectives: what is happening to rice consumption and its role in the food security of poor households, and how the diminished role of rice in the overall economy affects political approaches to food security. These questions are addressed in the following sections.

The Politics of Rice

It was noted in the 1980s that a successful structural transformation has always been painful for rural households (Timmer 1988). Although the structural transformation seems to offer the only sustainable pathway out of poverty in the long run, it can be a very challenging process for the poor in the short run. Is there any way to manage the process without hurting the poor? To answer the question, a historical perspective on the structural transformation is essential, especially on the experiences in the countries of East and Southeast Asia that managed both rapid growth and stability or even improvement in income distribution during the process (World Bank 1993; Ravallion and Chen 2007 Timmer 2004a).

Analysis of research on pro-poor growth suggests that an Asian pattern of rural development and poverty reduction exists (Oshima 1987; Besley and Cord 2006; Grimm, Klasen, and McKay 2007). The common structure involves the evolution of the agricultural sector from a starting point of household subsistence production, through the adoption of new technologies that provide surpluses and rural food security, to more diversified farm activities driven by commercial forces, and finally to the full integration of the agricultural economy into the overall economy.

This structural pattern can be examined from the perspective of the main policy concerns shown by Asian countries at each stage, and the links between these policy concerns and the key economic drivers and mechanisms for change. Asia may have been unique in its early concern for food security, including for rural households, as the main policy focus that mobilized substantial resources on behalf of agriculture (Timmer 2005a). The importance of rice in Asian food security—it accounted for 38 percent of caloric intake in 1975—and the tenuous (and tense) relationship between domestic rice economies and the world market for rice, focused political and economic attention on agricultural productivity in ways not seen in other parts of the world.

For Asia, the Green Revolution technologies for wheat and rice transformed their potential for a domestic approach to food security. When this potential was fully realized—in Indonesia in the early 1980s, in India in the late 1980s, in Bangladesh and China in the early 1990s, and in Vietnam in the mid-1990s—the policy concern turned to supporting farm incomes in the face of declining world prices for cereals. The efficient way to do this was through the next structural phase, that of diversification and specialization. Bangladesh seems to be moving in this direction. The more advanced regions in China are already well along this road. The alternative approach, however, is to maintain farm incomes by protecting the rice sector, using subsidies to keep inputs cheap, and thus to slow the diversification process. Both India and Indonesia are caught in this expensive and distortionary approach. It is impossible to move on to the stage of rapid productivity growth and integration into the overall economy as long as the diversification phase is postponed.

The structural transformation gradually closes off policy options for the agricultural sector. It is simply not possible to keep a third of the labor force employed growing rice and also have a modern industrial and service economy. Policy makers who fight the forces of structural transformation are fighting against the tide.

At the same time, the structural transformation opens new options to policy makers to cope with the distributional consequences of structural transformation. Making rice expensive in East Asia, when it was 6.8 percent of the entire economy, would have been a fiscal fiasco. In 2010, doubling the price of rice in China to increase farm income might not have been a wise economic policy, but since rice was less than 1.0 percent of the economy, it was no longer fiscally impossible. The degrees of freedom for policy, wise or unwise, were greater.

In 2013, rice is still important on both counts in Asia, and it is rising, not falling, in importance in other parts of the world, especially Africa. In Bangladesh, for example, rice still provides about two-thirds of daily caloric intake, and the average for all of Asia has just fallen below 30 percent. In much of Asia, rice is now the food of the poor. Price volatility and market shortages have a direct impact on poverty.

In nearly all of Asia, rice farmers (whether part-time or full-time) are the single largest identifiable interest group, a fact not lost on political leaders. It is no accident that political elections in 2009 in India and Indonesia were won by leaders who provided sharply higher prices to rice farmers than prices in the world market in the years leading up to the world food crisis in 2007. They were then able to buffer domestic consumers from the panic-driven prices in world markets in early 2008. Stable rice prices, even at high levels to support farmers, seem to be a winning political strategy. Only a successful structural transformation makes such a strategy financially feasible, even if it remains economically inefficient. But economists have not been very effective in designing efficient food price stabilization programs. These are programs that politicians need to stay in power (Dawe and Timmer 2012).

Thus the structural transformation has been a two-edged sword. It reduced the importance of agriculture, and rice, to the overall economy. At the same time, it also created the resources to spend on making the rice sector successful in contributing to the goals society has held out for it for generations: food security for consumers and satisfactory income for producers.

Dietary Transformation

As with the agricultural transformation, no single measure captures the complexity of dietary changes, and much is specific to local customs and tastes. In general, two basic regularities have been observed in food consumption patterns as countries have become richer:

- Engel's law: The share of food in budget expenditures falls with higher incomes, thus providing a buffer against the welfare impact of sudden changes in food prices.
- Bennett's law: The share of starchy staples in the diet falls with higher incomes, as a deep, perhaps hard-wired desire for diversity in the diet can be expressed (Bennett 1954).

Less well-established regularities also suggest that long-run changes in relative prices and changing demographics, as well as exposure to "foreign" eating patterns, have an impact.

Figure 11 illustrates the complex changes in Southeast Asia, a rapidly developing part of the world. This dietary transformation is in a region that has made substantial progress in reducing hunger, as noted in Chapter 3. Below each pie chart is shown the average energy intake per capita for each of the years from 1961 to 2009.

The Dietary Transformation in Southeast Asia

Four things are striking in Figure 11. First, total caloric intake has risen steadily, by 0.8 percent per year. In 1961, when average food availability per

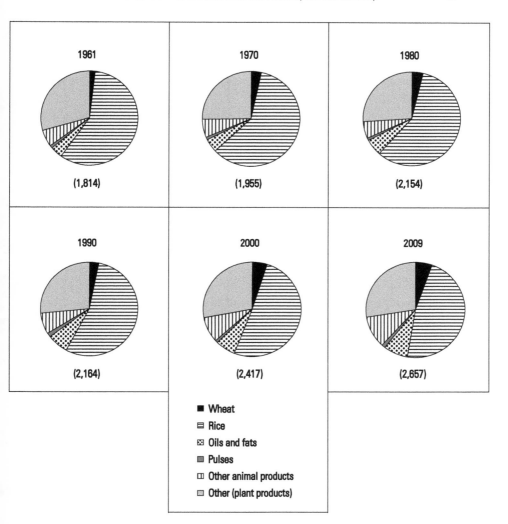

Figure 11. The Dietary Transformation in Southeast Asia (average calorie intake per day)
Source: FAO Food Balance Sheets.

capita was just 1,814 calories per day, most citizens of Southeast Asia would have been chronically hungry. By 2009, the most recent year for which data are available, food available per capita per day reached 2,657 calories.[5] At that level, hunger would not be common, and obesity would be a rising problem.

Second, the starchy staple ratio—the share of calories coming from cereals and starchy roots—fell from 74.8 percent in 1961 to 62.1 percent in 2009. In roughly forty years, intake of animal protein nearly tripled. The quality of the diet in nutritional terms improved markedly, although the doubling of fat in the diet is a worrisome sign.

Third, rising consumption of animal products will require a modern feed industry to supply domestic producers of poultry, livestock, and aquaculture products, unless imports of final goods increase drastically. Domestic farmers have a rapidly growing market for feedstuffs, but at the moment, a very large proportion of Southeast Asia's feed ingredients, especially corn and soy meal, is imported. This is true of the rest of Asia as well.

Fourth, calories from wheat increased 8 percent per year, and this consumption of wheat was more than a tenth of rice consumption. Southeast Asia imports all of its wheat. Indonesia surpassed Egypt in 2013 as the world's largest importer of wheat. A volatile world market for wheat will increasingly be seen as a threat to food security in Southeast Asia, but national agricultural development strategies cannot be used to cope with that threat. Since rice is becoming less important to food security in the region, and wheat and feed grains are becoming more important, management of food security will increasingly be a trade and macroeconomic issue rather than an agricultural issue.

Finally, the demand for livestock feed to enable the dietary transition raises an obvious issue presented in earlier chapters: all of these "feedstocks" also serve as fuel stocks. The potential for commodities—especially corn, sugar, palm oil, and cassava—to be grown as raw materials for production of biofuels needs to be seen as in direct competition with their use as feed for livestock (and fish). Continued political support for production of biofuels is a challenge to the dietary aspirations of hundreds of millions of households with new discretionary incomes that permit livestock and aquaculture products on their table. The consequences for food security are highly uncertain.

Diet Transitions and Changing Rice Consumption

As previously noted, momentous changes are under way in rice consumption, especially in Asia. New data, extensive econometric analysis, and a historical perspective help build an understanding of the underlying dynamics

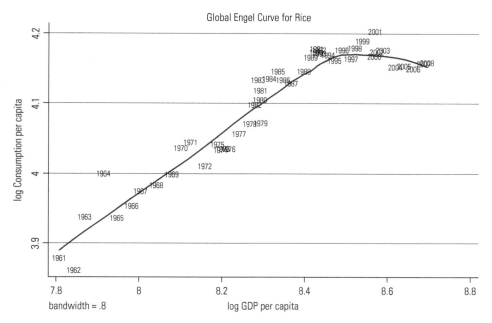

Figure 12. Nonparametric Engel Curve for Rice Consumption Per Capita, 1961–2008
Source: Timmer, Block, and Dawe (2010).

of these changes. The result is surprising. Projections that result from these analyses suggest a significant decline in global rice consumption by 2050; the global decline starts between 2020 and 2030. Rapid income growth in Asia, accompanied by a massive shift of labor from rural to urban areas, contribute to this decline. With more open trade and the globalization of tastes, a shift to more balanced diets in Asia—less rice and more wheat, animal products, fats and oils, and vegetables and fruits—means a decline in rice consumption. The foundations of this decline have been apparent in the global data since the early 1990s, when the aggregate income elasticity of demand for rice turned negative. Consumption of rice per capita peaked about the same time (see Figure 12 and Timmer, Block, and Dawe 2010, for details).

By their very nature, aggregate time series data of the sort used to construct Figure 12 conceal the possibly wide heterogeneity of rice consumption among individual households.[6] This heterogeneity is indeed very wide, at least in most of the countries for which disaggregated data are available. The heterogeneity is driven by household incomes, by whether the household lives in urban or rural areas, and by many other factors, including tastes.

To understand this heterogeneity, a unique set of data was assembled—rice consumption by income (or expenditure) quintile, usually for rural and urban households separately, often for several time periods, for a total of eleven countries. China, India, and Indonesia alone account for 60 percent of world rice consumption. Disaggregated data for these countries are essential to understand the underlying dynamics of rice consumption. The Philippines and Vietnam are also large consumers of rice. The Philippines has on occasion been the world's largest importer, and Vietnam has routinely been the second largest exporter. Bangladesh is both a major rice producer and consumer. Nearly 70 percent of its daily intake of calories still comes from rice.

Patterns of Change

Six patterns stand out from these data. First, there is an overwhelming diversity of rice consumption levels across countries and among regions within a country. In China alone, in 2005, for example, rice consumption in rural Shandong—China's second most populous province with 94 million inhabitants—averaged less than 0.07 kilograms (kg) per capita per week, whereas in rural Jiangxi Province, with 44 million inhabitants, rice consumption averaged over 4.3 kg per capita per week.

Second, there can be major differences in rice consumption by income class for a given country or region at one point in time, especially if they are quite poor. In rural Java-Madura in 1963–64, rice consumption by the top income quintile was 2.552 kg per capita per week, more than three times the level of the bottom quintile. At that time, of course, rural Java was desperately poor. The ratio was 2.2 for rural India in 1983 and 1.7 for rural Anhui province in China in 2005.

Third, large differences between rural and urban consumption of rice are common, but the differences change substantially over time and by income class. For example, in 1963–64 Java-Madura, rural consumption of rice in the bottom quintile of income was only about half that of the same urban quintile, but in the top income quintile, rural consumption of rice was slightly larger than urban (Figure 13). In 2004–5 India, rice consumption in

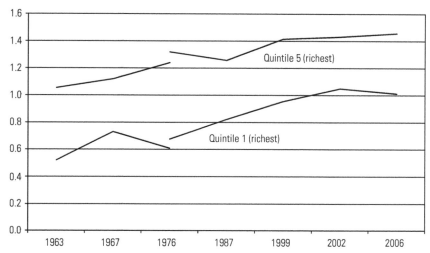

Figure 13. Ratio of Rice Consumption in Rural Areas to Consumption of Rice in Urban Areas for Top and Bottom Quintiles, Indonesia
Note: There are two data points for 1976, one for Java and Madura and the other for all Indonesia. Data in the figure for Java and Madura cover 1963–1976, while data for all Indonesia cover 1976–2006.
Source: Timmer, Block, and Dawe (2010).

the top rural quintile was about half again as large as in the top urban quintile. The rural-urban differences were especially large in China in 2005. In Jiangxi Province, rural consumption of rice was more than 3.3 times higher than urban consumption of rice, when averaged across income quintiles, and it was 3.7 times higher in the top income quintile. In most important rice-consuming areas, rural rice consumption is significantly higher than urban rice consumption. These patterns have direct implications for future levels of rice consumption when a larger share of the population works in urban areas.

Fourth, the income elasticity of demand for rice from these cross-sectional data depends on whether the household lived in a rural or urban area. Most income elasticities for urban households were zero or negative. The rotation of Engel curves that had taken place over time in urban Indonesia is particularly striking. Not only was rice consumption progressively less responsive to higher incomes, but over time the midpoint of the curves was also falling (Figure 14). For urban China in general, the rule held, but

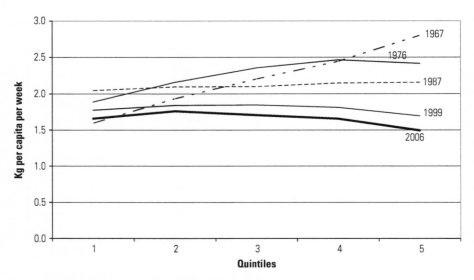

Figure 14. Engel Curves over Time for Urban Indonesia
Note: Data for 1967 refer to Java and Madura.
Source: Timmer, Block, and Dawe (2010).

several poorer provinces showed a positive response of rice consumption to higher incomes in urban areas—Anhui, Henan, Tibet, Shaanxi, and Gansu, for example (these provinces tend to be in traditional wheat-eating areas).

Income elasticities were more positive in rural areas, no doubt because incomes in these locations were lower on average. There was still at least a modest increase in rice consumption across income quintiles in all countries and most provinces of China. Even this effect dropped significantly over time. In Indonesia, for example, the ratio of rural rice consumption in the top income quintile to that of the bottom quintile dropped from 3.29 in 1963–64 (for Java-Madura) to 2.50 in 1976 (all Indonesia) and to just 1.30 in 2006. In India, the same ratio dropped from 2.21 in 1983 to 1.07 in 2004–5. Continued growth of incomes in rural Asia is likely to cause the consumption of rice in these households to fall.[7]

Fifth, there was a dramatic convergence of rice consumption patterns across income classes in those countries for which we have multiple observations— Indonesia, India, and Bangladesh. This convergence was partly a result of flattening Engel curves across income classes as overall levels of income rose

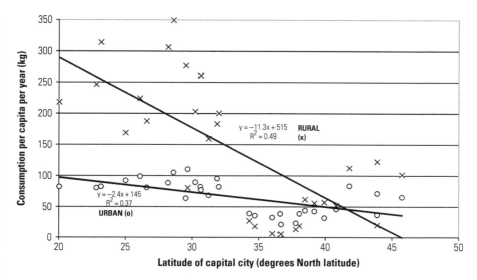

Figure 15. Annual Rice Consumption Per Capita as a Function of Latitude of the
Capital City and Urban and Rural Areas, China 2005
Source: Timmer, Block, and Dawe (2010).

(Figure 14), but it is also possible that tastes were changing in ways that made
patterns of food consumption more uniform across households, whatever
their levels of income and place of residence.

Finally, the argument that tastes are changing to become more homogeneous, especially in urban areas, seems especially relevant in China. In rural
areas in China, the latitude of the capital city was a strong determinant of
per capita consumption of rice. In low latitudes, rice has long been the traditional staple crop. In high latitudes, wheat is the traditional staple, and rural
dwellers stuck to traditional patterns of consumption (based on the data from
2005). Thus, a one-degree decline in latitude increased annual rice consumption per capita in rural areas by 11.3 kg (Figure 15).

As shown in Figure 16, rural consumption of rice was directly corre-
lated with production in the same province—a function of latitude, of
course. But in urban areas, this relationship was breaking down. The coefficient in urban areas showed that a one-degree decline in latitude increased annual rice consumption in urban areas by just 2.4 kg, and
provincial production of rice had relatively little impact on urban consumption. Thus, tastes were becoming more homogeneous in urban China.

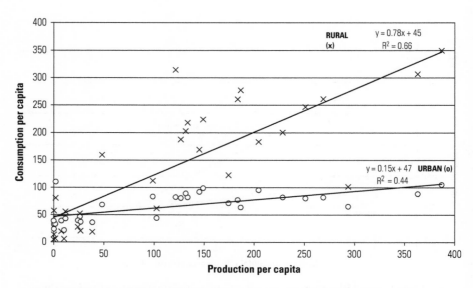

Figure 16. Rural and Urban Rice Consumption Per Capita as a Function of Rice
Production Per Capita, by Province, China 2005
Source: Timmer, Block, and Dawe (2010).

Traditional rice eaters reduced rice consumption, and traditional wheat eaters increased rice consumption.

These results from analyzing the disaggregated data on rice consumption
strongly support findings from the time series analysis of rice consumption.
Except marginally in rural areas, growth in income was no longer an important driver of higher consumption of rice. In most areas, future moves
from rural to urban jobs would mean lower consumption of rice, perhaps significantly lower. In several important rice-consuming countries in Asia, there
has been a steady drift downward over time in the whole Engel function, after
it peaked in the mid-1990s (or later, depending on the country).

As noted above, these are momentous changes in rice consumption,
both driving and being driven by the broader transition of diets. Underlying
the dynamics of these changes is the desire of most Asian consumers to have
a more balanced diet than that which has traditionally been available to
them, especially in rural areas. Historically, it was not unusual for rural
Asian households to get 70 percent of their daily calories from rice. It was the
only food staple that could be grown intensively in their agro-climatic environment, and trade opportunities were limited. Furthermore, Asia is the

only region in the world where a single staple grain so dominates patterns of consumption. As rising incomes, more open trade, and global communications present Asians with the opportunity to diversify their diets, we should not be surprised that they respond.

Transformation of the Food Marketing System

Food marketing systems need to move commodities from the plow to the plate. The ability of particular systems to do this efficiently varies widely from country to country and even within countries. Some systems have modernized rapidly; others remain quite traditional. The pace and impact of change also varies widely within countries and regions, but in Asia and Latin America the majority of food in urban areas is now purchased from modern retail establishments, especially supermarkets. As this chapter has emphasized, the structural transformation has been the historical pathway out of poverty. Two other transformations discussed in this chapter—agricultural and dietary changes—accompany the structural transformation. They also have lives of their own. Accompanying these three basic transformations, and helping them along, have been rapid changes in the entire food marketing system.

The food marketing system is the arena for all three functions which markets must perform if economic growth is going to be both efficient and sustainable—transforming food commodities in time place and form; providing price discovery to determine which resources are scarce and which are abundant; and signaling to farmers and consumers, via these prices, efficient choices of what to produce and what to buy and eat.

Modern supply chains have evolved primarily to provision supermarkets. Concerns for food safety and origin are increasingly reflected in the purchasing decisions of affluent consumers in urban areas. As Chapter 5 emphasizes, the development of modern supply chains, which change the nature of farm, market, and consumer interactions, can be an important source of income growth and job creation in both rural and urban areas. But the spread of modern supply chains can also be a challenge to food security (Reardon et al. 2003; Reardon 2010).

The experience of Asia offers the best evidence and shows the diversity of these complex relationships. Quantifying the linkages and interactions in Figure 17 is complicated at best, but many interactions are reflected in the changing role of rice in production and consumption in the region. So far,

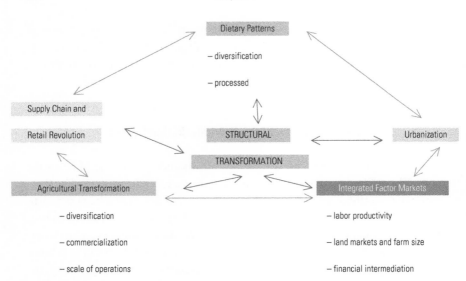

Figure 17. Conceptualizing the Structural Transformation as the General
Equilibrium Process of Integrating Five Key Components of the Food System

this chapter has used the changing role of rice as a story line to carry the
analysis of structural, agricultural, and dietary transformations as they foster improvements in food security.

Traditionally, farmers were connected to consumers by a number of marketing steps, often locally by small traders operating with minimal capital
and primitive technology (Reardon and Timmer 2007, 2012). The goal of
modern supply chains is to reduce the number of transactions between the
farmer and the consumer as a way to reduce costs and increase the efficiency
of the marketing system. Four important trends emerge from this process.

First, within a particular commodity system, such as for rice or corn, the
different levels in the marketing system are increasingly connected by market *and* nonmarket forces. Suppliers of technology in the private sector cannot expect effective demand for inputs unless farmers are able to sell surpluses
into the market. Successful efforts to reduce the transaction costs of incorpo-
rating small farmers into modern supply chains can simultaneously pay dividends by making these same farmers more accessible to suppliers of modern
input.

Second, emphasis on marketing starchy staples as the primary source of
food security has shifted to the diversified foods sector. This shift reflects

Bennett's law (Bennett 1954). Diversification of diets tends to improve the nutritional quality of the diet, although more processed foods and industrialized production of meat raise nutritional, environmental, and food safety concerns.

Third, this increasingly diversified, market-driven food economy is more reflective of supply chain dynamics and consumer demand than in the past. The food marketing system is more sensitive to rapid income growth and somewhat less sensitive to population growth. Population growth is slowing quickly in most of Asia, and income growth continues at a rapid pace. In such environments, understanding how demand for individual items responds to growth in incomes will be necessary for effective planning of investments—by both the public and private sectors—all the way back the chain to input supply. Other factors that shape consumer demand for food will also be important, such as advertising, age structure, urbanization, and globalization of tastes.

Fourth, as consumers increasingly use supermarkets as the source of their purchased food staples, some surprising implications arise for food security. Traditionally, staples have been purchased in small retail shops with multiple grades and varieties available. Prices fluctuated according to local supply and demand conditions and often changed daily during periods of instability. The concentration of purchasing power into a handful of supermarket chains raises the possibility that procurement officers for food staples will encourage (force) their suppliers to maintain large enough stocks so that supplies will be reliable and prices can be kept reasonably stable. Indeed, it is easy to imagine supermarkets, especially in East and Southeast Asia, where unstable rice prices remain a threat to food security, beginning to compete for customers with a promise of safe, reliable rice supplies at a stable, fair price. Stable rice prices could become a private good rather than the public good they have been historically (Timmer 1989, 2010a). When most food is purchased in supermarkets, the debate over how to provide food security—even in settings where volatile food prices can threaten it—will be transformed. We are a long way from that situation in 2014, but supermarkets are increasingly important as a supplier of basic food staples—and hence food security—in developing countries.

From a long-run perspective, these changes are simply part of the process of economic growth and are "the natural course of things," to quote Adam Smith's observation in the eighteenth century.[8] The structural transformation causes entire societies to undergo the wrenching changes associated with agricultural modernization, migration of labor from rural to urban areas, and the emergence of urban industrial centers. As part of this process, both effect and cause, the demographic transition moves a society from an equilibrium of high birth and death rates to a "modern" equilibrium of low birth and death rates. The center of gravity moves from rural to urban areas. The structural transformation has taken as long as three centuries in England and the United States (and is still continuing) and as little as a century in Japan and its East Asian followers. The process takes a long time. That said, modern food supply chains are changing very rapidly.

Modern Supply Chains and the Marketing Sector: Complements or Substitutes?

The primary functions of the marketing sector are inherently coordination tasks. They require an adroit combination of public and private investments if they are to be carried out efficiently because there are substantial public goods dimensions to a smoothly functioning marketing system (see Chapter 2). Historically, these investments have been made very gradually as farmers evolved from subsistence activities toward a more commercial orientation. Now that commercial activities are the norm, even in economies in which efficient marketing networks have not had time to emerge, policy makers are actively seeking new models and approaches to speed the creation of these networks. Supermarkets might already be performing this function, with little input from the public sector. This is an example where private supermarkets are supplanting the public sector in the (suboptimal) provision of public goods.

The agricultural sector as a whole is likely to become much more diversified over the course of the agricultural transformation, when compared with a representative individual farm, but significantly less diversified than patterns of food consumption. This increasing specialization of farms (decreasing diversification) is consistent with *greater* diversity at more aggregate levels because of the commercialization of agriculture.

> Commercialization of agricultural systems leads to greater market orientation of farm production; progressive substitution out of non-traded inputs in favor of purchased inputs; and the gradual decline of integrated farming systems and their replacement by specialized

enterprises for crop, livestock, poultry and aquaculture products. The farm level determinants of increasing commercialization are the rising opportunity costs of family labor and increased market demand for food and other agricultural products. Family labor costs rise due to increasing off-farm employment opportunities, while positive shifts in market demand are triggered by urbanization and/or trade liberalization. (Pingali and Rosegrant 1995: 171–72)

Likewise, patterns of food consumption become more diversified than patterns of domestic agricultural production because of the rising significance of international trade—that is, globalization.

The growing roles of commercialization and globalization in connecting diversity of production at the farm level with diversity of consumption at the household level spawn new problems, however. In particular, increased commercialization requires that farmers learn how to cope with a type of risk that is of little concern to subsistence farmers: the risk of fluctuating prices. At the same time, specialization in crop production increases their risk from yield fluctuations. Mechanisms for coping with risk, including contractual arrangements with supermarkets, thus play an important role in understanding the commercialization of agriculture and the government's role in it. The interplay among price fluctuations, increasing reliance on international trade, specialization of farmers in production for the market in response to profitable new technology, and continued failure of market-based mechanisms for risk management in rural areas accounts for much of the policy interest of governments in the process of rural diversification. Such diversification is impossible without a modern food marketing system.

Most countries want to speed up the gradual process of regional specialization and the development of efficient marketing systems, but they have found that government investments alone are inadequate. Well-developed, low-cost marketing systems require sufficient supplies of the specific commodities being marketed to justify the full investments needed to capture any economies of scale in the system. The process of achieving this balance has meant historically the simultaneous and gradual evolution of both the supply and demand side of the market. Supermarkets are internalizing this coordination process and speeding the rate of specialization. A private marketing system that is closed to outside parties will expand in a coordinated way to stimulate specialized production in a region, but it will be less of a public good. The lower costs generated by specialization can confer very significant competitive advantages on regions that are both low-cost producers of a commodity and have an efficient marketing system that has adequate volume to capture the economies of scale implicit in the forward and backward linkages.[9]

The increasing dominance of modern supply chains raises concerns for both the efficiency and equity of price formation, as more and more transactions are internalized by supermarket procurement officers. Such transactions are not open and transparent, and hence concern will grow over the shift in market power toward a few large buyers, and over the likely exclusion of disadvantaged suppliers from these arrangements. Second, however, and partially offsetting the first concern, supermarkets can also internalize consumers' desires for price stability and food safety, and hence can manage procurement contracts with stability and safety in mind. Finally, supermarkets in developing countries will tend to be as competitive as in rich countries because much of the competition is provided by transnational corporations themselves. Fears about monopoly control and market power seem to be ill founded. The market for the food consumer's dollar is highly contestable, even when only a small handful of players are able to survive the cost competition.

Macroeconomic and Growth Issues

Most effects of modern supply chains in developing countries are likely to play out at the firm and sector level, but macroeconomic effects will not be trivial, especially as lower food costs translate into greater real purchasing power for consumers. By passing on lower costs or improving food quality and convenience, supermarkets can actually speed up the structural transformation as well as the agricultural dietary transformations that are part of it (Timmer 1988).

There will also be significant efficiency effects. The mantra of supermarket procurement officers is to "drive costs out of the food marketing system." Although these "costs" are also someone's income, especially that of farmers and traders in the traditional agricultural marketing chain, lowering costs of food marketing not only allows lower costs to the consumer but also frees up productive resources that can be used in more profitable activities. This is the process by which total factor productivity improves, and this improvement is the basic long-run source of economic growth (Timmer 2002).

A final growth effect might in the long run be the most important: the effects from technology spillovers that result from the use by supermarket managers of imported information technology and modern management techniques honed in the fierce competition of food markets in rich countries. Most of this technology arrives as part of foreign direct investment, which has been the main vehicle of rapid penetration by supermarkets into developing countries (Reardon et al. 2003; Reardon and Timmer 2007, 2012). The technology is often proprietary, and supermarket owners go to great lengths to keep it internal to the company. But like most technologies, the knowledge that these tools and techniques exist is the key to rapid emulation, as local managers trained by the first wave of foreign supermarkets leave to establish their own companies and consulting firms. Thus the spillovers from introducing modern information technologies and management techniques can occur fairly rapidly and have widespread effects across the entire economy, not just in food retailing.

Modern supply chains will affect not only the efficiency of the food marketing chain but also the distribution of benefits from the value added in the process. In general, it is very difficult to say whether these distributional changes will be positive or negative—that is, whether income distribution will improve or not.

There are two important offsetting effects. On the negative side, rapid penetration of supermarkets into traditional food marketing systems can quickly displace family-run, often informal retail shops, traders in traditional wet markets, and small-scale wholesalers. The people displaced usually earn relatively low incomes and will have to make significant adjustments to find new livelihoods. The distributional effect is likely to be negative and can be substantial if these small-scale food marketing firms are numerous and widely visible. Their imminent demise can also generate significant political resistance to the spread of supermarkets, an effect already seen throughout Asia and with historical antecedents in the United States, Europe, and Japan.

The impact of supermarket penetration on the farm sector has tended to be the most vocal issue. Experience suggests that small farmers can rapidly lose access to supermarket supply chains and thus be cut off from the growing value-added component of retail food baskets (Reardon et al. 2009). These farmers might fall further into poverty. But this experience is not uniform. There are circumstances in which small farmers have gained profitable access to modern supply chains. Keeping a significant number of small farmers in the supply chain of supermarkets in the short to medium run is likely to be essential for poor countries to reap widespread social benefits from the rapid domination by modern food supply chains. The impact on the traditional food marketing sector will be small relative to this impact on small farmers.

Potential social benefits also have positive distributional effects. The extraordinary spread and speed of supermarket penetration suggests that affluent consumers find them time-saving and convenient. Low-income consumers do not benefit differentially, at least initially. But lower real costs of food across the board (corrected for quality, safety, and convenience, all of which consumers value) have an impact of greatest importance to the poor. Efforts to slow the penetration of supermarkets on behalf of small farmers and traditional agents in the food marketing system need to keep this widespread consumer benefit in the calculus. At the same time, significantly more evidence is needed on whether poor consumers have access to these benefits (Asfaw 2007; Michelson 2013).

The fate of small farmers has been a source of policy concern well before the supermarket revolution gained speed in the early 1990s in Latin America, but there is no question that the issue is squarely on the policy agenda. In the short run, finding income opportunities for small farmers is essential, but in the longer run, the structural transformation requires that they need to have other options, including migration to urban jobs.

Transformations and Food Security

Policy makers need to be careful not to choose winners or reward losers. The process of economic development is dynamic and unpredictable, full of "creative destruction" (McCraw 2007). There will be winners and losers in the process, but only innovation and technical change can raise living standards in the long run.

The drivers of change in modern food systems might now be multinational corporations rather than domestic marketing boards. The policy levers might be nutritional education and emphasis on activity levels in schools to prevent childhood obesity. Agricultural choices may be more influenced by quality standards and relationships with procurement officers than price policies and extension agents. These changes require that policy analysts and policy makers also have a broader perspective—and a broader set of skills—than before.

The food system is more consumer driven than before. The marketing system is even more important as the efficient vehicle for transmitting desires of consumers back to farmer opportunities. There are fewer players in the new marketing system. However, the old problems—building human capital through education, improving the institutional environment for risk management, and stimulating technical change while managing its consequences—remain front and center on the agenda.

The central role of the structural transformation has been understood for some time: the long-run, integrated modernization of the agricultural, industrial, and service sectors underlies economic growth. The convergence of labor productivity in the agricultural and nonagricultural sectors, as that productivity increases over time, provides higher standards of living in both sectors.

The endpoint of the structural transformation—the full integration of factor markets between rural and urban areas—is now within sight in the richest transition countries, but remains a challenge for poor- and middle-income countries. A failed structural transformation, where many poor rural households move to slums in cities because productive work is no longer available on their farms or there are too many mouths to feed from the small amount of land controlled by the household, has been characteristic of many countries in sub-Saharan Africa as well as several in South Asia (Badiane 2011; Binswanger-Mkhize 2012). Failed structural transformations are always accompanied by failed agricultural transformations.

Historically, the structural transformation has been the only sustainable pathway out of poverty. I have made that argument forcefully, but I am not alone. Most of the early development economists and economic historians took this process as an historical inevitability. I studied under Alexander Gerschenkron and co-taught development economics with Hollis Chenery! From this intellectual perspective, it is very hard to understand how a sustainable escape from hunger into modern economic growth and food security can be accomplished without these transformations taking place in a more or less orderly fashion. But what if they do not?

CHAPTER 5

When Pro-poor Growth and Structural Transformation Fail

It is no secret that sub-Saharan Africa and South Asia remain the epicenter of concerns about ending hunger in the reasonably near future. Even rapid economic growth in India since 1990 has brought only modest reductions in hunger and malnutrition. Rapid growth in a number of countries in Africa since the commodity booms of the early 2000s have brought riches to some but little reduction in hunger and poverty on that continent. In view of the rapid reductions in hunger and poverty experienced in East and Southeast Asia, and earlier reductions in Western Europe and North America, the question has to be why.[1]

What Goes Wrong?

In a book stimulated by extensive interaction with Bruce L. Gardner before his untimely death in 2008, Isabelle Tsakok identifies five essential ingredients for a successful agricultural transition:

> This book is the result not of the search for correlations, but of the effort to identify conditions that are common to all successful transformations. It tests these conditions by looking at experience worldwide. The five conditions that survive these tests are the following:
> First, a stable framework of macroeconomic and political stability. The central and local governments are able to enforce peace and order.
> Second, an effective technology-transfer system. Research and extension messages reach the majority of farmers.

Third, access to lucrative markets. The majority of farmers face expanding markets of paying customers. To them, investing in agricultural and rural production is good business.

Fourth, an ownership system, including a system of usufruct rights that reward individual initiative and toil. It is feasible for farm/rural families to gain monetarily for risk taking and hard work.

Fifth, employment-creating non-agricultural sectors. As agriculture becomes more productive, it must shed labor, which unless absorbed in non-farm jobs that pay as well as agriculture would simply constitute exporting farm poverty to other sectors.

While these may seem obvious as stated, what is not obvious is how some governments have been able to maintain them over decades. How governments have succeeded in maintaining them has varied from country to country. However, there is a common thread. Underlying all five conditions is *sustained government investment in and delivery of public goods and services over decades.* (Tsakok 2011: xxi–xxii)

The story so far has mostly been about countries that have been able to deliver the conditions that Tsakok describes. But what happens when they fail? The answer depends to a large extent on why they fail, and there are at least three basic possibilities—a poor resource base, weak institutions, and/or the problems stemming from being a latecomer in a world of increased global competitiveness.

The Resource Base and Agricultural Productivity

Development specialists and economic historians have known for a long time that some ecological and geographical settings are more suitable for rapid growth in agricultural productivity than others (Djurfeldt et al. 2005; Jones 1981; Diamond 1997; Hayami and Ruttan 1971).The sharp difference in starting points for agricultural development in sub-Saharan Africa and in Asia provides a focus for Jones's cogent summary of why development has lagged on the continent (Jones 1981).

If we cast around for continents and cultures to set aside European experience and turn first to Africa, we find that the general level of development and the size and density of population lagged well behind in the historic period. . . . There were towns of some size in West Africa and stone buildings of moderate skill in Zimbabwe and in the chain of fortifications across southern Africa. . . . But no wheel, no plough, and no stable combination of powers that could erect a common front against Arab or European slavers. . . .

In the wet Africa, notably West Africa, living was easy but infant mortality was horrendously high. In the dry Africa hunting and gathering were not unrewarding, but the agriculture was not productive by world standards. Soils are ancient and poor, having been leached to the poverty line. Rainfall is adequate over vast areas but there is always a dry season. Shifting cultivation over the centuries may have lowered the productivity of forest areas everywhere. Huge tracts of forest are underlain by the charcoal layers and pottery fragments of previous shifting cultivators. Fire and grazing pressure encourage thickets of unpalatable shrubs. Indeed, but at the opening of the modern period there were no great virgin tropical forests left in Africa. . . .

Where there were denser populations within Africa they were connected only by long overland routes which made freight charges a large part of the final price of goods. This restricted the market. Land was in general neither a scarce resource nor a particularly rich one. There was scant incentive or pressure for development or invention. Not even the wheel was forthcoming—and to overcome its problem of a small and very widely dispersed market, Africa probably needed not only the wheel but the motor-driven vehicle as well. (Jones 1981: 153–55)

Weak Institutions Lead to Poor Governance and Bad Policy Choices

It is hard to disentangle the emergence of strong institutions that foster growth in agricultural productivity from the presence of a good environment for such growth, although a substantial wing of economic history and modern development economics is engaged in that search.[2] Still, agricultural development specialists have identified the key linkages, from weak institutions to poor governance and from there to bad policy choices (North 1959; Bates 1981; Bates and Block 2013; Mellor forthcoming). Because a successful agricultural transformation is hostage to poor governance and bad policy, these linkages matter (Tsakok 2011).

> When the high yielding varieties hit Asia they were preceded by a long history of development of agricultural institutions and an immediately prior period of foreign aid assistance on a large scale to the key institutions of research, extension, and finance. Concurrently large foreign assistance went to higher agricultural education to train the large numbers of personnel to staff those institutions and a rapidly growing private sector as well. Thus, the institutional structure for quickly modifying and adapting through applied research, extending knowledge farmers, and financing the inputs was well-established. The new high yielding varieties walked into a very hospitable institutional environment (Mellor et al. 1968).
>
> In Africa, there was a similar, early period of foreign assistance to institutional development in a few countries e.g. Michigan State in Nigeria, Oklahoma in Ethiopia developing quite good agricultural universities and through them research and extension. But by the time independence had been generalized and a green revolution could be thought of, foreign aid was already turning away from agriculture, away from the non-poor small commercial farmer who accounts for the bulk of growth, and most importantly away from national scale development of institutions by governments and towards small scale unintegrated private sector and NGO efforts with little national impact (Mellor 1989; Mellor, Delgado, Blackie 1987; Lele 1991). The abandonment of assistance to higher agricultural education was most striking and most damaging. As a result the institutional structures, particularly the central public sector component is still way short even now of the Asian standard when the green revolution struck. Even now there is little sign of a massive effort. (Mellor forthcoming: 5)

Bates and Block (2013) note that significant progress in building institutions which support the rural economy has been made in Africa since the spread of democracy, and Radelet agrees: "Local actions, courageous leadership and smart policies have been the central drivers of Africa's progress, with foreign assistance playing a supporting role. . . . Development is hard. Businesses, governments, aid agencies and small farmers all sometimes succeed and too often fail. Those involved must constantly strive, experiment and learn" (Radelet 2013: A32).

Globalization and Agricultural Competitiveness

The notion that nations compete with each other is highly controversial. Michael Porter's hugely influential book explains how nations can compete more effectively, but many trade economists feel that companies compete, not nations (Porter 1990; Neary 2003). The general issue cannot be resolved here. Porter's concept of "competitive advantage" is broader but less concrete than trade economists' notion of comparative advantage. It does seem clear that governments can provide a more or less supportive environment for both the private sector and public institutions to support smallholder farmers and the rural economy. The outcome affects farm productivity and the competitiveness of agricultural commodities in both local and world markets.

The challenge to latecomers in the development process has been stressed in an empirical analysis of rural transformation, built on an extensive new statistical database, conducted by Bruno Losch and his colleagues in the RuralStruc Project with the support of Agence Française de Développement and the World Bank (Losch, Fréguin-Gresh, and White 2012). Their analysis and conclusions are especially sobering for much of rural Africa, which they see as trapped in highly traditional agrarian structures. These societies face mounting pressures from local demographics and global competition for both rural and urban goods.

> In 2050, North America and Europe combined will account for only 15 percent of the global population. Asia will remain the world's most populous region, but the relative weights of the populations of Sub-Saharan Africa (SSA) and Europe will be reversed compared with 1960 (10 percent for SSA and 20 percent for Europe in 1960, and the reverse in 2050). This major population realignment will exacerbate existing inequalities in access to resources.
>
> Meanwhile, despite continued urbanization, 2.8 billion people will still live in rural areas in 2050. Rural populations will still be massive and will still earn their living primarily from agriculture. Regional differences in urban dynamics will strongly affect the

distribution of rural populations: South Asia and Sub-Saharan Africa will together account for nearly two-thirds of world's rural population, and uniquely, in SSA the rural population will continue to grow.

These trends are of major importance because they challenge the prospects for development in much of the world. Agriculture is more than just the production of food. Because agriculture is the core activity and main source of livelihood for billions of rural people, its evolution will shape the process of economic, social, and environmental change. The situation is especially challenging in SSA, where the lack of economic diversification—reflected most notably in the region's anemic rate of industrialization—limits options for employment outside agriculture and the informal sector. . . .

Today, the situation for developing countries in the early stages of structural transformation is drastically different [from the conditions facing Europe, North America, Latin America, and Asia]. Sub-Saharan Africa—the last region of the world to embark on the structural transformation process—faces the challenges of an incipient economic transition and an unachieved demographic transition in the context of a global open economy and under the constraints of climate change. (Losch, Fréguin-Gresh, and White 2012: 1–4)

This perspective of a challenged, even failed, structural transformation in sub-Saharan Africa is also the topic of Badiane's address to the Stanford Symposium Series on Global Food Policy and Food Security in the 21st Century (Badiane 2011).

Different Outcomes of the Structural Transformation

As was stressed in Chapter 4, the central role of the structural transformation has been understood for some time. The convergence of labor productivity in the agricultural and nonagricultural sectors, even as that productivity increases over time, provides higher standards of living in both sectors. Historically, the structural transformation has been thought to be the only sustainable pathway out of poverty.

But developments in recent decades have not been so supportive of that broad historical pathway followed by industrial and transition countries.

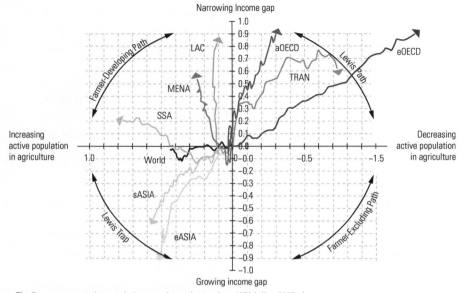

The figure represents the cumulative annual growth rates from 1970 (=0) to 2007 of:
-the active population in agriculture (x-axis) (FAO, 2010),
-the income differential between agricultural and non-agricultural workers (y-axis) measured with the Labour
Income Ratio (LIR, eqation 4) in 1990-US$ (UNSTAT, 2010)

Figure 18. The Agricultural Transformations
Source: Dorin, Hourcade, and Benoit-Cattin (2013). Paper with regional details
available: http://www.centre-cired.fr/spip.php?article1508.

Consider Figure 18, which is reproduced from a paper by Bruno Dorin and
colleagues at Montpellier (Dorin, Hourcade, and Benoit-Cattin 2013). There
are other possible pathways of structural transformation, several of which
do not lead out of poverty. Indeed, much of Asia seems to be headed into a
"Lewis trap," with a growing income disparity between agricultural and nonagricultural workers. Sub-Saharan Africa is moving steadily toward smaller
farms rather than the (modestly) larger ones needed for a successful structural transformation.

Many countries are not following the standard, historical path of structural transformation. The "middle-income trap" seems to have captured a
number of countries in Asia and Latin America. After initial periods of rapid
growth and convergence with rich economies, these countries have slower
growth and are no longer converging. To break out of this trap, governments
need to help farmers on very small plots raise their incomes. Do they move

to the city or do they raise productivity on their tiny plots of land? What can governments do so that this process moves quickly and smoothly, with a minimum of hardship on households that are already barely getting by? And how can all of this be accommodated by the need to have a "green" revolution in agricultural production techniques so that food supplies become more sustainable?

Ousmane Badiane directly raised these issues in his analysis of Africa's agricultural problems, its structural history, and the possible ways forward (Badiane 2011). The task is "getting agriculture moving" (the title of Art Mosher's influential 1966 book) but also getting industry moving. Badiane maintains that part of the failure of Africa's agriculture is because of an even more depressing failure of its industrial sector.

When the Kenyan parliament tabled its first white paper on food policy in 1980, it was easy to observe on even a short field trip the vast differences in multicrop farming systems in Kenya from the much more uniform, rice-based farming systems on Java. My conclusion at the time was that agricultural development would be more difficult in Africa, even in such favored regions as Kenya, because of the great diversity of the farming systems and the complexity of developing profitable new technologies for them.

More troubling, however, was the policy approach being followed by the government. Michael Lipton coined the term "urban bias" in 1977 to describe antirural policies of governments (Lipton 1977). The term accurately described the Kenyan situation. Despite significant success in raising agricultural output between 1970 and 1980, the economic framework for agriculture was highly exploitive and urban oriented, especially because of macroeconomic policies and marketing regulations. It was hard to imagine how the country could continue to develop its smallholder agriculture with such an antirural bias.

As the 1980s played out, this concern seemed amply justified. Africa went through a series of economic crises and more or less forced structural adjustment programs imposed by the donor community (Eicher 1992). Agricultural productivity fell in many countries (Block 1995). At the same time, Asia struggled with low commodity prices but continued to invest in its smallholder agriculture, especially rice and such labor-intensive export crops as rubber, coffee, palm oil, and cocoa.

Within Asia, agricultural productivity continued to rise during the 1980s, the structural transformation was quite rapid, and poverty was significantly lower in most of Asia in 1990 than it was in 1980.

By the end of the 1980s, it became fashionable to seek "lessons from Asia for Africa." USAID sponsored a series of conferences on the topic, engineered mostly by Dick Cobb, with assistance from Winrock International. As a lead commentator in this series, I laid out three major concerns for Africa's agricultural development from the perspective of Asia's historical record (Timmer 1991a).

First, and somewhat paradoxically, wages in Africa were not low enough to compete with Asian workers in either labor-intensive manufactured goods or agricultural export crops. It was hard to see how Africa could develop a dynamic urban economy that would help pull up labor productivity in rural areas as well. At this time, hundreds of millions of surplus workers in China had not yet entered the world labor market as additional competitors.

Second, Africa had lost the capacity to do state-of-the-art agricultural research on either food crops or export crops. Asia was making rapid progress on both. As a consequence, Africa was simply no longer competitive in world markets for many of its agricultural products—especially palm oil and rubber. New Asian producers also threatened Africa's exports of coffee and cocoa.

Third, the serious governance issues that were apparent in Kenya in 1980 showed no signs of being resolved. If anything, antirural bias was becoming stronger, reinforced by the availability of cheap food in world markets to provision the major coastal cities. Much of this imported food was made even cheaper through aggressive food aid policies pushed by the OECD countries. Easy availability of food aid had a distinct disincentive impact on the policy environment for agriculture, even if the econometric evidence indicated little short-run impact on local market prices and incentives for farmers (which were very low already).

While some parts of Asia were coping with the middle-income trap after the 1990s, and despite significant signs of economic growth on the African continent, Asia continued to pull away. The structural transformation in East and Southeast Asia has continued to proceed rapidly, with absolute levels of population in rural areas beginning to decline (South Asia continues to lag in this process). This fact has important implications for the startling finding that the structural transformation in Africa has been "backward"— that is, it has lowered labor productivity rather than raising it. Migration of labor has been from relatively high-productivity farming activities to very low-productivity jobs in the informal rural and urban service sectors (Badiane 2011).

This push of labor out of agriculture into the service sector has important implications for the nature of the development strategy that should be pursued. In the classic labor-surplus model developed by W. Arthur Lewis, the basis for much of Asia's strategic approach, low productivity ("surplus") labor is pulled out of agriculture and employed at higher productivity in a rapidly growing industrial sector. Wages are low in both sectors until the surplus labor runs out (the Lewis "turning point"), and these low wages permit the industrial sector to make large profits that are reinvested in expanding factory capacity, which leads to more industrial employment.

If the Badiane story is right, the surplus labor in Africa appears increasingly to be in the informal service sector. A strategy of raising labor productivity on farms, thus freeing up food and labor for the industrial sector, will not have the same impact it had in Asia, because there are few high-productivity industrial jobs in Africa. Raising productivity in the informal sector would seem to be a much trickier task. No obvious technological innovations are available for the informal service sector that would match the impact of the Green Revolution on agricultural productivity and its subsequent stimulus to the entire development effort. Microfinance schemes and ready access to cell phones are not the answer. These concerns are similar to those raised by the RuralStruc research program (Losch, Fréguin-Gresh, and White 2012).

The potential importance of this informal service sector thus highlights the concern of many development analysts for the role of social services in poverty alleviation. If social services focus on safety net provisions based on entitlement mechanisms, the resources will not be available for the kind of social services needed in the health and education sectors that will build human capital and raise the productivity of workers in the informal service economy. This outcome would be a perverse structural transformation. Much hunger will remain decades from now if this pattern continues.

The South Asian Challenge

South Asia has more poor people than Africa, more pervasive child malnutrition, and significantly greater hunger. Yet South Asia has been a primary beneficiary of the Green Revolution, and agricultural development has proceeded much more rapidly than in Africa. Why this disconnect? In Pakistan and Sri Lanka, it is easy to blame widespread ethnic and religious conflicts as impediments to broad-based economic growth and structural transformation.

Bangladesh has a surprisingly successful record of reducing hunger and malnutrition, despite being written off as a "basket case" during the food crisis in the early 1970s (Hardin 1974). The big (in every sense of the word) enigma is India.

In fact, India has been an enigma to several generations of development specialists. The "Hindu rate of growth" of 2 percent per year per capita, when East and Southeast Asia exceeded 5 percent, was an early issue. The surprisingly rapid response to economic liberalization in the 1990s resolved that issue but raised another. In an increasingly globalized and competitive world, would India's economic policies be adequate to meet the new challenge from China? And from the perspective of 2014, another important puzzle has emerged: why has rapid economic growth not transformed the diets and health of India's poor, especially in rural areas?

India in Chinese Perspective

Rapid economic growth in China and India is the envy, and worry, of the world.[3] Never in history have so many people been pulled out of poverty so quickly. But the newly emergent middle class in both countries has familiar desires: better diets, more comfortable housing and places to shop, and more convenient transportation, including personal automobiles. These rapidly expressed desires are placing demands on global resources, which have stirred new Malthusian fears. Is there enough food and fuel for people in China and India to live like those in Europe and the United States?

This India-China comparison has been taken on directly by Gulati and Fan (2007). Their edited volume is the product of a massive collaborative research effort which was difficult to arrange and manage. The International Food Policy Research Institute, home base at the time for Gulati and Fan, deserves credit for pulling it off.

Gulati and Fan do not address the global resource dimensions of the Chinese and Indian growth successes. Instead, they seek to understand the foundations of the successes themselves. Not surprisingly, success stems from efforts in both countries to revitalize their rural economies. Such revitalization was essential, the various authors argue, if the massive and impoverished populations in each country were to have any hope of higher living standards, including enough food to eat. The specter of hunger was a basic driver of reform policy in both China and India.

Three main themes drive the story of rural reforms in China and India. First, China started well behind India in 1950 in terms of poverty, institutional infrastructure, and mechanisms of governance. Both countries struggled for thirty years to find a path to inclusive modernization, where "inclusive" refers to the distribution of economic gains, not to the political institutions that bring them about. But to most observers' surprise, China found the path sooner, exploited it faster, and has roared past India in nearly all indicators of economic success. Only India's democratic form of governance (flawed as it is) holds promise for convergence in the future, and even this promise depends to a significant degree on China's political elite ultimately being unable to reform the institutional foundations of its rapid growth (Acemoglu and Robinson 2012). The Chinese leadership selected in 2012 seems determined not to let this happen.

Second, and no doubt controversially, China's initial conditions laid down during the Maoist era are now seen to provide substantial advantages in managing rapid, inclusive growth. Greater gender equality, investments in rural human and physical capital, even the capacity to control policy from the center, now make the Maoist experiment with collectivization and rigid central planning seem not quite the disaster it appeared to be in the late 1970s. Rozelle (2013) argues that China's starting point for rapid growth in 1978 looks remarkably like Africa's starting point in 2013. Both have the potential to build on decades of catastrophic economic policies.

Third, details matter. They matter at both a strategic level and at the level of commodity-specific, region-specific approaches to agricultural development. A rich literature, to which Gulati and Fan (2007) add substantially, testifies to significant contrasts in China's and India's approaches to the big rural reform issues. In trade policy, China opted early on for a much more open approach. To alleviate poverty, China opted for rapid growth in rural areas, whereas India retained a state-provided safety net that has become increasingly cumbersome and expensive. In the rural nonfarm economy, which stimulated development in China since the 1970s, India is only beginning to facilitate the natural vibrancy of its rural entrepreneurs, who are investing to service their agricultural neighbors (Perkins et al. 1977 Reardon et al. 2012).

For the future, it is hard to miss the pessimism of Indian authors and analysts as they look at their country's rural reforms and progress compared with China's. The chapter in Gulati and Fan (2007) by V. S. Vyas, the dean of agricultural economists in India, is titled "Market Reforms in Indian Agriculture:

One Step Forward and Two Steps Back" (Vyas 2007: 264–82). The not-so-hidden agenda of this massive comparative research project by Gulati and Fan is apparent in the final sentence of the acknowledgments: "We are most grateful to Indian Prime Minister Manmohan Singh, the architect of economic reforms in India, who inaugurated the first conference in New Delhi and is still keen to know what each country can learn from the other" (Gulati and Fan 2007: xxii). Competition works in powerful ways, even in the world of political economy (Timmer 2008b: 642).

The Outlook for India: Prospects for Ending Poverty and Hunger

Whether India can make substantial progress in ending poverty and hunger is hotly debated both inside and outside the country. Gaiha, Jha, and Kulkarni (2014) seek to answer the question directly, within the broader context of the evolution of India's economy and policy arena.[4] The authors, three of the most respected academics working on Indian food policy and poverty dynamics, bring a breadth of analytical techniques to rich data sets and then place their analysis in the context of India's perplexing political economy.

Befitting its large role in the developing world, India's approaches to solving these problems have attracted high-profile attention. An intense focus on the massive health and education problems facing India comes from two of its best-known analysts, Amaryta Sen and Jean Drèze (Drèze and Sen 2013). A review of the Drèze and Sen book in the *Economist* (2013) highlights the issues:

> As a conundrum it could hardly be bigger. Six decades of laudably fair elections, a free press, rule of law and much else should have delivered rulers who are responsive to the ruled. India's development record, however, is worse than poor. It is host to some of the world's worst failures in health and education. If democracy works, why are so many Indian lives still so wretched?
>
> Social indicators leave that in no doubt. A massive blackout last summer [2012] caught global attention, yet 400m Indians had (and still have) no electricity. Sanitation and public hygiene are awful, especially in the north: half of all Indians still defecate in the open, resulting in many deaths from diarrhoea and encephalitis. Polio may

be gone, but immunization rates for most diseases are lower than in sub-Saharan Africa. Twice as many Indian children (43%) as African ones go hungry.

Many adults, especially women, are also undernourished, even as obesity and diabetes spread among wealthier Indians. Despite gains, extreme poverty is rife and death in childbirth is all too common. Prejudice kills on an immense scale: as many as 600,000 fetuses are aborted each year because they are female. Compared even with its poorer neighbours, Bangladesh and Nepal, India's social record is unusually grim. (*Economist*, June 29, 2013: 74)

Against this record, Gaiha, Jha, and Kulkarni (2014) offer documentation of the problems as well as insights into solutions. Three basic forces drive their empirical investigations. Incomes, prices, and gender each have direct consequences for how policies might be brought to bear in bringing about improvements. The authors are understandably cautious in claiming to have understood these problems well enough to offer full-blown policy recommendations. Great uncertainties remain in understanding causal relationships among key economic and social variables as determinants of hunger and malnutrition. Thus an incremental approach to policy formulation, learning from evidence-based analysis as experience unfolds, is essential to sustaining progress (Timmer 1997b, 2004b).

The analysis by Gaiha, Jha, and Kulkarni shows that, first, incomes at the household level are directly related to nearly all of the problems under analysis: demand for nutrients, the dietary transition from reliance on starchy staples to a much more diversified diet, the measurement of malnutrition, the prevalence of poverty traps in rural areas and prevalence of child malnutrition, the increasing incidence of noncommunicable diseases and health problems of the aging and affluent, even the prevalence of leakages from targeted programs for subsidized food intake or guaranteed work opportunities.

Incomes are the leading driver of nutritional outcomes. Choice matters, and higher incomes provide greater freedom of choice. The importance of continuing to increase incomes per capita in India—not just on average but among the poor, where it really matters—cannot be stressed too much.

Second, absolute and relative prices matter to food consumption and to nutritional outcomes. To someone who published a book on "getting prices right" in 1986, the continued relevance and significant impact of food prices

is not surprising (Timmer 1986). Market economies depend on price formation to send signals to producers and consumers about what to grow and
what to eat. If these signals are distorted or ignored, the market paradigm
falls apart. State planning of crop production and rationing of consumption
goods cannot replace it. Prices need to work.

Finally, incomes and prices do not come even close to being the whole
story in explaining India's perplexing patterns of dietary choices, malnutrition, and disease. Many other variables are at play, and the authors are good
at teasing them out, even when measurement is difficult—for example, individual nutritional requirements.

Still, there are powerful and easily measurable forces at work. Perhaps
the most important and visible is gender. It is well established that the quality of home care for children, in particular their nutrient intake and health
care, is greatly conditioned by the empowerment of the mother. In turn, this
role of women is characterized by a multitude of cultural factors (which economists often take as fixed); but in reality, the woman's role in the household
can often be enhanced, quite significantly, by educational opportunities and
access to family planning services.

Knowledge of good nutritional practices seems to be acquired mostly by
observational learning. But we now know that it can be taught in school. The
result is significant improvement in children's nutritional status (Webb and
Block 2004). Any society that cares about the welfare of its children will be
working hard to guarantee that women attend school and learn about health
and nutrition.

The bleak status of children's nutritional status, especially in rural India,
has its parallels in China as well. A team from Stanford University working
with Chinese scientists has documented the depth of malnutrition among
school-age children in rural China and has started a campaign to mobilize
additional resources and policy attention from the government. Early malnutrition can cause severe cognitive impairment, permanently damaging the
ability to learn and think creatively: "China's stability and prosperity, and
that of the region and the globe, depends on how well today's youth master
the knowledge and skills that enable them to thrive in the technology-driven
globalized world of the mid-twenty-first century. Resilient public and private sector leaders of the future must be able to think creatively. Therefore,
China's government should respond to population aging by acting now to
invest more in the health and education of youth, especially the rural poor"

(Eggleston et al. 2012). India does not face China's immediate problems of an aging population or hollowed-out rural villages. Still, the extent and severity of childhood malnutrition documented by these recent studies surely call for similar initiatives to guarantee that the next generation will have the cognitive abilities and skills to contribute to India's modernization and productivity growth (Gaiha, Jha, and Kulkarni 2014; Drèze and Sen 2013).

Reducing Poverty and Hunger in Africa and South Asia: Elements of Success

The main elements of successful approaches to reducing poverty and hunger have been known for some time (Mosher 1966; Hayami and Ruttan 1971; Mellor 1966, 1995; Timmer 1988, 2002; Tsakok 2011). Without exception, historical experience shows that an agricultural transformation has been part and parcel of a broader structural transformation that raises productivity of labor in both rural and urban areas. This higher productivity of labor, and the higher incomes that it supports, is then the main vehicle for reducing poverty and hunger. More active interventions by governments determined to speed the process can help—such as stabilization of food prices, safety nets for vulnerable households, public investments in rural infrastructure, support for agricultural research, and outreach programs to deliver modern inputs and knowledge to farmers. None of these specific measures to stimulate the farming sector work, however, in the absence of broad-based economic growth. So far, this chapter has focused on how hard it is to put all these pieces together in a sustainable approach to reducing poverty and hunger in Africa and South Asia (Losch, Fréguin-Gresh, and White 2012; Binswanger-Mkhize 2012). But the elements of success in this endeavor are also beginning to take shape.

Finding the Appropriate Farm Size

Finding the appropriate farm size, and type of farmer, on which public investments can be focused is an important issue that needs to be resolved before further elements of strategies for poverty alleviation become clear. The tiny farms emerging in much of Africa and throughout Asia seem not to be large enough to access and utilize modern agricultural technology efficiently. They certainly cannot produce enough income to keep the household out of poverty.

Part of the farm-size debate spills over to the service and industrial sectors. If farm size needs to increase, jobs will need to be found for labor exiting agriculture. In both Africa and South Asia, the record of job creation outside agriculture has been poor. The issue is how labor-intensive, competitive manufacturing and service jobs can be created in the nonfarm economy. Here, Africa seems to be at a very significant disadvantage.

The small-farm/large-farm debate is largely misfocused. Increasingly, the issue seems to be whether all the currently farming households, no matter how small their plots, should be supported as a way to alleviate poverty. The main alternative presented is to attract large-scale (usually foreign) investment into land purchases that will be organized and managed as highly mechanized, capital-intensive farms, often with output destined for other countries. Pingali (2012) and the Bill and Melinda Gates Foundation (2012) are vigorous and forceful advocates of a smallholder strategy, especially in Africa and South Asia. In sharp contrast, Dercon (2012), Collier (2007), and Collier and Dercon (forthcoming) are the most prominent voices rejecting the exclusive focus on smallholder farmers. They contend that only large farms can bring the capital, management skills, access to new markets, and economies of scale that now are required of modern agriculture.

Both historical lessons and the actual facts get in the way of this debate. At least a third of African smallholder farmers now have less land to till than will support their families' food needs, even with higher productivity. The fraction is higher in South Asia. These are not commercially viable farmers, either now or going forward, no matter what technologies become available or what the market price is for their output (Mellor forthcoming). Most of these farmers operating tiny plots must exit agriculture for alternatives elsewhere if there is to be a successful agricultural transformation—higher productivity for agricultural labor—and from that a successful structural transformation and a sustainable pathway out of poverty. The perspective offered by Byerlee and Haggblade (2013) seems sensibly grounded in the facts with a clear recognition of the alternative commercial farm models which will be viable going forward.

Over time, as agricultural growth and structural transformation proceed, Africa's rural households must navigate one of three primary pathways to the future. The first path centers on agriculture and involves transitioning from low-productivity agriculture into high-productivity commercial farming. The second pathway focuses on rural nonfarm businesses, including value added transformation of agricultural products, and wage labor in rural areas. The third pathway involves exit from rural areas and migration to Africa's growing cities (World Bank 2007). Perhaps surprisingly, agricultural productivity growth offers a powerful stimulus facilitating transitions along all three of these pathways. Although two-thirds of Africans currently work primarily in agriculture, probably only a minority possess the management skills, asset endowments, financial resources and social capital required to succeed as commercial farmers along pathway one. Instead, the majority of today's subsistence farmers will need to transition out of agriculture over the coming generation along pathways two and three. To do so, they will require a boost in agricultural land and labor productivity, especially for women, that enables them to free their children from farm labor obligations, deploy oxen or hired labor in their stead, and use agricultural earnings to finance school fees that will prepare their children for successful careers in the rural nonfarm or urban economies. (Byerlee and Haggblade 2013: 2)

This is the only approach in which some smallholder farmers remain commercially viable, while many of their neighbors find jobs in the nearby nonfarm economy or in urban areas. Such an agricultural transformation, as part of a broader economy-wide structural transformation, remains the best hope for successful pathways out of poverty.

The answer will not be large-scale, mechanized, and "capitalistic" farms managed by absentee landowners using hired labor. With a few narrow exceptions, these have never worked anywhere, and they will not work in Africa or South Asia. At the same time, raising agricultural productivity—both of land and labor—will require a continuous increase in the size of the median farm in both regions. Within a generation, median farm size in India needs to be closer to five hectares than the current two hectares; in Africa the median size for commercially viable farms needs to be about ten hectares. Such substantial increases in median farm size—roughly a doubling—will be accomplished only if there are suitable, and productive, exit options for surplus agricultural labor. Poverty and

hunger will remain as significant problems until this track is well established in both regions.

Labor-Intensive, Competitive Industrialization

As the editor and main intellectual force behind the influential volume on
the changing role of agriculture "on the road to industrialization," John W.
Mellor (1995) has long been an articulate voice for recognizing the interaction between higher productivity in agriculture and vigorous growth in the
nonagricultural sectors. The failure to establish this connection in Africa
and South Asia is clearly at the heart of problems there in reducing hunger
and poverty, even as a commodity boom has stimulated growth in per capita incomes in many countries.

The question then is how to stimulate broad-based economic growth outside of agriculture to absorb the workers that need to leave low-productivity
jobs on family farms. If the question seems far from a concern about how to
end hunger and poverty—mostly concentrated in rural areas—it is not. No
conceivable increase in farm productivity can accomplish this goal without
a commensurate increase in job openings and labor productivity in the nonfarm economy.

Ramachandran, Gelb, and Shah (2009) have examined why this process
has been so slow in sub-Saharan Africa. They attribute the weak business
environment to poor infrastructure, especially the electrical grid for small
and medium enterprises, significant uncertainty about land rights, and quite
burdensome regulations of the formal sector. In further research, Gelb,
Meyer, and Ramachandran (2013) note that Africa's industrial labor costs—
wages relative to productivity—are significantly higher than those in competing countries, a problem which has existed for some time and which
seems not to have an easy solution.

Supply Chains Connecting Commercial Farmers to Urban Consumers

An encouraging development in both Africa and South Asia offers significant hope for creating some of these jobs. The "missing middle"—modern
supply chains that connect small-scale but commercial farmers with growing purchasing power in urban areas—is undergoing a quiet revolution that

has so far escaped the notice of most policy makers. At some point, modern supply chains will need active government support to reach their potential.

This potential will depend on continued developments at both ends of the supply chain. Urban incomes and the middle class will provide the demand, but more productive commercial farmers will need to respond with increased supplies. Effective and appropriate agricultural technologies can be developed for these farmers, even in lagging regions (and small nations) in Africa. But the task will not be successful if donors, governments, and research scientists focus on the wrong agents, which is why the farm-size debate is so important.

By leveraging urbanization and diversification of the diet, both rural-urban supply chains and the rural growth they generate offer solutions to poverty and hunger. Broad-based rural economic growth offers Africa's best opportunity for overcoming these problems. Rural suppliers need to sell to sources of dynamic, growing demand. Typically, rural purchasing power is too limited to propel a rural area out of poverty by rural suppliers just producing for themselves and their local market alone.

African farmers face an opportunity, via newly developing rural-urban food supply chains, to link to the growing and diversifying urban food market. These supply chains are two-way roads, bringing food and fiber one way and a flow of financial resources (and modern inputs) the other way. The money flows to producers at every step in the chain—to the farmers, truckers, and wholesalers, operators of warehouses and cold storage facilities, and processors. This income fuels grassroots investments (much of it in rural areas or rural towns) by millions of small and medium producers in the rural-urban supply chains, in farming, and in the input supply chains. This rural growth spreads out in ripples to the poorest of those in the dynamic areas and, over time, to the hinterlands. African policy makers have an emerging opportunity to encourage this development (Reardon et al. forthcoming; Reardon and Timmer 2014).

Urban areas are now the majority of the African food economy, a surprise to many analysts and policy makers. The new feature of African urbanization is that it is accompanied by rapid growth in urban incomes and the middle class itself, and by diversification of the diet. These trends are similar to those found in Asia, which is somewhat ahead in these developments (see Chapter 4). Diversification of diets goes beyond basic grains into animal products, vegetable oils, and fruits and vegetables. It includes diversification into processed foods and into shopping at supermarkets.

Rural-urban food supply chains are developing rapidly to meet this growing urban demand. The small-to-medium companies which are the main investors in this sector are the "missing middle" in the African food debate. Their success is the key to African competitiveness in both the rural and urban food economies, and to rapid reductions in poverty and hunger.

New Agricultural Technologies

After decades of neglect, considerable resources are now being devoted to raising the yield potential of many of Africa's staple food crops (Bill and Melinda Gates Foundation 2012; Block 2013). India has long had considerable scientific expertise in agricultural research and extension. New energy and resources are being devoted to breaking constraints on farm-level yields, especially for rice in Eastern India (Pingali 2012). These investments are likely to have high social and economic returns in the form of greater crop production in the future.

At the same time, raising yield potential, and even actual yields, alone will not solve the massive problems of poverty and hunger unless the other components of a successful agricultural transformation are also put in place (Tsakok 2011; Byerlee and Haggblade 2013). Solving the availability dimension of food security is necessary but not sufficient. Access, utilization, stability, and sustainability remain on the agenda.

Foreign Assistance Is Problematic

The role of foreign assistance in helping developing countries with strategies and investments to reduce poverty and hunger is significantly larger than the financial flows or extent of advisory services might indicate. Donors provide key signals on priorities and access to the best knowledge of what works and what does not. Historically, the donor community has been prone to fads that had no lasting impact or, worse, diverted attention and resources away from where they were needed. A serious rethink about the role of donors in the development process is needed.

The debate over the role and effectiveness of foreign assistance has been going on for a long time and is largely unresolved, no doubt because the issue is complex and fraught with political dimensions, which are hard to measure and evaluate and often highly specific to context. To some extent, the debate is diffuse because there are so many different dimensions that foreign assistance might address. There are instances in which emergency relief has saved millions of lives and other instances in which billions of dollars have been spent supporting friendly governments in a lost cause against their own people. No single answer to whether foreign assistance "works" or not is possible in such confusing and complex circumstances.

A narrower question is perhaps more addressable: can foreign assistance speed efforts to end poverty and hunger? Even here, the debate rages. Easterly (2004) is scathing about the empirical record, but Mellor (forthcoming) notes a long history of foreign assistance to building agricultural development institutions, which was successful as long as agricultural productivity stayed on the development agenda.

Foreign assistance has returned to supporting agricultural development, but the institutional bases no longer exist to support the country-specific efforts needed to address the issues. The very short-term focus of most foreign assistance almost rules out this resource—both financial and advisory—as a path for successful impact on raising agricultural productivity (much less speeding the rate of growth of incomes of the poor).

Experience with aid to help Africa improve its food security is especially troubling.

> This growing problem of hunger, linked in Africa to low farming productivity, has until recently brought forth surprisingly little in the way of development assistance from the outside world. Donor governments have responded to Africa with more food aid rather than more aid to farmers. The United States allowed its official development assistance to agriculture in Africa to fall from more than $400 million annually in the 1980s to only $60 million by 2006, a decline of approximately 85 percent. During that same time, America's food aid budget more than doubled in real terms, up to $1.2 billion. In other words, the United States was spending roughly 20 times as much giving away food in Africa as it was spending to help Africans do a better job of producing their own food. (Paarlberg 2010: 187–88)

More fundamentally, there is no evidence that foreign assistance can address the serious governance issues that have so bedeviled efforts to raise productivity on small farms in Africa and South Asia (and elsewhere). Radelet

(2010) notes that foreign assistance can have a significant payoff when it becomes available to new governments keen on economic reform, if the aid comes quickly and with flexible terms. But these windows of opportunity almost always open outside of the purview and vision of traditional aid donors. Improving donor capacity to act quickly and flexibly in such circumstances is probably the best we can hope for.

Better Training, Better Analysis

Both donors and countries need better policy analysts. Unique circumstances dictate unique analyses, even if the broad approaches are visible from history (and this book). Several questions arise in the analytical arena, which is the main focus of this book: who will do the analysis; where will they be trained; and what is the appropriate institutional base for such analysts?

Substantial investment in human capital is needed to train skilled food policy analysts. It is hard to find the educational institutions capable of providing this training. A successful food policy analyst needs an unusual blend of technical skills, mostly economic, and a broad vision of the interactions within food systems and their evolution over time. University Ph.D. programs have basically stopped doing this kind of training. Economics programs, for example, increasingly focus on microeconomic decision making that needs to be understood through careful experimental design of the data needed for analysis. Some extraordinarily smart students have come out of these programs with field experience in rural settings, and their journal articles are technical gems. But it is rare for these students to be trained in the macroeconomics of growth and development, much less economic history. Such students have little intuition about the functioning of complex food systems and changes within them. Undergraduates seeking graduate programs to train them have nowhere to go.

The failure of academic programs to provide coherent training in policy analysis is partly due to the lack of visible career tracks for such analysts. Just where are the jobs? What institutional base provides the best opportunities for analysts to do good work and be effective advocates for sound policies and programs? The historical record is quite fuzzy, as successful policy units have functioned in planning agencies, food logistics agencies, trade and commerce ministries, ministries of health, even ministries of agriculture. No single institutional base provides the best opportunities for high-quality analysis that is effectively plugged into the policy process. Serendipity and leadership are part of such success.

Finally, the need for empirical research to identify appropriate interventions in specific circumstances means that general diagnostic frameworks will have limited usefulness apart from their pedagogical role. This book offers several such frameworks for organizing analysis of food security—see Figure 4 in Chapter 2, for example. But they can provide guidance only on how to think about a problem, not what the answer will be. For that, good data, appropriate research methodologies, and a clear sense of the relevant questions will, in the hands of a talented food policy analyst, provide the necessary answers.

It is perhaps pessimistic to close this section on elements of success by noting how difficult it is to put them in place. The message, however, is that "difficult" is not "impossible." By knowing what needs to be done, we can concentrate our resources and analysis on bringing these elements of success into existence. These are all highly controversial issues and subject to extensive debate in the development community. Still, the elements of success are visible and provide significant hope that rapid progress can be made in reducing poverty and hunger in Africa and South Asia despite the disappointing historical record.

CHAPTER 6

The Political Economy of Food Security: Food Price Volatility and Policy Responses

The basic premise of this book is that an early escape from hunger—achieving food security at the societal level—is not just the result of one-way causation from economic growth generated by private decisions in response to market forces. Improved food security stems directly from a set of government policies that integrate the food economy into a development strategy that seeks rapid economic growth with improved income distribution, as explained in Chapter 3. With such policies, economic growth and food security mutually reinforce each other. Countries in East and Southeast Asia offer evidence that poor countries using this strategy can escape from hunger in two decades or less—that is, in the space of a single generation.[1] At the macro level, policy makers created the aggregate conditions in which households at the micro level gained access to food on a reliable basis through self-motivated interactions with local markets and home resources.

The Asian countries that have been most successful at providing food security to their citizens have based their strategies on two elements of their domestic food system over which they have some degree of policy control: the rate of income growth in the agricultural sector and stability of food prices. The sectoral dimensions of pro-poor growth are now well established (Timmer 1997a, 2005; Ravallion and Datt 1996; Warr forthcoming). At the same time, the development profession has ignored the role of stable food prices in food security. The spikes in prices of food grains in 2007–8 and again in 2010–11 (except for rice) directly support the main argument in this chapter: food price stability needs to be on both research and policy agendas.

Food Security: Market Outcomes or Government Action?

The modern escape from hunger to food security would not have been possible without the institutional and technological innovations that are at the heart of modern economic growth (Kuznets 1966; Deaton 2013). The record of economic growth for developing countries since the 1950s, however, indicates that even in countries with relatively low levels of income per capita, governments can intervene to enhance food security.[2] The countries most successful at this task are in East and Southeast Asia, although the experience in South Asia has been instructive as well (Timmer 2000, 2004a).

Because they are poor and devote a high share of their budget to food, consumers in poor countries are continually exposed to hunger and are vulnerable to shocks that set off famines (Anderson and Roumasset 1996). Still, several poor countries have taken public action to improve their food security. The typical approach, modeled and explained in Chapter 3, reduces the numbers of the population facing daily hunger by gradually raising the incomes of the poor while simultaneously managing the food economy in ways that minimize the shocks that might trigger a famine—shocks that are usually felt as rapidly rising food prices. These countries have managed the same "escape from hunger" that Fogel (1991) documented for Europe during the nineteenth and early twentieth centuries. Stabilizing domestic food prices was a key part of the European strategy.

Particularly since 1960, Asian governments sought to stabilize domestic rice prices. Engel's law ensures that success in generating rapid economic growth that includes the poor is the long-run solution to food security. In the language of Drèze and Sen (1989), such economic growth provides "growth-mediated security." In the meantime, stabilization of food prices in Asia ensured that short-run fluctuations and shocks did not make the poor, with their low incomes, even more vulnerable to inadequate food intake (Timmer 1991b, 1996). Essentially, food price stabilization functioned as a safety net, and Asian governments viewed it as such, although the academic literature did not.

The Logic of Market Outcomes

Most economists are highly dubious that such stability of food prices is financially feasible or even economically desirable. Price stabilization is, therefore, not a key element of the "support-led security" measures outlined by Drèze and Sen (1989). The standard objections to using trade restrictions to stabilize food prices are familiar to most economists, but they are relevant in only special circumstances. Four theoretical objections are prominent.

First, trade restrictions reduce economic efficiency and aggregate welfare in the short run. In order to maximize economic welfare, prices must fluctuate freely. These efficiency gains are realized, however, only in a world without market failures—not the world of developing countries. Further, if producers, consumers, and policy makers actually prefer stable prices, the short-run welfare gains posited by trade theorists are illusory (Timmer 2012a).

Second, trade restrictions are not targeted to the poor and thus waste scarce resources. This objection misses the key point of stabilizing food prices. A policy to protect the poor should not be evaluated on whether it also delivers benefits to the nonpoor but rather on the costs of reaching the poor. If there is a low-cost policy that delivers benefits to the poor, and at the same time that policy happens to deliver benefits to the nonpoor at zero or low marginal cost, then the benefits to the nonpoor (that is, the lack of targeting) should not be considered a disadvantage.

Instead, the policy should be evaluated on the basis of its total costs relative to the benefits delivered to the poor. A well-implemented trade policy could have very low costs, and in an economy with reasonably well-functioning markets such a policy would deliver benefits to nearly all of the poor. It makes sense, when costs are low, to maximize the number of poor people who are included in its benefits, even if many nonpoor also reap some benefits. Indeed, there might be political benefits from having so many beneficiaries, and these political benefits might be valued very highly by the government in charge.

Third, shocks to world prices often last for several years; it is not possible to stabilize domestic prices without substantial fiscal costs. This objection assumes that the target price remains unchanged from year to year. If the target price is allowed to adjust (slowly) to changes in world prices, then fiscal costs can be managed and domestic prices can follow the long-run trend of world prices without being subject to sharp variability from year to year.[3]

Impact on the World Market

Finally, trade-based domestic stabilization policies destabilize the world market. Consumers in other countries without stabilization policies are worse off, at least relative to a hypothetical world with no trade restrictions (see Anderson 2012). But instability must be absorbed somewhere when there are exogenous shifts in supply or demand in the world food economy (Dawe 2010b). There are only a few possible shock absorbers: world market prices, stocks, safety nets (which simply shift the adjustment costs from recipients to taxpayers at large, or to donors), or welfare of consumers and producers. Strong arguments can be made that, in poor countries, welfare of consumers and producers should not serve as the shock absorber.

If safety nets that include all of the poor are difficult to implement in a cost-effective manner, then the remaining possible shock absorbers are stocks and world market prices. The choice between them should depend on costs and benefits. Since stocks are expensive to hold, trade policies deserve consideration, even if they destabilize world prices. One possible approach to this problem would be to allow only the poorest countries to implement policies for stabilization of food prices under the auspices of the World Trade Organization (WTO). This might already be happening, by default. No country has issued a WTO challenge to actions by a poor country to stabilize their domestic food prices, even though the World Bank and International Monetary Fund often object.

The most serious objection to programs designed to stabilize food prices is the practical difficulty that many governments have in implementing them in a cost-effective manner without destabilizing expectations among market participants. Anderson and Roumasset (1996) essentially dismiss efforts to stabilize food prices by using government interventions, because poor implementation often causes greater, not less, instability. Their condemnation of national price stabilization schemes might well be appropriate for much of the developing world (Jayne 2012).[4] As noted in Chapter 2, the vastly more complicated food systems in Africa make stabilizing domestic food prices much more difficult, at least in ways that minimize costs and stabilize the expectations of private traders. The historical contribution to inclusive economic growth from reasonably stable food systems in Asia might thus not be available to African countries. Economic growth on the continent might be more difficult to stimulate in an environment of unstable food prices.

The Economic Case for Government Intervention

The dominance of rice in the diets of most Asians, coupled with the extreme price instability in the world market for rice, caused all Asian countries to buffer their domestic rice price from the world price despite the theoretical objections. Policy makers, particularly in East and Southeast Asia, sought to design and implement interventions that would stabilize the prices of rice in domestic markets while allowing the private sector to procure and distribute 90 to 95 percent of the crop (Timmer 1996). For food security in this region, the stabilization of domestic rice prices was in fact feasible in the context of an expanding role for an efficient private marketing sector. The resulting stability was not an impediment but was actually conducive to economic growth (Timmer 2002). The stabilization scheme and economic growth worked in tandem to achieve food security as quickly as possible.

Rice typically accounts for half the income of farm households that produce rice. On the consumption side, especially for the rural landless, farm households that grow other crops, and the urban poor, rice often accounts for 25 to 40 percent of household expenditures (Dawe 2000; Timmer, Block, and Dawe 2010). Changes in rice prices, therefore, cause large changes in the purchasing power of the poor, some positive and some negative. All government leaders recognize these impacts, and most Asian countries have felt the need to stabilize their rice economies and lend some stability to the lives of the poor by keeping domestic prices for rice more stable than prices at the border.

The Time Horizon: Rice Prices in the Short Run and Long Run

In the short run, fluctuations in rice prices have large effects on the purchasing power and nutrition of the poor (Block et al. 2004; Torlesse, Kiess, and Bloem 2003). Any government concerned about poverty and food insecurity needs to stabilize (or stop destabilizing) rice prices and connect the poor to rapid economic growth.

In the long run, however, the impact of stabilizing rice prices can be complicated and perverse. For example, by implementing a simple policy objective of stabilizing the real domestic price of rice—the operational definition of food security in these societies—most Asian countries saw the level of protection of their rice farmers rise sharply from the 1970s to the mid-1990s (Timmer 1993). The main drivers of this unexpected result were the steady appreciation of these countries' exchange rates against the U.S. dollar (in which world rice prices are denominated) and the steady decline in the world rice price over the time period. Neither driver was caused, or even anticipated, by the efforts to stabilize domestic prices of rice.

High levels of agricultural protection and failure of countries to diversify and modernize their agricultural sectors were largely unanticipated side effects of the strategy of growth with stability. Efforts to reduce these high levels of agricultural protection, especially for rice farmers, by directly confronting the political forces defending this Asian approach to food security have been repeatedly rebuffed since the 1980s. Any political economy approach must explain this key historical reality. On the other hand, if world food prices reverse their long-term decline over the next few decades and increase in real terms, the opposite outcome could in fact occur. Domestic price stabilization would lead to future taxation of the rice sector (relative to international prices).

Rice Price Stabilization During the World Food Crisis of 2008

Much of the importance attached to stabilization of domestic rice prices stems from the fact that international rice markets have been historically thin and unstable, causing all Asian countries to buffer their own farmers and consumers from fluctuating world prices. This buffering requires that governments actively control the flow of rice across their borders. This intervention to stabilize rice prices directly contradicts free trade.

During the world rice crisis of 2008, China, India, and Indonesia—the three most populous developing countries in the world—successfully insulated their domestic rice economies from the turmoil in world markets. Rice price stability in these large countries was one reason why the food and financial crises pushed fewer people into poverty and undernourishment than was initially feared (FAO 2011). All three of these countries used trade controls. They did not allow the private sector to eliminate the large difference between domestic and world prices by exporting supplies. These trade controls were no frantic response to sudden turmoil in the world market for rice—they existed well before the crisis. They were part of a long-term strategic vision that recognized the importance of stable prices.

Two important caveats to the use of such trade controls should be emphasized. First, trade controls sometimes fail to work, especially if they are accompanied by actions that destabilize the expectations of private traders and consumers. The Philippines and Vietnam had trade controls in place as well (also dating to before the crisis), but they witnessed substantial price increases during the crisis. Inappropriate statements by government officials induced speculative hoarding. Farmers decided to delay sales; traders engaged in hoarding; and consumers decided to stockpile an extra week or two of supplies (Timmer 2010c). Second, refusal to export supplies has negative effects on countries not directly engaged in the specific trade deals, but that rely on imports for a substantial proportion of domestic supplies (as is true for many countries in sub-Saharan Africa). Bangladesh was especially hard hit by the ban on rice exports from India in 2007–8 (Dorosh and Rashid 2013).

The case for domestic food price stabilization has not become part of mainstream development thinking but it has strong economic underpinnings. The benefits of stabilizing prices of staple foods can be divided into three categories: microeconomic benefits for consumers, microeconomic benefits for producers, and macroeconomic benefits (Timmer 1989).

Benefits for Poor Consumers

Rice is a major share of expenditures for the poor in Asia. In the absence of stabilization, sharp price increases can cause hunger for those who are not wealthy enough to maintain consumption levels at the higher prices. And even relatively moderate increases in price can cause significant hardship for major subsets of the population that have enough income to maintain rice consumption but need to make cutbacks on other expenditures. For example, rice accounts for more than 20 percent of expenditures for the poorest quarter of the urban population in Bangladesh (Bangladesh Bureau of Statistics 2011). For these people, a 30 percent increase in rice prices would lead to about a 6 percent decline in effective income. This is a large shock and is equivalent to their entire expenditures on health and education.

Thus, one choice is to forgo expenditures on education and medical care. Alternatively, a consumer might reduce intake of foods high in protein, vitamins, and minerals, such as meats, dairy products, and vegetables. Even temporary reductions in the intake of these foods can cause problems (for example, stunting or anemia) that have permanent effects, especially for young children and pregnant women (Block et al. 2004). These hardships, even when temporary, can have permanent effects by reducing cognitive capacity as adults or by pushing people into debt burdens that become poverty traps (Carter et al. 2007; Hoddinott 2006; Maccini and Yang 2009).

Stabilization of rice prices can thus serve as a complement to a program of social safety nets. By preventing sharp fluctuations in prices in the first place instead of merely reacting to price increases when they occur, successful programs to stabilize rice prices eliminate the need to hastily implement a food distribution program. This is an obvious example of "an ounce of prevention is worth a pound of cure."

Benefits for Producers

Farmers also benefit from stable rice prices because stable prices protect them from periods of abnormally low prices. Since many farmers are poor, this effort is to some extent an issue of avoiding poverty traps, as is the case with consumers. In addition, however, price stabilization can enhance efficiency in the farm sector. To understand the efficiency effects, one must view the farmer as an investor in an uncertain biophysical environment in which risk markets are imperfect and cannot guarantee access to credit when needed (Timmer 1989). Were credit markets more reliable, farmers would be more likely to increase productive investment, especially investment with long gestation periods. As it stands, however, the supply response of farmers is hindered by price volatility (Subervie 2008).

One response of many governments is to remedy this lack of credit by intervening directly to supply more credit. These interventions often take the form of subsidized credit, loan targeting, or a variety of other measures. The problems with such strategies have been well recognized for some time (Von Pischke, Adams, and Donald 1983). They include, among others, reduced savings mobilization because of negative real interest rates, increased rent-seeking behavior because of the fact that not everyone is able to gain access to the subsidized interest rates, and decreased efficiency of financial intermediation because of the numerous bureaucratic requirements of loan targeting.

Stabilizing prices attacks this problem from a different direction. Instead of increasing the supply of credit to rice farmers, price stabilization reduces their demand for credit by protecting them from periods of very low prices that could cause cash flow problems. This approach avoids the large costs and inefficiencies associated with subsidized credit programs, although it does not eliminate the need for a well-functioning rural financial system in the long run.

Benefits for the Macro Economy

Aside from these microeconomic benefits to consumers and producers, there are also likely to be significant macroeconomic benefits in terms of investment and growth, especially in poor countries in which rice (or other important staple foods—for example, corn in Malawi) is an important share of economic output. These macroeconomic benefits arise for a number of reasons. Newbery and Stiglitz (1981: 441) posit such benefits when wages and prices are sticky instead of adjusting immediately to shocks, and they conclude from their analysis that "there are some significant macroeconomic benefits that might be derived from price stabilization."

Various market failures provide a microeconomic foundation for macroeconomic benefits from stabilizing prices of staple foods.[5] These market failures all tend to reduce levels of investment from what they would otherwise be in a more certain world, and reduced investments lead to slower economic growth. The most important market failures include imperfect credit markets, partially irreversible investment, and signal extraction problems because of fluctuating prices under conditions of imperfect information (Dawe 2001).

Instability in rice prices can lead to instability for other commodities in the economy because of the large share of rice in consumer budgets. Changes in expenditures on rice, due to price changes, spill over to changes in expenditures on other commodities. These effects are noticed by and of concern to policy makers. A former coordinating minister for the economy in Indonesia noted complaints from garment retailers that changes in rice prices created uncertainty for sales of garments and affected investment decisions (Saleh Afiff, personal communication, 1996). Consistent with this observation, Dawe (1996) found that instability in export earnings has a large negative effect on the efficiency of investment and hence on the rate of economic growth.

These spillovers and their macroeconomic consequences will be large only if the price elasticity of demand is low (in absolute value) and if the budget share of the commodity is large for most consumers. These conditions are jointly satisfied only for staple foods in low-income countries. Under such conditions, the macroeconomic benefits can be quantitatively significant. Timmer (2002) estimated that stabilization of rice prices added 0.5 to 1.0 percentage points of growth in GDP per year to the Indonesian economy in the 1970s, when rice was still a large share of the economy and when the world rice market was particularly unstable. These estimates are consistent with the work of Rodrik (1999), who stresses the importance of macroeconomic stability for investment and growth, and Dawe (2001), who argues that food (rice) price stability is a key ingredient of macro stability in Asia. Thus, stabilization of food prices—as a policy measure—can bring about and sustain stable conditions for private investment and growth.

Social and political stability can also be affected by food price volatility. Arezki and Bruckner (2011) have found that surges in international food prices lead to an increased frequency of antigovernment riots and demonstrations, as well as a weakening of democratic institutions. Strictly speaking, their argument is about the level of international food prices, but as a practical matter, countries can adapt to slow increases in international prices over time. Sudden surges in prices (which are common during periods of price instability) are more difficult to adjust to, and they constitute a genuine problem for governments concerned with providing food security.

Limits to Food Price Stabilization: Which Commodities Need Stable Prices, and for How Long into the Development Process?

Staple foods are the most promising commodities for cost-effective price stabilization, primarily because of the greater potential benefits to stabilizing these prices. Export crops can be important to certain economies, but because they are exported, they are of little importance to domestic consumers. Oil is often viewed as a strategic commodity, but it is not produced by small, risk-averse farmers. Its share of the budget for the poor is an order of magnitude less than for staple foods. In contrast, staple foods are important for both poor producers and poor consumers and thus also for the macro economy.

How long should staple food prices be stabilized? The benefits of stabilizing prices of a staple food depend directly on the share of the staple food in consumer budgets, farm incomes, and the overall economy. As economic development and structural transformation proceed, all of these shares will decline (Chapter 4). The importance of stabilizing prices of staple foods will be less as economic growth proceeds. Put another way, programs to stabilize food prices will need to incur lower costs if they are to remain cost-effective during the transition from low- to middle- to high-income status. This transition has always been politically challenging to manage because of the changing role of agriculture and the food economy during the process.

A Behavioral Perspective on the Political Economy of Food Security

People are not food secure until they *feel* they are food secure.[6] This basic reality of behavioral psychology adds an important expectational dimension to the traditional definition of food security. A standard definition includes availability of food at all times, access by households to this food, and effective utilization within the household through adequate diet, water, sanitation, and health care (USDA 1996: 2).

Each of these three dimensions can be affected by instability in food prices, but more recent thinking has stressed the risk and vulnerability of poor households to catastrophic and irreversible changes in their food security (Webb and Rogers 2003; Barrett and Lentz 2012). The behavioral dimension of food security extends this line of thought by illuminating the origins of the welfare losses that accompany sharp spikes in food prices. A better understanding of these losses is important to food security because it can help policy analysts design more effective interventions to prevent future food crises.

Although not common—on average there are three world food crises per century—food crises do enormous damage to the poor when they hit. Equally devastating, food crises almost always give rise to antimarket and antitrade policies in a beggar-thy-neighbor approach to building national food reserves at the expense of trade. The panicked response of dozens of countries to the spike in rice prices in 2007–8 is ample witness to this effect (Slayton 2009; Dawe 2010a). National food autarky has not been a reliable way to improve food security or broader economic welfare in the long run. If climate change adds to production variability, greater trade, not self-sufficiency campaigns and autarky, will be needed to even out supplies across regions and countries.

Preventing food crises through better understanding of their fundamental causes, thus allowing implementation of better food policies, is a high priority. Once a food crisis hits, coping with its consequences becomes the main task at hand. Emergency food aid and other forms of safety nets are hastily brought into play. But preventing food crises in the first place, especially by preventing sharp spikes in food prices, is obviously a superior alternative if a way can be found to do it. Integrating new insights from behavioral economics into the reasons governments should stabilize prices of basic food grains leads to a better understanding of how to design and implement stabilization policies.

Highly unstable prices for food—sharp spikes and price collapses—are undesirable for two separate reasons. First, as argued in this chapter and increasingly recognized by economic analysts, unstable prices for staple grains have serious consequences for the welfare of poor households (Timmer 1989, 1991b; World Bank 2005; Timmer and Dawe 2007; IFPRI 2008; Dawe and Timmer 2012). Second is a factor little recognized by the economics profession. Spikes in food prices universally evoke a visceral, hostile response among producers and consumers alike. This response has deep behavioral foundations. The experimental and psychological literature shows that individuals strongly prefer stable to unstable environments.[7]

Kahneman and Tversky (1979), for example, in their treatment of decision making under risk, establish "reference points" for individual decisions as the basis for widespread "loss aversion," which is the foundation of what they call "prospect theory." The pervasiveness of loss aversion among individual decision makers has immediate implications for our thinking about welfare losses from unstable prices for food. Equal movements in prices up and down over time leave society worse off because the welfare losses from higher prices always outweigh the welfare gains from lower prices. The asymmetry of welfare losses caused by loss aversion means that the gains from trade possible when prices are unstable will be less than the losses. This result alone explains much of the empirical political economy of food prices (K. Anderson and Hayami 1986).

Although this behavioral response is part of the reason that individuals tend to be risk averse, the implications are actually more profound. It is conceptually possible to hedge the risks from unstable food prices or to mitigate their welfare consequences for the poor using safety nets, but there are no markets in which to purchase stability in food prices directly. The message is clear. Citizens would willingly go to the market to buy food price stability, but such a market does not exist. Food price stability is a public good, not a market good.[8] Understandably, then, citizens turn to the political market instead. Under current institutional arrangements, only political action and public response from governments can provide stable food prices. Thus food becomes a political commodity, not just an economic commodity, and we will need a behavioral political economy to understand policy approaches to food security.

Governments that fail to stabilize food prices have failed in the provision of a quite basic human need that is rooted in behavioral psychology—the need for a stable environment. Governments that are successful in stabilizing prices of food are usually rewarded politically; witness the landslide victories for Prime Minister Singh in India and of President Yudhoyono in Indonesia in early 2009. Both candidates campaigned openly on their ability to bring their countries through the world food crisis with minimal impact on domestic food prices.

The challenge, of course, is to provide stability in domestic food prices at low cost to economic growth and participation by the poor. By and large, Asia has figured out how to do this as a domestic endeavor, but there are large negative spillovers to world markets (Timmer 2009c). For understandable reasons, African countries do not have the same options for stabilizing their domestic food prices. The instability in world markets transmitted from the Asian approach to food price stabilization has a disproportionately harsh effect on Africa (Jayne 2009). Finding alternatives to stable food prices as a way to stabilize and extend domestic investment horizons is one of the major policy challenges in Africa.

Understanding the Behavioral Dimensions of Food Crises

Price behavior in late 2007 and early 2008 showed that speculative price bubbles can be a serious problem. The question is what stabilizing actions might be taken to make the world rice market a more reliable venue for imports and exports, with price signals that reflect long-run costs of production and demand from consumers rather than panicked behavior in the short run.[9]

The formation of rice prices in world markets has long interested scholars and policy makers.[10] International trade is approximately 30 million metric tons out of a global production of nearly 440 million metric tons (milled rice equivalent). Only 7 to 8 percent of rice produced crosses an international border. Despite this small share, the world market for rice provides essential supplies to importing countries around the world, and the prices set in this market provide signals to both exporting and importing countries about the opportunity costs of increasing production and/or consumption. It is disconcerting to exporters and importers alike if these market signals are highly volatile.

Part of the long-standing interest in the world rice market has been precisely because it has been so volatile. The coefficient of variation of world rice prices has been higher than that of wheat or corn for decades at a time. Understanding this volatility has been difficult because much of it traces to the residual nature of the world rice market, as both importing and exporting countries stabilize rice prices internally by using the world rice market to dispose of surpluses or to meet deficits via imports. Thus supply and demand in the world market are a direct result of political decisions in a large number of countries. Rice was an important economic and political commodity in the mid-1970s (Timmer and Falcon 1975). It remains important politically for behavioral reasons even while its economic importance has fallen dramatically (see Chapter 4).

But volatility in rice prices is also driven by the structure of rice production, marketing, and consumption in most Asian countries—that is, by the industrial organization of the rice economy. Hundreds of millions of small farmers; millions of traders, processors, and retailers; and billions of individual consumers all handle a commodity that can be stored for well over a year in a consumable form. The price expectations of these market participants are critical to their decisions about how much to grow, sell, store, and consume. Because there are virtually no data available about these price expectations or their marketing consequences, the world rice market operates with highly incomplete and imperfect information about short-run supply-and-demand factors. In this, rice is a very different commodity from the other basic food staples, wheat and maize.[11]

When the political dimensions and the different market structure for rice are integrated into actual price formation, extreme volatility can result. Understanding the proximate causes of unstable rice prices requires understanding both politics and markets and their contribution to the formation of price expectations on the part of market participants. These expectations can drive destabilizing speculative behavior among millions, even billions, of market participants, such that price formation seems to have a large destabilizing and speculative component.

The emphasis here on destabilizing expectations and subsequent speculative price behavior is meant to contrast with the normally stabilizing role that routine speculative activities play. If speculators did not buy during the harvest, store grain, and sell during the short season, seasonal price movements would be much larger than they are. Of course, seasonal prices must rise from their harvest lows to their peak just before the new harvest, or these stabilizing speculative investments would not be made. It is difficult to define precisely the difference between stabilizing and destabilizing speculation. Even agents who engage entirely in the financial derivatives of commodities, such as futures, options, and swaps, can contribute to the liquidity of the underlying markets and thus help support the stabilizing function of speculation. But when herd behavior sets in and most financial speculation is in only one direction, the potential to generate bubbles and less stable prices is clear. Much more analytical and empirical work needs to be done on the role of financial instruments as they influence commodity prices in spot markets (Robles, Torero, and von Braun 2009; Galtier 2009; Galtier 2013a; Munier and Briand 2012).

The Role of Price Expectations

The two most recent world food crises—in 1972–73 and 2007–8—were instrumental in understanding the behavior of a wide range of economic agents in the food system. In particular, understanding how price expectations for basic food grains are formed by farmers, traders, and consumers, and how these agents act on those expectations, is essential to knowing what policy actions will stabilize food prices and keep consumers more food secure (Timmer 2009c, 2010a).

To address this issue, understanding the behavioral foundations of formation of price expectations will be important. In particular, the dynamics of herd behavior and the tendency of bad news—about terrorism, wild fires, or a sudden rise in rice prices in local markets—to serve as a focusing event in stimulating simultaneous, spontaneous behavior that results in panics, provide robust insights into how individuals form price expectations and respond to them (Tversky and Kahneman 1986).[12]

As explained in Chapter 3, a model of the supply of storage, a staple of commodity market analysis for more than half a century, has been used to understand the factors affecting price expectations, and price formation, in the short run. This model builds primarily on the behavior of profit-maximizing firms engaged in storage activities and is quite successful when virtually all the commodity storage is in commercial hands, as with cocoa or wheat, and when stock levels for such commodities are reported regularly or can be estimated fairly accurately (Brennan 1958; Houthakker 1987). For a commodity such as rice, however, which is mostly grown by smallholders, marketed by a dense network of small traders and processors (many with limited access to credit), and purchased by consumers in a readily storable form (milled rice), stock levels can change at any or all levels of the supply chain, and there are virtually no data available on these inventory levels (Timmer 2009c).

For rice, in fact, most inventories are held by individuals (farmers, small traders, and consumers) or by governments. Neither of these types of inventory holders have behavior that is explained by the supply-of-storage model. The behavior of individuals, whose short time horizons (or time-inconsistent utility functions) impede rational savings decisions and storage investments, does not lead to optimal storage decisions. The tendency in many peasant economies for there to be a "hungry season" shortly before the harvest is a particularly relevant example of this short-term decision making (Thaler and Benartzi 2004). Governments hold rice stocks to stabilize domestic prices, despite this being a loss-making activity in financial terms. At least for the rice economy, we need behavioral explanations—for individuals and for governments—to explain storage decisions and their simultaneous impact on price expectations.

As concerns grew in 2007 that world food supplies were limited and prices for wheat, corn, and vegetable oils were rising, several Asian countries reconsidered the wisdom of maintaining low domestic stocks for rice.[13] Fears of shortages spread and a cumulative price spiral started that fed on the fear itself. On March 28, 2008, rice prices in Thailand jumped $75 per metric ton. Prices continued to skyrocket until rice cost over $1,100 per ton in April. Rice had cost just $375 per ton at the start of the year. Panic had set in. Everyone was hoarding rice.[14]

The psychology of hoarding behavior is important in explaining why rice prices suddenly shot up starting in late 2007. Financial speculation seems to have played only a small role (partly because futures markets for rice are very thinly traded). Instead, as apprehension spread about the impending world food crisis, governments stepped up their actions to stabilize rice prices within their borders. Not all of these actions were credible, of course, and decisions by millions of worried households, farmers, and traders sparked a sudden surge in demand for rice. This surge changed the gradual increase in rice prices from 2002 to 2007 into an explosion.

A rough calculation of the effect of household hoarding of rice shows the potential. With a 25 percent increase in short-run demand on the world market—about what would happen if rice-consuming households doubled the amount stored in their pantries—the world price will have to rise by over 150 percent to get a new equilibrium. That is what happened: panicked hoarding caused the rice price spike.

Fortunately, a speculative run based on herd psychology can be ended by "pricking the bubble" and deflating expectations. Once the price starts to drop, the psychology reverses on hoarding behavior by households, farmers, traders, and even governments. When the government of Japan announced in early June 2008, after considerable international urging, that it would sell 300,000 tons of its surplus WTO rice stocks to the Philippines, prices in world rice markets started to fall immediately (Slayton and Timmer 2008). By late August, medium-quality rice for export from Vietnam was available for half of what it had sold for in late April, as dishoarding gained momentum (Dawe 2010a).[15]

The announcement by Japan that it would release some of its rice stocks to world market participants came only after strong urgings from the U.S. government. These urgings in turn came only after pressures from policy analysts, Congress, and the press (Slayton 2010). In the rice market, at least, a worse food crisis was prevented through understanding and action. Food crises need to be prevented. They have terrible short-run and long-run consequences for the welfare of the poor. Poverty traps and irreversible effects from childhood malnutrition (on learning, stature, or mortality) stem from even temporary loss of access to food. Preventing food crises requires two separate, but integrated, approaches—a market-oriented approach to economic growth and structural transformation (see Chapter 4), and a stabilization approach to policy initiatives that prevent sharp price spikes for staple foods. Both approaches benefit from a behavioral perspective.

Structural transformations have always been primarily market-driven processes. Markets process billions of pieces of information on a daily basis to generate price signals to all participants. No other form of institutional organization has evolved that is capable of the necessary information processing required for individuals and firms to make efficient allocation and investment decisions, and thus to raise long-run productivity.

The dilemma, of course, is that markets often fail at tasks that society regards as important, such as reducing poverty or promoting nutritional well-being or food price stability. We now understand that these failures are not just for technical reasons—externalities, spillovers, monopoly power, or asymmetric information, for example—but that they also have deep behavioral roots based in loss aversion, widespread norms of fairness, and the regularity of "other-regarding preferences." Fixing market failures is not easy unless these root causes are incorporated into the policy analysis, design, and interventions (an example is in Thaler and Benartzi 2004).

Mechanism Design in Policy Analysis

The key to effective public action is to get the mechanism design right. That is, policy initiatives must worry about the incentive structures set up so that they are compatible both with respect to government budgetary and bureaucratic capacity and with respect to self-interested behavior on the part of market participants who are exposed to the results of policy changes. This may seem an arcane and theoretical point (and worthy of the Nobel Prize in Economics in 2007), but failure to think through the nature of incentives being set up by policy initiatives is almost a sure way to guarantee an unsuccessful outcome.

One of the obvious complexities in mechanism design arises from the difficulty in predicting behavioral responses to policy changes. Further, most models of policy evaluation assume that if at least one person is better off and no one is worse off—the Pareto criterion for welfare improvement—the policy is worth pursuing. But if some groups are relatively worse off, even if absolutely better off, there can be sharp political ramifications. Actions that are Pareto improvements in the sense of neoclassical economics might not be politically improving.

Equally, policy design needs to be clear on whether the initiative is meant to be a temporary palliative for the problem at hand or a long-run cure. There is nothing wrong with palliatives, especially if they build support for longer-run approaches that solve the problem. But it is important not to confuse palliatives with cures. Thus, bridges between short-run approaches and long-run impact become the essence of successful food policy design and implementation. The time inconsistency of much human behavior—a heavy focus on the here and now—makes building these bridges very complicated.

The reality of human behavior means that these bridges must be built from real policy instruments, not theoretical ones based on models of revealed preference. The distinction lies in understanding how realistic the assumptions are that underlie the expected behavioral responses to policy initiatives. A policy that assumes poor people have unimpeded access to financial markets to hedge risks will fail, as will one that assumes rational savings behavior. But equally, a policy that assumes poor people will not change their consumption behavior in the face of price subsidies will also be challenged by unexpected results.

For a sustainable end to food crises, policy initiatives must stress the importance of economic growth that is both cause and effect of the historical process of structural transformation. When this process includes the poor, with rising labor productivity for unskilled workers, the access dimension of food security is largely solved, and political tensions are reduced. Without these long-run economic dynamics working reasonably smoothly, policy initiatives become an exercise in permanent and expensive palliatives. Even when the long-run economic dynamics are working smoothly, however, a set of transitional issues for health and nutrition begin to loom large for analysts. A new food policy that focuses on the exclusion of vulnerable groups from market-provided food supplies, on obesity and chronic diseases that are directly food related, and on the safety of food supplies when food origins are often quite distant from food consumers, is emerging to complement the traditional policy analysis that has focused primarily on reducing poverty and hunger (see Chapter 1). Just as people might not be food secure until they feel they are food secure, they might not feel healthy unless they feel that their diet is nutritious, safe, and environmentally friendly.

Good intentions in policy design do not inevitably lead to good outcomes. The concern for appropriate mechanism design is one reflection of this potential disconnect, but that concern is primarily a technical one. A broader concern is also an issue—the potential (indeed, likely) disconnect between political rhetoric and effective public action. The problem is that political rhetoric can generate expectations that cannot be met. The government loses credibility. Because credibility is often essential to successful implementation of government policies—in activities to stabilize prices in the short-run, for example, or in regulating food safety—this loss is potentially serious. Understanding the roles of government credibility and effective leadership is at the core of behavioral political economy.

A way must be found to make markets work to deliver long-run growth, but political survival requires that this growth be stable and equitably distributed.[16] No alternative exists to organizing economies around market-based transactions if societies are to reach their goals of greater material welfare and broad political freedom. Markets produce both. But markets also fail in important social tasks. Responsible governments must find a way to prevent those failures through careful regulation and to alleviate them when innocent workers and consumers cannot participate in the promises of market outcomes.

Why Is Good Economics Often Bad Politics?

This behavioral perspective raises a set of questions around the political economy of food policy. If politics is in command, which is often the state of affairs in developing countries, how do efficiency issues stay on the agenda?[17] Good economics can easily be derailed by bad motivation on the part of policy makers and project managers. Corruption and diversion of funds are obvious examples, but political interference in the location of development investments, or over who controls the fertilizer distribution centers, can also convert an otherwise sensible policy into a fiscal disaster. Poor institutional capacity, almost inevitable in a poor country, can derail the implementation of good projects. Part of mastering the political economy of development is learning to appreciate the limitations of government action.

But the converse is also an issue. If markets are in command, how do distributional and welfare issues stay on the agenda? Because much of the policy advice from the donor community focuses on increasing the role of markets in allocating resources, do donors also have an obligation to address the adverse effects of markets? Do NGOs and other interest groups devoted to ending poverty have a special responsibility?

The World Trade Organization (WTO) has been a focal point for such concerns as part of the Doha Round of trade negotiations, which were launched in November 2001 with a broad development agenda. At the Ninth Ministerial Meeting of the Doha Round held in Bali, Indonesia, in December 2013, agreement was reached to allow developing countries to implement wide-ranging subsidies on behalf of food security and distributions of food to the poor. Somewhat ironically, India was the lead speaker on behalf of this issue. The Indian approach—using massive subsidies to both farmers and consumers—is politically visible but relatively ineffective and highly wasteful (see Chapter 5). It cannot possibly serve as a sustainable model for other countries.

Thus the broader question becomes how we educate politicians and policy makers as well as analysts. In democratic societies, it would seem to require educating citizens so that they can be informed voters. If ever there has been a market failure, it is here.[18] And yet the lesson to be taught does not seem all that difficult. Asia's economic success shows that there is no substitute for agricultural development in societies that have a substantial rural sector. Providing food security is an important rationale for investing in agriculture. Widespread confidence in food security, made manifest by stable food prices, can then be translated through extensive externalities and linkages into rapid economic growth.

Conclusions: Toward a Behavioral Political Economy

Economists are often upset when politicians reject their optimal policy designs to enhance social welfare. Traditionally, these designs have been based on the Pareto criterion that at least one individual is better off and no one is worse off. But if most individuals care more about their relative status than absolute levels of income or consumption, the Pareto criterion spells political trouble. Only a new behavioral focus on the design of policy interventions can help real policy makers bring about real improvements in welfare.

The neoclassical solution to unstable food prices, for example, has been to allow full expression of price volatility in markets because of the information content of prices. Any problems for firms in the supply chain can be managed with financial instruments to hedge risks from price movements. Problems for poor consumers can be managed by implementing safety nets that kick in when prices of food spike.

This approach fails at both ends (Galtier 2009, 2013a). The financial instruments are themselves highly volatile and subject to outside speculative pressures. They are not widely accessible to most market participants. They fail to exist at all in many developing countries.

Safety nets face their own problems of transactions costs and behavioral responses that make effective implementation quite difficult. Using community-based information and organizations to target resources to the poorest of the poor often runs afoul of the widespread sense of fairness in these communities that requires external resources to be shared equally. Targeting is thwarted and fiscal costs rise, or the poor do not get the resources they need to cope with shocks to their welfare. Either way, safety nets have a poor record of coping with sudden price shocks.

What can be done? First, far more analytical and financial resources need to be aimed at preventing food crises by preventing sharp spikes in food prices. Many Asian countries have managed to stabilize their rice prices for decades at a time. We can learn from those experiences while making interventions more efficient and with fewer international spillovers.

Second, finding a way to allow governments to deliver effective and efficient safety nets is both a moral and political imperative. These safety nets allow markets to deliver their long-run promise. Designing and implementing them is the essence of effective policy making. New tools using modern information and communication technologies offer substantial hope that targeting can be improved and transfers made at lower real costs. But governments, like the poor, live in the short run. Their vision and strategic design for inclusive, stable, long-run growth must survive the day-to-day challenges of managing power. Only input from behavioral political economy, broadly for development policy and more narrowly for food policy, can help governments link their short-run political mandates—to provide effective safety nets in times of crisis—to the investments and policies that lead to rapid, inclusive economic growth.

The characteristics of rice-based food systems have helped forge a strong link between politics and economics, a link that policy makers, elected or not, see as a public mandate to deliver food security. Without understanding this link, it is impossible to understand Asia's record of economic growth—driven historically by dynamic rural economies—and the subsequent, seemingly inevitable, rise of agricultural protection. Although some of the forces driving this protection are similar to those in Europe and the United States, the speed, level, and early onset are unique to Asia.

The way forward is to make rice less "different" to consumers, farmers, and in world markets by making it more of an economic commodity and less of a political commodity. Much progress has actually been made in this direction since the 1980s, but that progress has not been widely recognized or incorporated into new, politically viable strategies for food security in Asia and beyond.

Still, the ingredients of such a strategy are apparent: greater investment in rural human capital to improve labor productivity and mobility; more efficient rural financial markets to facilitate farm consolidation and even rural exit; and coordinated international efforts to open the world rice market to freer trade in order to deepen and stabilize price formation. Given likely future demand for biofuels, increased natural resource scarcity in some areas, and the impacts of a gradual rise in temperatures, among other fac-tors, agricultural research to increase productivity and lower the long-run level of food prices is imperative.

Progress on these fronts will ensure higher incomes and lower prices, the key drivers of improving access to food over the long term. But in the meantime, development of lower-cost strategies to stabilize domestic prices of food in a way that creates stable expectations for private sector traders will also be essential. The level of food prices is certainly important, but so too is the stability of those prices. Making rice a normal commodity is a big agenda, to be sure, but implementing it, even gradually, will ensure a more prosperous and equitable future for Asia's farmers and greater food security for its consumers. And the lessons from this progress can inform food secu-rity strategies for other regions as well.

CHAPTER 7

The Way Forward: The Time Horizon Matters

There is no shortage of proposals to improve food security and reduce poverty. The most useful ones are regional or even country-specific, although important global issues need to be solved as well. To have a significant and sustainable impact on food security, particularly in Asia, the main arenas in which changes are needed are these:

- higher productivity for smallholder farmers;
- a dynamic rural economy with rising real wages, stabilized by a concern for volatile food prices;
- design and funding of safety nets that protect the vulnerable from chronic poverty and a volatile economic environment; and
- support for the regional (and global) public goods that will be essential going forward to sustain adequate food supplies, access to that food, and adequate nutritional outcomes in households.[1]

Perhaps the most visible of the recent proposals is the book by Gordon Conway, *One Billion Hungry: Can We Feed the World?* (2012). My rather unsympathetic review of this book for the *Wilson Quarterly* was a significant stimulus to drafting my own volume (Timmer 2012b). I wanted to explore why ending hunger is so hard. The answer—because governments and markets need to work together around an agenda of pro-poor growth, agricultural development, and stable food economies—has been the main theme of this book.

At a global level, the focus needs to be on the time horizon over which policies and investments must be designed and implemented. By their very nature, some of the most important investments needed to guarantee enough food for all in the future have very long gestation periods and payoff horizons. Rural infrastructure, including irrigation facilities, schools and health centers, basic agricultural research and development, even the basic institutions of effective governance, all take decades to design, build, and deliver benefits. A good policy idea in 2013 might, with effective political support, become a new policy initiative by 2015. Implementation could come within a few years, with effects visible in the field within a decade. Discouraging as this process sounds for those seeking immediate solutions to hunger, in the world of developing agriculture, reducing poverty, and ending hunger, this is the short run. A main theme throughout this book has been the importance of an historical perspective. Doing things right takes time. As *Food Policy Analysis* argued three decades ago, "crash programs tend to crash" (Timmer, Falcon, and Pearson 1983: 288). Only policies that recognize this basic reality have a chance of working.

This historical perspective suggests that the basic time horizons in the arena of food security that are useful for policy analysis, design, implementation, and evaluation are

- the short run (less than a decade), when the task is to manage volatility of food prices;
- the medium run (two to three decades from now), when the task is to manage demand for food (especially for biofuels, and to a less pressing extent, for livestock feed), and;
- the long run, when the task is to manage the sustainable increase in supplies of food, subject to increased risks from climate change and a depleted resource base in many regions.

Of course, as Keynes said, in the long run we will be dead—but our children and grandchildren will be alive and facing a legacy that we will bequeath to them.

The Short Run to 2020: Coping with High and Volatile Food Prices

The important policy agenda in the short run is coping with food price volatility and the increased frequency of spikes in food prices. Three basic approaches to coping with the impact of high food prices once they hit world markets are domestic price stabilization; increasing supplies available in local markets, and providing safety nets to poor consumers. All of them must be managed by individual countries. Donors and international agencies, however, can play a substantial role in coordinating activities and providing resources, both financial and technical assistance.

Policy Approaches to Food Security in a Volatile Price Environment

The first approach is for individual countries to use market interventions to stabilize their domestic food prices. Such stabilization requires some capacity to isolate the domestic food market from world markets and can be implemented only through government actions (although private traders can handle most of the actual logistics).[2] Such isolation runs directly against the spirit and, for many countries, the letter of World Trade Organization (WTO) agreements. But it is a very widespread practice. Demeke, Pangrazio, and Maetz (2009) count thirty-six countries that used some form of border intervention to stabilize their domestic food prices during the 2007–8 crisis.

Such policies can have a large impact on the level of food insecurity, even at a global level. India, China, and Indonesia stabilized their domestic rice prices during the 2007–8 food crisis by using export bans (or at least very tight controls), thus protecting well over two billion consumers from sharply higher prices. The policies pursued by these three countries demonstrate the importance of understanding local politics in forming policy, especially food policy. Although the end results were similar—food prices remained stable throughout the crisis—the actual policies pursued in each country were quite different (Slayton 2009; Dawe 2010a).[3]

India, Indonesia, and China are big players in the global rice market, even if their actual trade is limited. As Dawe (2010b) emphasizes, there is a case to be made simply in terms of aggregate global welfare that stabilizing domestic rice prices in these large countries using border interventions might be both an effective and an efficient way to cope with food crises, even after considering the spillover effects on increased price volatility in the residual world market. Dawe points out that unstable supply and demand must be accommodated *somewhere*, and passing the adjustment to the world market might be both equitable and efficient in a second-best world in which fast-acting and well-targeted safety nets are not available. One important advantage of successful efforts to stabilize rice prices in Asia is that they also stabilize price expectations among the many participants along the entire rice supply chain and thus prevent the disastrous hoarding behavior that can generate extreme market shortages and severe price spikes, as emphasized in Chapter 6 (Timmer 2010, 2012a).

An important paper by Dorosh and Rashid on how Bangladesh coped with the rice crisis in 2007–8 concludes as follows:

> Finally, the Bangladesh experience has important implications for other rice importing countries that attempt to stabilize prices through public distribution. Private sector rice imports can provide major benefits to net rice purchasers, especially in periods when international prices are relatively low and stable as was the case from 2000 to 2006. But in periods of unstable international markets and rising prices, timely interventions and clear policy messages are needed to avoid precautionary buildup of private stocks that can greatly exacerbate domestic price increases. The analysis in this paper suggests that a relatively small increase in private stocks can lead to a large price increase; conversely, timely distribution of readily available public stocks could offset these effects. In summary, the Bangladesh experience suggests that private sector rice import trade has much potential for enhancing welfare of consumers in rice importing countries, but careful monitoring of market conditions and the capability for limited, timely market injections are still needed to prevent international rice price spikes from having severe negative effects on domestic consumers. (Dorosh and Rashid 2013: 110)

The second basic approach to coping with a food crisis is to stimulate additional supplies through fast-acting programs. Nearly all countries tried to do something along these lines during the 2007–8 crisis, whether by subsidizing fertilizer to get a quick production response or encouraging planting of short-season crops, even urban gardens. If the high prices for food seen in the crisis actually get to farmers, they have strong incentives to search out these options themselves, but government assistance in gaining access to inputs or proper seed varieties can also help. In Asia, the short-run response of rice farmers to high prices was surprisingly vigorous, partly because of the availability of short-duration rice varieties and irrigated farming systems with multiple-cropping potential (Slayton 2009). In Vietnam, for example, which has three distinct cropping seasons for rice, production increased 6.3 percent in 2007 and 5.3 percent in 2008, compared with average annual increases of just 3.3 percent per year between 2005 and 2011. All of this increase in production, a total of 1.2 million metric tons, was put on the export market.

Countries can also hold emergency food stocks as part of a broader strategy for providing food security to their citizens. Expectations of higher and more volatile food prices in the future should lead authorities to invest in larger food stocks than in the past. The design rules for adding to and disposing of these stocks, and their day-to-day management to avoid large storage losses, will be essential to making emergency food stocks a sustainable and cost-effective approach (Timmer 2009b). Clear rules on management of public stocks minimize the displacement of private storage, a point also emphasized by Dorosh and Rashid (2013).

One crucial element of these rules will be to use international trade in the commodity as part of the provisioning mechanism, thus avoiding the extraordinarily high costs that can come from a strategy of total self-sufficiency. Even in countries as large as Indonesia, India, and China, where a high degree of food self-sufficiency is required simply because of the limited size of world grain markets, some interaction with these markets through a managed trade regime can lower the costs of food security. Managed trade regimes can be open and transparent, with clear rules on the nature of interventions, thus allowing the private sector to handle actual trade logistics.

The third approach to coping with a food crisis is to provide safety nets to poor consumers, either in cash or through the direct provision of food aid. This was the immediate and almost only response of the donor community to the food crisis in 2007–8. The safety net approach figures prominently in best-practice recommendations from the World Bank, FAO, and the World Food Program (World Bank 2005). The logic is clear: let high prices be reflected in local markets to signal the necessary changes in resource allocations to both producers and consumers, but protect the very poor from an irreversible deterioration in their food intake status. Efficiency is maintained, and the poor are protected.

The difficulty is that food crises are relatively short-lived events (as opposed to chronic poverty). Effective safety nets take a long time to design and implement, and they are very expensive if the targeted poor are a significant proportion of the population. Unless a well-targeted program with adequate fiscal support is already in place when the crisis hits, it is virtually impossible for a country to design and implement one in time to reach the poor before high prices for food threaten their nutritional status. Even when a program is in place and can be scaled up quickly, as with the Raskin program of rice distribution to the poor in Indonesia, operational inefficiencies and simple corruption in deliveries might mean that the poor are reached only at exceptionally high cost (Olken 2006).

Global Agreements or National Self-Interest: The Case for National Food Reserves

It may seem strange that countries wishing to hold larger national food reserves to protect themselves against sudden price shocks from the world market or significant production shortfalls in their own economies face substantial obstacles in doing so because of binding WTO rules on the aggregate measure of support (AMS) that countries can provide to their agricultural sectors. Purchases of grain for domestic food reserves count in a complicated and perverse way as part of the AMS. The G33 countries, a group of developing countries led by India, have proposed a revision to the rules for developing countries (DCs), and Galtier (2013b) has offered an analysis and recommendations for a sensible way forward.[4]

> Buffer stocks play a decisive role in policies aiming to hold the price above a floor and/or below a ceiling. Of course, other measures can be used for this purpose: the quantity available on the domestic market can also be regulated through border measures regulating imports and exports. However, these measures are likely to increase the instability of international markets (as happened in 2008 on the rice market). National buffer stocks are likely to have the opposite effect: by increasing the global level of stocks, they are likely to reduce the frequency and the magnitude of price spikes on international markets. Price spikes only occur when the level of global stock is low. . . .
>
> Yet the use of buffer stocks by countries (including DCs) is strongly limited by current rules of the WTO. . . .
>
> The G33 proposal states that "acquisition of stocks of foodstuffs by developing country members with the objective of supporting low-income or resource-poor producers shall not be required to be accounted for in the AMS." In other words, countries would be free to authorize their public stocks authorities to acquire the quantity they want at the price they want without any limitation, so long as they buy from "low-income or resource-poor producers" (who are

sometimes defined as farmers holding less than 10 hectares—a definition that would include the vast majority of producers in DCs).

This proposal is extremely important. It clearly goes in the right
direction as it would allow DCs to build the public stocks they need to
guarantee their food security both in the short term (by allowing poor
consumers to have access at any time to basic food products) and in
the long term (by boosting investments in the production of grain and
other basic foods). It would also contribute to an increase in the level of
global grain stocks and thereby reduce the frequency and the magnitude of spikes on international markets (as already noted, in the past,
international price spikes only occurred when the level of global stock
was low and the increased instability of international markets since
2008 is to a great extent due to the lack of stocks). (Galtier 2013b: 3–5)

Galtier's recommendations are to not give all countries a completely free
hand in determining the size of their publicly owned and managed stocks
but rather to fix the rather bizarre method of accounting for public stock
purchases in the AMS. The Ninth Ministerial Meeting of the Doha Round,
held in early December 2013 in Bali, Indonesia, basically dodged the issue by
agreeing to allow developing countries to subsidize procurement of stocks
for purposes of food security, but only for four more years. After further study,
a recommended solution will be offered. Clearly, if such a sensible step turns
out not to be feasible during the current Doha Round of trade negotiations,
individual countries are likely to take matters into their own hands and act
unilaterally on behalf of stabilizing their domestic food economies by holding
larger grain reserves. Either way, larger reserves are needed as one component
of domestic food price stabilization efforts.

The Medium Run from 2020 to 2050: Managing Demand

Several medium-term policy approaches to improving food security at the
country level need to be considered. Which is best will depend on which
global food price regime emerges over the coming quarter century. The historical path of structural transformation with falling food prices leading to
a "world without agriculture" is an obvious possibility (Timmer 2009a). But
continued financial instability, coupled with the impact of climate change,
could lead to a new and uncertain path of rising real costs for food with a

reversal of the structural transformation (Timmer and Akkus 2008, and Chapter 4). Management of food policy in the medium run, and the outlook for sustained poverty reduction, will be radically different depending on which of these global price regimes plays out. It will depend on how food demand grows in relation to growth in supply. In the medium term—up to 2050 or so—there is more scope to influence growth in demand than growth in supply.

Three basic sources of demand for staple food grains—the main source of food energy for the poor—drive the overall level of production needed to keep food prices reasonably stable. As Chapter 3 demonstrated, population and income growth are relatively stable and predictable factors. Demand for food to produce biofuels is much less predictable and depends as much on political forces as on economics. Left unchecked, however, growth in demand for food grains to produce biofuels could swamp growth in demand from regular sources—population and income growth.

The main impact of a growing population is to expand demand for traditional diets. For this demand to be realized, the household must have income, or land on the farm, to translate need into effective demand in food markets. The more challenging dimension of income growth is its impact on the dietary transition, especially rapidly growing demand for meat and other livestock products whose production is increasingly grain intensive (Webb and Block 2010; Naylor and Falcon 2008. The surge in Chinese demand for pork and poultry, for example, has led to a massive increase in demand for livestock feed, especially soymeal as a high-quality protein ingredient and corn as a high-quality energy source.

This demand for feed then translates fairly directly into broader demand in markets for food grains. Low-quality wheat competes directly with corn in many feed rations, and world prices for wheat have had a stable long-run relationship with prices for rice (Mitchell 2008). Will rich(er) consumers starve poor consumers? Perhaps yes if (new) rich consumers aspire to an American-style diet, but probably not if the full economic, health, and environmental costs of such a diet become better understood. There is significant scope for improved diets without these heavy costs.

Changing Diets

Dietary patterns are determined by four basic forces: incomes and general living standards; prices of various foods available to households, relative to their incomes and other costs of living; culture and tastes of the household and the society at large; and the specific nutritional knowledge of the main cook or food preparer—typically the mother in a household with children.

Which of these factors are subject to informed policy initiatives and which will play out as basic outcomes of market forces? There is much that individual, informed consumers can do to shape their diets and consequent health outcomes, but it is also true that nutritionally informed decisions can be very hard to make in today's commercial environment. The global obesity epidemic has not developed so quickly just because consumers have higher incomes, food has been cheap, and nutrition training in schools is woefully inadequate. The food industry has been working very hard for decades to encourage the behavior and expenditures that lead to obesity. It is hard to resist.

That said, the issue is what can be done to make consumers chose healthier diets, with substantially lower resource demands on food production and reduced impact on the environment. There are three possible drivers in this direction:

- better knowledge by consumers of the health and environmental consequences of their dietary choices;
- informed policy initiatives that tax (or prohibit) bad dietary choices while rewarding good choices; and
- a market process whereby environmentally friendly and healthy food choices become relatively cheaper in relation to their livestock-intensive, "junk food" competition.

It is already apparent that well-educated, informed consumers choose healthier diets. Controlling for incomes, college-educated households are much less obese, consume less red meat and processed foods, and lead healthier lifestyles. Individuals in these households also have longer life expectancies, partly because of their diet and lifestyle choices, but also because they are more knowledgeable about maintaining other dimensions of personal health and have the education and income to act on that knowledge. These are empowered households, and they offer some hope that targeted health and nutrition education can make the dietary transition both healthier and more environmentally friendly.

At a global level, of course, these households are a speck of sand.[5] China, with its newfound ability to afford pork or chicken every day, or India, with an enormous taste for dairy products, eggs, and fish, are not even close to a dietary transition that will emphasize small amounts of livestock products, greater reliance on fresh fruits and vegetables, and continued reliance on starchy staples to provide healthy diets. It seems likely that only when livestock-intensive diets become prohibitively expensive even for the emerging middle class will the dietary transition become more environmentally sustainable. Unfortunately, these high prices will also tend to price basic food grains out of the reach of the poor. Either grain production will need to speed up substantially or more aggressive programs to modify the current trends of dietary transition in emerging economies will be needed if continued progress on hunger in the medium term is going to be possible.

Fortunately, consumers in wealthy countries eat so much meat and other grain-intensive animal products that there is substantial scope to reduce meat consumption, and the associated grain consumption, through desirable lifestyle and dietary changes.[6] Gradually reducing use of grain for feed in rich countries would allow an increase in livestock production in developing countries. Admittedly, moving dietary patterns in this direction will take active engagement from a wide variety of players—health professionals, enlightened public policy makers, and the food industry itself. Supermarkets—the most informed agent about consumer preferences (and how to change them)—perhaps can be enlisted in the drive for healthier diets.

There is cautious hope that global food supplies can keep up with demand from population growth and higher incomes, especially if diets in rich countries start a transition away from grain-intensive livestock products because of health risks.

Biofuels and Food Policy

The outlook for meeting demand from growth in biofuel production is not so promising. High prices for liquid fuels that keep most of the transportation system moving have also made it possible to convert agricultural commodities, especially sugar, corn, and vegetable oils, into ethanol or biodiesel. Many rich countries have encouraged this process by subsidizing the costs of conversion technologies and by mandating the use of the output. Biofuels have become a significant source of demand for several food commodities.

The role of biofuels going forward, and their impact on agriculture, will depend on the structure of agriculture in individual countries. In the extreme, the demand for biofuels in rich countries to power automobiles has the potential to raise the price of basic agricultural commodities to such a level that the entire structural transformation could be reversed. If so, the growing use of biofuels has alternative possible results. It could spell impoverishment for much of the world's population because of the resulting high prices for food, or it could spell dynamism for rural economies and the eventual end of rural poverty. Which result turns out to be the case depends fundamentally on the location, technology, economics, and politics of biofuel production.

The potential devastating effects of biofuels are easy to conceptualize (Naylor et al. 2007; Naylor 2012). The income elasticity of demand for starchy staples (cereals and root crops for direct human consumption) is less than 0.2 on average, and falling with higher incomes. It is already negative in much of Asia. Adding in the indirect demand from grain-fed livestock products brings the average income elasticity to about 0.5, and this relationship is holding steady in the face of rapid economic growth in India and China. Potential supply growth seems capable of managing this growth in demand.

But the demand for biofuels is almost insatiable in relation to the base of production of staple foods. The income elasticity of demand for liquid fuels for automobile and truck fleets, not to mention power generation, is greater than 1.0 in developing countries. The average for the world is rising as middle-class consumers in China, India, and beyond seek to graduate from bicycles to motorbikes to automobiles. One simple calculation shows the dimension of the problem. If all the corn produced in the United States were used for ethanol to fuel automobiles, it would replace just 15 percent of current gasoline consumption in the United States. Something has to give.

If this were a market-driven process, it is easy to see what would give. High grain prices would make it uneconomic to produce ethanol. Demand would fall, as would returns on investments in ethanol processing plants. Greater profitability of grain production would stimulate a supply response, although this increase in output might take several years if improved technologies are needed. Grain prices would reach a new equilibrium. Demand from the biofuel industry would have only a modest impact.

This is not the scenario most analysts see. Instead, political mandates to expand biofuel production in many countries will continue to drive investments in processing facilities. Large public subsidies will be required to keep these investments profitable in the face of high prices for raw material. Rich countries will be able to afford these subsidies more easily than poor countries. A combination of inelastic demand for fuel and a willingness to pay large subsidies would keep grain prices very high (Naylor 2012; de Gorter and Just 2010).

If this scenario plays out, the consequences for economic growth, poverty reduction, and food security in developing countries depends on the role of agriculture in individual countries, the pattern of commodity production, and the distribution of rural assets, especially land. It is possible to see circumstances in which smallholder farmers respond to higher prices for grain by increasing output and reaping higher incomes. These incomes might be spent in the local, rural nonfarm economy, stimulating investments and raising wages for nonfarm workers. In such environments, higher grain prices could stimulate an upward spiral of prosperity. Rozelle (2013) argues that China might pursue this strategy. So far, however, China seems to be importing most of the raw material for its nascent biofuel industry.

An alternative scenario seems more likely, however, partly because the role of smallholder farmers has been under so much pressure in the past several decades. If only large farmers are able to reap the benefits of higher prices for grain and their profits do not stimulate a dynamic rural economy, a downward spiral can start for the poor. High prices for food cut their food intake, children are sent to work instead of school, and an intergenerational poverty trap develops. If the poor are numerous enough, the entire economy is threatened and the structural transformation comes to a halt. The share of agriculture in both employment and GDP starts to rise, and this reversal condemns future generations to lower living standards. One could expect much more "structural" poverty. Countries determined to cope with such poverty would find themselves supporting expensive and long-term safety nets for the poor.

This grim scenario is not inevitable. Policy interventions could limit the scope for converting food into fuel. The first step would be to stop subsidizing such conversions and the mandates that require the use of biofuels in automobiles and trucks. Next, explicit taxes on the use of food-based biofuels would restrict their impact on food prices and, at the same time, provide incentives to develop new technologies that provide more efficient ways to convert solar energy into liquid fuels. Agriculture, as society's most efficient way to capture solar energy for human use, would likely play an important role in this process even as food crops would be disconnected from their potential use as fuel.

From this perspective, it is important to remember that biofuels are not new. Although coal was known in China in prehistoric times and was traded in England as early as the thirteenth century, it was not used widely for industrial purposes until the seventeenth century. Until then, biofuels (mostly wood and agricultural waste) were virtually the only source of energy for human economic activities. For many poor people they remain so today. But the widespread use of fossil fuels since the Industrial Revolution has provided a huge subsidy to modern economic activities—because coal, petroleum, and later natural gas were so cheap—a subsidy which seems to be nearing an end for reasons of both supply and demand.

Agricultural productivity also benefited from this subsidy, as fertilizer costs were kept low and cheap fuel for farm machinery, processing, and transportation made modern supply chains feasible. With that era of cheap energy from fossil fuels about to end, the agricultural transformation will also be under threat. And without the dynamic of a modernizing and more productive agriculture, the entire structural transformation as the main pathway out of poverty would be much less feasible.

A reversal of the structural transformation as the regular path to economic development and reduced poverty would be a historic event, countering the patterns generated by market forces over the past several centuries. Such an event would have stark political consequences, as populations do not face the sustained prospect of lower living standards with equanimity.

It is possible, of course, that new technologies will come onstream quickly and reduce energy costs across the board. This would allow the biofuel dilemma to disappear quietly. But it looks like a rocky couple of decades before that happens.

The Long Run After 2050: The Supply Challenge

Even with sensible actions to manage growth in food demand, the reality is that food supplies need to double between now and when global population stabilizes, probably shortly after 2050, at a level likely to exceed nine billion people. Many commentators seem to think that population growth itself is driving the pressure on food supplies, but it is population coupled with increased purchasing power that drives most of the increased demand.

Population

In fact, there is no politically feasible way to stabilize the global population without an increase in the welfare of the poor. This is a good thing, of course, because the alternative is that without higher incomes, the curb on population growth will be Malthusian. Mortality rates will increase because of limited access to food. The scenario with higher incomes, with fertility dropping to replacement levels as couples see the value of investing in the quality of their children rather than the quantity, is vastly to be preferred.

Even with this preferred scenario, of course, food supplies will need to increase over the next half century at roughly the same pace as they did since 1950. This increase will have to come in the face of these factors:

- seriously depleted resource bases in many major food basins;
- increased weather extremes, and higher average temperatures, caused by climate change; and
- greatly increased demand for water for nonagricultural purposes at the same time that many groundwater resources are nearly gone.

In the past, rapid technological change has stimulated growth in food supplies, and real prices fell over the long run (Timmer 1995). Perhaps that era is past.

Improving the Supply Outlook

Several authors treat various dimensions of increasing agricultural output and food supply (see Gready [2013] for a comprehensive, if provocative, overview). This cursory discussion focuses mostly on the challenges facing that task as they relate to food security. In keeping with the basic framework of the book, there are short-run and long-run dimensions, and issues at the micro, macro, and global levels. Only the global and long-run topics are treated here.

In the long run, the supply response, made up of varied national responses, has to meet the outlook for rapid growth in demand, especially at the global level. In the past, when food prices spiked and talk of an impending Malthusian crisis arose, output responded to bring world food prices back to their long-run downward trend, though with a lag. Three basic reasons now suggest that such a benign output response may not be forthcoming:

- limited land available for expanding area;
- stagnant growth in yields; and
- high-cost inputs.

Malthus might be wrong, of course, and higher prices might yet again induce a significant enough supply response to bring down food prices. The recent experience with rice, in which real world prices are now below their 2007 levels, provides modest encouragement on this front. But rice consumption has been falling in Asia, thus relieving pressures to increase supplies.

A quarter of a century ago, Hayami and Ruttan (1985) pointed out that area expansion as a source of increased agricultural production was drawing to a close. Future increases would need to come from higher yields on existing farmland. More than a decade into the twenty-first century, there is little high-quality, unutilized agricultural land available for farming. Where there is good land available for expansion, especially in Africa and a few areas in Southeast Asia, vigorous competition, especially from foreign companies and sovereign investment funds (land grabs), has the potential to make that land inaccessible to local farmers.

Yields at research stations of existing agricultural technologies have essentially been unchanged for decades because of the paucity of investment in research during this time. Raising yields from actual farmer practices to the potential of present technology—closing the "yield gap"—is the only source of increased output until new agricultural technologies are developed. New technologies, however, are at least a decade away. Moreover, the yield gap has largely been closed, except in Africa.

The costs of essential inputs—fuel, fertilizer, and water—to obtain greater yields are high and growing rapidly. In addition, prolonged periods of high prices for grain are likely to raise land rents and rural labor costs. High prices for grain also raise the payoff to increased investment in basic agricultural research and development, and these investments are beginning to take place after almost three decades of neglect. There is considerable optimism that technologies and farm management practices can meet the long-run challenge of feeding nine billion better-nourished people. But in the short and medium run, most of the action will be on managing the volatility of food systems and limiting the growth in demand that stems from diets intensive in grain-fed animal products and from biofuel production using food grains as the feedstock.

Responding to Climate Change

The biofuel challenge to policy analysts stems from efforts to mitigate climate change. Equally challenging will be efforts to adapt agriculture to the dual effects of climate change—higher temperatures and greater variability in rainfall. In pulling together their final thoughts on the impact of climate change on the three main factors that determine food security—availability of food, access to food, and healthy utilization of food—Lobell and Burke make the following observation: "One thing appears almost certainly true in the twenty-first century; if agriculture and food security are to thrive, they will have to do so in a constantly warming world. The level of climate stability that has been experienced since the dawn of agriculture is a thing of the past; the future will be one of constant change. This need not spell disaster for food security, but we would be wise not to underestimate the enormity of the challenge at hand" (Lobell and Burke 2010: 1960).

Behavioral Dimensions of Food Security

Perhaps the most important element of food security in the minds of most citizens is the fear of a food crisis in which prices spike or staple foods (especially rice) disappear from the market. Accordingly, preventing food crises through better understanding of their fundamental causes, thus allowing implementation of better policies, should be a high priority for policy analysts. As argued in Chapter 6, an approach to political economy that utilizes insights from the rapidly developing field of behavioral economics is likely to provide far more realistic policy initiatives than have been generated by the standard neoclassical paradigm.

Unfortunately, moving beyond this paradigm requires a different approach to development than is currently in vogue in academia and the donor community. Ending hunger is hard because it is so complicated and deeply entwined with the organization of economic activities and their regulation through public policies. Still, history provides grounds for optimism. As Kenny (2011: 204) notes:

> In fact, governments and civil society organizations have been central to improved outcomes across the developing world. These all too often corrupt and usually inefficient organizations have nonetheless played a role in a widespread, unprecedented revolution in quality of life over the last fifty years. Governments and civil society organizations have been key to expanding educational opportunities, to improving access to infrastructure, to providing basic health care. This success, rather than continued failure leading to crisis, is surely the reason that developing country governments and their development partners deserve continuing, growing support.

Part of this support will come through academics contributing a better understanding of the historical roots of the complications that make effective policy interventions so difficult. Part will come through more informed donor support to countries seeking ways to improve food security for their citizens. These efforts—by academics and policy makers—will mostly be at the national level. They will be successful only in environments in which political determination is coupled to good governance, high-quality data, and analysis to illuminate and guide effective policy. Only in those societies able to put all three pieces together—political determination, good governance, and effective policy—will it be possible to end hunger.

NOTES

Chapter 1. Setting the Stage

1. One debate is over the efficiency of taxing fats in foods, taxing fat people, or taxing the health consequences of being fat.

2. Because agricultural development has turned out to be so important to the overall rate of economic growth and to reductions in poverty, very considerable attention has been devoted to bringing it about. It is impossible to do a full literature review in this note, but efforts to develop a theory of agrarian change would include at least the following contributions: Mosher (1957, 1966, 1978), Schultz (1964), Boserup (1965), Mellor (1966), Geertz (1966), Wharton (1969), Hayami and Ruttan (1971, 1985), Johnston and Kilby (1975), Timmer, Falcon, and Pearson (1983), Eicher and Staatz (1984), Ellis (1988), Tomich, Kilby, and Johnston (1995), Fafchamps (2004), Lipton (2005), Poulton, Dorward, and Kydd (2005), and Barrett, Carter, and Timmer (2010). Some of these works are more descriptive of "what things need to be done" than theoretical in terms of "why things need to be done," but all are useful milestones in our understanding of agrarian change and the challenges in bringing it about.

3. See chapter 3 of Timmer, Falcon, and Pearson (1983) for use of a farming system tableau to analyze multiple farm activities, and see the references for further details.

Chapter 2. Learning to Manage Food Security

1. This section draws on Timmer (2000).

2. Defining food security is an exercise in itself, especially when both macro and micro dimensions are included in the definition. The goal of this chapter is to understand the economic context in which food security is no longer a personal or a policy concern. Almost any definition that is intuitively plausible will do for that purpose. A formal definition that is widely used is from the United States position paper for the 1996 World Food Summit: "Food security exists when all people at all times have physical and economic access to sufficient food to meet their dietary needs for a productive and healthy life. Food security has three dimensions: AVAILABILITY of sufficient quantities of food of appropriate quality, supplied through domestic production or imports; ACCESS by households and individuals to adequate resources to acquire appropriate

foods for a nutritious diet; and UTILIZATION of food through adequate diet, water, sanitation, and health care" (USDA 1996: 2). This definition is obviously an ideal that no country could hope to reach in fact.

3. See chapter 4 of Timmer, Falcon, and Pearson (1983) for further analysis of the importance of an efficient marketing system and the role of price policy in developing one.

4. For a review of the importance of externalities in the development process, see Stewart and Ghani (1991).

5. By the early 1990s, a number of factories had been built on former rice paddies along the road from Jakarta to Karawang.

6. A good early review of this approach was produced by the CIMMYT Economics Staff (1984). Mellor (forthcoming) emphasizes that many upland regions in Asia are most productive growing tree crops rather than food staples, and the successful countries in the region, especially Malaysia, recognized this diversity in ecosystems as a core part of their development strategy.

7. For a particularly eloquent statement of the lack of investment in African agriculture, see Eicher (1992). Block (1995) demonstrates how serious the productivity problems have been in agriculture, but he has also documented the recent gains in agricultural productivity on the continent (Block 2013). Pardey (2011) also reviews trends in agricultural productivity in sub-Saharan Africa.

8. The rather long period required for price integration to occur may be a significant impediment to such a single-commodity stabilization policy. Three months of highly unstable prices for substitutes may impose very heavy burdens on consumers who depend on these commodities for most of their caloric intake. Similarly, prices can collapse at harvest for these commodities for as long as three months even if maize prices are stabilized, thus providing to producers few of the benefits of stable prices. The difficulties of stabilizing prices in the African context, and the costs of doing to, are modeled in Pinckney (1988).

9. Imported rice is increasingly important in several West African countries.

10. The political economy dimensions of the argument are explained in Bates (1981) and Bates and Block (2013).

11. Several countries in East Africa fluctuate around self-sufficiency for white maize, their staple grain. In good years exports are possible, and in bad years imports are needed. For landlocked Malawi, the swing between the CIF and FOB prices can be very wide indeed—from negative prices for exports to more than $300 per ton for imports.

Chapter 3. Understanding Food Security Dynamics

1. Although the math may look formidable, the model really is quite simple. Skipping to "Why the Analytics Matter" is permissible but not recommended.

2. There is an entire body of literature devoted to estimating the calorie-income relationship illustrated in panel A of Figure 3.3 and to examining the significance of any relationship between calorie intake and severe health consequences, such as infant mortality or shortened life expectancy (Srinivasan 1981; Poleman 1981; Behrman and Deolalikar 1988; Gaiha, Jha, and Kulkarni 2013). The perspective here draws on Reutlinger and Selowsky (1976); Alderman (1986); and Alderman and Paxson (1992).

3. For convenience, all individuals in each income quintile are assumed to have the average income of that quintile. However, income distribution in panel B is drawn continuously after the first quintile to reflect the smooth distribution likely after incomes rise above a subsistence floor.

4. The extensive land reforms carried out in East Asia after World War II can be considered as a strategy of immediate income distribution. They were carried out in revolutionary circumstances or at the instigation of foreign powers, and the reforms established a distribution of assets from which equitable growth was possible. The conditions for similar reforms in other countries have not been widely applicable since the 1960s (Tomich, Kilby, and Johnston 1995).

5. It should be noted that the income gap between rich and poor continued to widen in Indonesia between 1970 and 1995, despite the faster growth rate of the incomes of the poor during that period. In the bottom quintile, for example, per capita incomes increased by $336 (in 1995 U.S. dollars) in the twenty-five-year period, whereas incomes of the top quintile increased by $1,374. Even highly successful poverty alleviation does not necessarily solve the problems of income distribution, especially in the political arena, a topic discussed in Chapter 6.

6. The methodology is a variant of that developed by Reutlinger and Selowsky (1976) and used in this chapter (see Figure 7).

7. By definition, the supply variable makes no allowance for the state of nutrition of the population. The measure of population-normalized food deficit indicates how much food energy would be needed per capita to bring the undernourished population up to the minimum energy requirement. The relative importance of food availability or food access in driving the extent of undernutrition can be seen when the two measures are compared. The food security gap in Table 3 does this in a simple way.

8. The statistical relationships used to calculate the rate of diminishing returns are based on annual data for individual countries in each of the regions.

Chapter 4. Structural Transformation as the Pathway to Food Security

1. Both of these cases have been documented in the Stanford Symposium Series on Global Food Policy and Food Security in the 21st Century (Badiane 2011; Binswanger-Mkhize 2012).

2. Alternatively, the convergence between labor productivity in the agricultural and nonagricultural sectors can be measured by the ratio of the two, which approaches

one when labor productivity is equal in the two sectors. This is the main approach used by Dorin, Hourcade, and Benoit-Cattin (2013).

3. This is not a temporal statement but one driven by movements in real incomes per capita. If incomes per capita fall over extended periods, as they have in Brazil or Nigeria, for example, the pathway back is not likely to track the pathway forward because of substantial stickiness in structural patterns of labor allocation.

4. It should be emphasized that these are production shares of rice to value added and do not include the value of processing and marketing. The share of rice at the level of consumption is probably about half again as large.

5. Caloric intake data are from FAO food balance sheets.

6. Aggregate time series data for rice consumption also rely on food balance sheet estimates of consumption per capita. In turn, food balance sheet data rely on rice production data, and these seem to be increasingly suspect in a number of Asian countries. A further problem with these aggregate data is their sensitivity to unrecorded changes in levels of rice stocks. Official data are lacking on these stock changes in China, where they are regarded as a state secret, and private stocks are not known anywhere. Household surveys of consumption avoid these problems.

7. In Indonesia and India, where data are available to disaggregate the top quintile of income into smaller increments, such as deciles or smaller, there is evidence of negative income elasticities for rice consumption in the top half of the top income quintile, even in rural areas.

8. The full quotation runs as follows. "Little else is requisite to carry a state to the highest degree of opulence from the lowest barbarism than peace, easy taxes, and tolerable administration of justice; all the rest being brought about by the natural course of things." Lecture by Adam Smith in 1775, cited by E. L. Jones (1981: 235). The perspective here also draws heavily on Jones's *Growth Recurring*, published in 1988.

9. This perspective on regional specialization has been generalized and formalized in Paul Krugman's work on economic geography. See Krugman (1993).

Chapter 5. When Pro-poor Growth and Structural Transformation Fail

1. A word of warning: this chapter takes me well beyond my personal range of experience as a policy analyst and advisor. Failed development efforts have many explanations, and there are few empirically based models. This chapter quotes extensively from many sources on what has gone wrong and how to fix things. Without necessarily agreeing with all of these arguments in their entirety, I cite them because of the authors' greater knowledge of these difficult environments and for their explanatory usefulness.

2. See the ambitious book by Acemoglu and Robinson (2012) for a summary of the methodological issues in asserting causality as well as for a powerful argument that

the quality of resulting institutions largely determines the path of welfare gains from economic growth.

3. This section draws on Timmer 2008b.

4. Some of the discussion in this section draws on my foreword to Gaiha, Jha, and Kulkarni (2014).

Chapter 6. The Political Economy of Food Security

1. The escape from hunger is part of the broader "great escape" that Deaton (2013) documents globally.

2. This section draws on Timmer (1989) and Dawe and Timmer (2012). A very useful introduction to the politics of food, as distinct from the economics, is in Paarlberg (2010).

3. Even if the target price adjusts, it is still inevitable that, given a large enough shock, the scheme will eventually collapse in the sense that it will become bankrupt or will fail to prevent a surge in prices. But such long-run inevitability is not necessarily a relevant guide to policy. Most producers, consumers, and policy makers have time horizons measured in months and years, not decades and centuries.

4. The dismissal by academic trade economists of efforts to stabilize food prices has little relevance to the design and implementation of interventions to stabilize rice prices in East and Southeast Asia (Dawe 2001; Timmer and Dawe 2007; Timmer 1989, 1991b, 1996, 2010c).

5. The basic references in the macro literature on these effects are McDonald and Siegel (1986), Pindyck (1988), Dixit and Pindyck (1994), and Lucas (1972, 1973).

6. This section draws from Timmer 2012a.

7. As Bernheim and Rangel (2009) point out in a review of "behavioral public economics," one of the most important contributions of behavioral economics has been in the analysis of provision of public goods. Their review focuses on the joint provision of a public good by government and charitable bodies. Behavioral research illuminates the motivations for individuals to make charitable contributions for causes and institutions that provide jointly produced public goods (such as public radio). Of direct relevance to the discussion here is evidence in these decisions of herd behavior and "keeping up with the Joneses," or other-regarding preferences.

Bernheim and Rangel also stress the seriousness of the challenge from behavioral economics to mainstream welfare analysis, which is based on the principle of revealed preferences, a challenge first presented by Duesenberry (1949) and revived by Kahneman and Tversky (1979). If revealed preferences from choices about consumption, income generation, and time allocation, for example, are not "really" what individuals prefer, or if they incorporate what others are doing, as the experimental evidence from behavioral economics confirms, the normative foundations of consumer theory no longer hold. Without these foundations, such stalwarts of applied welfare analysis as consumer surplus no longer have a theoretical basis. The consequences are obvious for the arguments in this chapter. Models that international economists use to prove the existence of gains from trade no longer hold, and theoretical arguments against stabilizing prices also disappear.

8. As noted in Chapter 4, the rapid emergence of supermarkets and modern supply chains might offer the possibility that stable prices for staple foods could become more of a private good.

9. A workshop at FAO Rome on October 26–27, 2009, discussed this topic in detail. See Gilbert (2009), Jayne (2009), Gross (2009), and Dart (2009) for a variety of contrasting views, and the rapporteur's report by Sarris, Gurkan, and Cummings (2009) for a synthesis of the divergent views of the participants.

10. The early standard works are Wickizer and Bennett (1941) and Barker and Herdt, with Rose (1985). This section of the chapter draws on Timmer 2009c.

11. This difference was pointed out clearly in Jasny's classic study *Competition Among Grains* (Jasny 1940: 7). He justifies his exclusion of rice from the study with the following observation: "The Orient is a world by itself, with its own climate, diet, and economic and social setup, and this makes it easy for us to omit it. The inclusion of rice would mean the discussion of two worlds. The writer would be satisfied to have mastered one." The sharp difference between rice-based economies and those based on wheat or corn is also stressed by Bray (1986) and Oshima (1987).

12. A major debate in the finance profession is the importance of self-fulfilling expectations that are driven by the psychology of herd behavior. Such behavior leads to the formation of price bubbles which are disconnected from the underlying fundamentals of commodity supply and demand, at least for short periods of time (Shiller 2003; Gilbert 2009; Munier and Briand 2012). The Nobel Prize in Economics awarded in 2013 to Robert J. Shiller (and two others working in finance) indicates the seriousness now given in the economics profession to the behavioral dimensions of price formation.

13. See Slayton (2009, 2010) for a detailed analysis and chronology of the "fire" in the world rice market from late 2007 until mid-2008.

14. I was guilty myself. As a close follower of the world rice market, I realized that my favorite rice varieties available at Trader Joe's would soon shoot up in price. I cleared the shelf. Two weeks later, the price had doubled. Hoarding can be entirely rational if it is based on accurate expectations of how others will behave.

15. As further evidence that psychology, rather than fundamentals, was driving prices in the world rice market, it was the announcement by the prime minister of Japan that rice supplies would be available to the Philippines, not their actual shipment, that pricked the price bubble and started the rapid decline in rice prices. After lengthy negotiations over the sales price and as world market prices kept falling, Japan never did ship any rice to the Philippines or to any other country seeking rice imports during the crisis (Slayton 2009).

16. The source of the measurable unhappiness of many citizens in the transition economies of the former Soviet Union can be traced primarily to unprecedented in-

stability in incomes, growing income inequality, and the loss of public goods (Guriev and Zhuravskaya 2009). Most Asian governments consciously tried to balance equity, growth, and stability during their early periods of rapid industrialization (Timmer 1995b).

17. This issue was highlighted at a conference in Singapore in late 2013. A high-level WTO official was lamenting the fact that politicians often gave in to populist pressures on food prices and food trade issues. I asked, "What do you call an official who gives in to these populist pressures?" The WTO official was quizzical; I responded, "Elected." In a democracy, it is important to understand what voters want, even if they are unrealistic in economic terms.

18. David Leonhardt (2013) makes a similar point in his review of Angus Deaton's book *The Great Escape*.

Chapter 7. The Way Forward

1. Asia Society/IRRI Task Force (2010). Because the International Rice Research Institute (IRRI) cosponsored the Task Force, the focus was on rice. I was the principal analyst and lead author of the report, which was unanimously approved by all members of the Task Force.

2. Isolation from the world market does not, of course, guarantee more stable prices. Indeed, for most countries, open borders to world markets lead to greater price stability, as local shortages and surpluses can be accommodated through trade. But completely open borders mean a country is exposed to world market shocks as well as domestic instability. Most large countries, at least for rice in Asia, find such openness to be politically impossible. An excellent review of the African environment and possible steps to stabilize volatile food environments there is in IRAM et al. (2013).

3. The pass-through of price increases in world markets to the domestic economies of China, India, and Indonesia from early 2007 to early 2008 were 4 percent, 8 percent, and −3 percent, respectively. In each case, however, domestic rice prices were already higher than world prices before the crisis hit (Dawe 2010a).

4. It is slightly strange that India is leading this charge because the country already maintains huge and costly food reserves, although having these reserves sanctioned by the WTO would be a big political plus. A recent right to food decision by the Indian Supreme Court has basically ordered that these reserves of rice and wheat, well beyond amounts needed for price stabilization efforts, should be used to increase the amount of food grains distributed at highly subsidized prices to the poor. Given the extraordinarily large costs of such a scheme, it remains to be seen if the rights approach to feeding the poor can be effective.

5. Economists are pretty pessimistic about changing the dynamics of food demand over the next several decades. Barrett (2013) has argued that almost all the demand changes between now and 2050 are "baked in," and if we want a better balance between

supply and demand over that time interval, virtually all of the action will have to come from significantly enhanced growth in agricultural productivity or from higher real prices for food.

6. Most aquaculture depends on grain-based diets, and virtually all increases in seafood consumption will need to come from aquaculture rather than wild fisheries.

REFERENCES

Abbott, Philip C., Christopher Hurt, and Wallace E. Tyner. 2008. Updated in 2010. "What's Driving Food Prices?" Farm Foundation Issue Report 37951. July. Oak Brook, Ill.: Farm Foundation.

Acemoglu, Daron, and James A. Robinson. 2012. *Why Nations Fail: The Origins of Power, Prosperity and Poverty.* New York: Random House.

Alderman, Harold. 1986. *The Effect of Food Price and Income Changes on the Acquisition of Food by Low-Income Households.* Washington, D.C.: International Food Policy Research Institute.

———. 1992. "Intercommodity Price Transmittal: Analysis of Food Markets in Ghana." Policy Research Working Paper WPS 884. April. Washington, D.C.: World Bank.

Alderman, Harold, and Christina H. Paxson. 1992. "Do the Poor Insure? A Synthesis of the Literature on Risk and Consumption in Developing Countries." Research Program in Development Studies Discussion Paper 164. Princeton: Princeton University.

Anderson, J. R., and J. A. Roumasset, 1996. "Food Insecurity and Stochastic Aspects of Poverty." *Asian Journal of Agricultural Economics* 2: 53–66.

Anderson, Kym. 2012. "Government Trade Restrictions and International Price Volatility." *Global Food Security* 1 (2): 157–66.

Anderson, Kym, and Yujiro Hayami. 1986. *The Political Economy of Agricultural Protection: East Asia in International Perspective.* Sydney: Allen and Unwin.

Anderson, Kym, Gordon Rausser, and Johan Swinnen. 2013. "Political Economy of Public Policies: Insights from Distortions in Agricultural and Food Markets." *Journal of Economic Literature* 51 (2): 423–77.

Arezki, R., and M. Bruckner. 2011. "Food Prices and Political Instability." International Monetary Fund Working Paper 11/62. Washington, D.C.: International Monetary Fund.

Asfaw, Abay. 2007. "Supermarket Purchases and the Dietary Patterns of Households in Guatemala." Discussion Paper 696. Washington, D.C.: International Food Policy Research Institute.

Asia Society/IRRI Task Force. 2010. "Never an Empty Bowl: Sustaining Food Security in Asia." Task Force Report, September. New York: Asia Society and International Rice Research Institute.

Badiane, Ousmane. 2011. "Agriculture and Structural Transformation in Africa." Stanford Symposium Series on Global Food Policy and Food Security in the 21st Century, April 7. Stanford University, Stanford, Calif.

Bangladesh Bureau of Statistics. 2011. Household Income and Expenditure Survey 2010. Dhaka: Bureau of Statistics. http://www.bbs.gov.bd.

Barker, Randolph, and Robert W. Herdt (with Beth Rose). 1985. *The Rice Economy of Asia*. Washington, D.C.: Resources for the Future.

Barrett, Christopher B. 1995. "Idea Gaps, Object Gaps, and Trust Gaps in Economic Development." Economic Research Institute Study Paper 95-16. August. Department of Economics, Utah State University, Logan, Utah.

———, ed. 2013. *Food Security and Sociopolitical Stability*. Oxford: Oxford University Press.

Barrett, Christopher B., Michael R. Carter, and C. Peter Timmer. 2010. "A Century-Long Perspective on Agricultural Development." In "Commemorating the Centennial of the AAEA." Special issue, *American Journal of Agricultural Economics* 92 (2): 447–68.

Barrett, Christopher B., and Erin C. Lentz. 2012. "Food Insecurity." International Studies Association Compendium Project. New York: Wiley-Blackwell.

Barro, Robert J., and Xavier Sala-i-Martin. 1994. *Economic Growth*. New York: McGraw-Hill.

Bates, Robert H. 1981. *Markets and States in Tropical Africa: The Political Basis of Agricultural Policies*. Berkeley: University of California Press.

Bates, Robert H., and Steven A. Block. 2013. "Revisiting African Agriculture: Institutional Change and Productivity Growth." *Journal of Politics* 75 (2): 372–84.

Behrman, Jere R. 1984. "The Analytics of International Commodity Agreements." In *Agricultural Development in the Third World*, ed. Carl K. Eicher and John M. Staatz, 362–77. Baltimore: Johns Hopkins University Press.

Behrman, Jere R., and Anil B. Deolalikar. 1988. "Health and Nutrition." In *Handbook of Development Economics*, ed. Hollis Chenery and T. N. Srinivasan, 1: 631–711. Amsterdam: North-Holland.

Bennett, Merrill K. 1954. *The World's Food*. New York: Harper.

Bernheim, B. Douglas, and Antonio Rangel. 2009. "Beyond Revealed Preference: Choice-Theoretic Foundations for Behavioral Welfare Economics." *Quarterly Journal of Economics* 124 (1): 51–104.

Besley, Tim, and Louise Cord, eds. 2006. *Operationalizing Pro-poor Growth: Synthesis and Country Experiences*. London: Palgrave Macmillan.

Bhargava, Alok. 2008. *Food, Economics and Health*. Oxford: Oxford University Press.

Bigman, David. 1985. *Food Policies and Food Security Under Instability: Modeling and Analysis*. Lexington, Mass.: Lexington Books.

Bill and Melinda Gates Foundation. 2012. "2012 Annual Letter by Bill Gates." Seattle: Bill and Melinda Gates Foundation.

Binswanger-Mkhize, Hans P. 2012. "India 1960–2010: Structural Change, the Rural Non-farm Sector, and the Prospects for Agriculture." Stanford Symposium Series on Global Food Policy and Food Security in the 21st Century, May 10. Stanford University, Stanford, Calif.

Birdsall, Nancy, David Ross, and Richard Sabot. 1995. "Inequality and Growth Reconsidered: Lessons from East Asia." *World Bank Economic Review* 9 (3): 477–508.

Block, Steven A. 1995. "The Recovery of Agricultural Productivity in Sub-Saharan Africa." *Food Policy* 20 (5): 385–406.

———. 2013. "The Post-Independence Decline and Rise of Crop Productivity in Sub-Saharan Africa: Measurement and Explanations." *Oxford Economic Papers* (March 23): 1–24.

Block, S. A., L. Kiess, P. Webb, S. Kosen, R. Moench-Pfanner, M. W. Bloem, and C. P. Timmer. 2004. "Macro Shocks and Micro Outcomes: Child Nutrition During Indonesia's Crisis." *Economics and Human Biology* 2 (1): 21–44.

Boserup, Ester. 1965. *The Conditions of Agricultural Growth: The Economics of Agrarian Change Under Population Pressure*. Chicago: Aldine Press.

Brahmbhatt, Milan, and Luc Christiaensen. 2008. "Rising Food Prices in East Asia: Challenges and Policy Options." Washington, D.C.: World Bank.

Bray, Francesca. 1986. *The Rice Economies: Technology and Development in Asian Societies*. Oxford: Basil Blackwell.

Brennan, Michael J. 1958. "The Supply of Storage." *American Economic Review* 47 (1): 50–72.

Byerlee, Derek, and Steve Haggblade. 2013. "African Food Systems to 2030: Toward Inclusive Business Models." Stanford Symposium Series on Global Food Policy and Food Security in the 21st Century, February 5. Stanford University, Stanford, Calif.

Carter, M. R., P. D. Little, T. Mogues, and W. Negatu. 2007. "Poverty Traps and Natural Disasters in Ethiopia and Honduras." *World Development* 35 (5): 835–56.

Chen, Yu-Chin, Kenneth Rogoff, and Barbara Rossi. 2008. "Can Exchange Rates Forecast Commodity Prices?" Working Paper 13901. March. Cambridge, Mass.: National Bureau of Economic Research.

Chenery, Hollis, Montek S. Ahluwalia, C. L. G. Bell, John H. Duloy, and Richard Jolly. 1974. *Redistribution with Growth*. London: Oxford University Press for the World Bank and the Institute of Development Studies (University of Sussex).

Chisholm, Anthony. 1982. "Commodity-Price Stabilization: Microeconomic Theory and Policy Issues." In *Food Security: Theory, Policy, and Perspectives from Asia and the Pacific Rim*, ed. Anthony H. Chisholm and Rodney Tyers. Lexington, Mass.: Lexington Books and D. C. Heath.

CIMMYT Economics Staff. 1984. "The Farming Systems Perspective and Farmer Participation in the Development of Appropriate Technology." In *Agricultural Development in the Third World*, ed. Carl K. Eicher and John M. Staatz, 362–77. Baltimore: Johns Hopkins University Press.

Collier, Paul. 2007. *The Bottom Billion: Why the Poorest Countries Are Failing and What Can Be Done About It.* Oxford: Oxford University Press.

Collier, Paul, and Stefan Dercon. Forthcoming. In "African Agriculture in 50 Years: Smallholders in a Rapidly Changing World?" Special issue, *World Development.*

Collins, Keith J. 2008. "The Role of Biofuels and Other Factors in Increasing Farm and Food Prices: A Review of Recent Developments with a Focus on Feed Grain Markets and Market Prospects." Supporting material for a review conducted by Kraft Foods Global, Inc. June 19.

Conway, Gordon. 2012. *One Billion Hungry: Can We Feed the World?* Ithaca, N.Y.: Cornell University Press.

Cootner, Paul H. 1960. "Returns to Speculators: Telser vs. Keynes." *Journal of Political Economy* 68 (4): 396–404.

———. 1961. "Common Elements in Futures Markets for Commodities and Bonds." *American Economic Review* 51 (2): 173–83.

Dart, Samantha. 2009. "Financial Speculators and Commodity Market Instability." Paper presented to the Experts' Meeting on "Institutions and Policies to Manage Global Market Risks and Price Spikes in Basic Food Commodities," FAO Trade and Markets Division. October 26–27. Food and Agriculture Organization of the United Nations, Rome.

Dasgupta, Partha. 1993. *An Inquiry into Well-Being and Destitution.* Oxford: Clarendon Press.

Dawe, David. 1996. "A New Look at the Effects of Export Instability on Investment and Growth." *World Development* 24 (12): 1905–14.

———. 2000. "The Contribution of Rice Research to Poverty Alleviation." In *Redesigning Rice Photosynthesis to Increase Yield*, ed. J. E. Sheehy, P. L. Mitchell, and B. Hardy, 3–12. Makati City, Philippines: International Rice Research Institute; Amsterdam: Elsevier Science B.V.

———. 2001. "How Far Down the Path to Free Trade? The Importance of Rice Price Stabilization in Developing Asia." *Food Policy* 26 (2): 163–75.

———. 2008. "Running Out of Steam." *Rice Today* (July–September): 41. Los Baños, Philippines: International Rice Research Institute.

———, ed. 2010a. *The Rice Crisis: Markets, Policies and Food Security.* London and Washington, D.C.: Food and Agriculture Organization of the United Nations and Earthscan.

———. 2010b. "Can the Next Rice Crisis Be Prevented?" In *The Rice Crisis: Markets, Policies and Food Security*, ed. David Dawe, 345–56. London and Washington, D.C.: Food and Agriculture Organization of the United Nations and Earthscan.

Dawe, David, and C. Peter Timmer. 2012. "Why Stable Food Prices Are a Good Thing: Lessons from Stabilizing Rice Prices in Asia." *Global Food Security* 1 (2): 127–33. http://dx.doi.org/10.1016/j.gfs.2012.09.001.

Deaton, Angus. 2013. *The Great Escape: Health, Wealth, and the Origins of Inequality.* Princeton: Princeton University Press.

de Gorter, Harry, and Dusan Drabik. 2012. "The Effect of Biofuel Policies on Food Grain Commodity Prices." *Biofuels* 3 (1): 21–24.

de Gorter, Harry, and David R. Just. 2010. "The Social Costs and Benefits of Biofuels: The Intersection of Environmental, Energy and Agricultural Policy." *Applied Economic Perspectives and Policy* 32 (1): 4–32.

Demeke, Mulat, Guendalina Pangrazio, and Materne Maetz. 2009. "Country Responses to the Food Security Crisis: Nature and Preliminary Implications of the Policies Pursued." http://www.fao.org/fileadmin/user_upload/ISFP/pdf_for_site _Country_Response_to_the_Food_Security.pdf.

Dercon, Stefan. 2012. "Agriculture and Development: Revisiting the Policy Narratives." Department for International Development, London, and Oxford University. http://www.scribd.com/doc/159933153/Narratives-in-African-agriculture.

Diamond, Jared. 1997. *Guns, Germs, and Steel: The Fates of Human Societies.* New York: W. W. Norton.

Dixit, Avinash K., and Robert S. Pindyck. 1994. *Investment Under Uncertainty.* Princeton: Princeton University Press.

Djurfeldt, Gören, Hans Holmén, Magnus Jirström, and Rolf Larsson, eds. 2005. *The African Food Crisis: Lessons from the Asian Green Revolution.* Wallingford, England: CABI.

Dorin, Bruno, Jean-Charles Hourcade, and Michel Benoit-Cattin. 2013. "A World Without Farmers? The Lewis Path Revisited." Working Paper 47-2013. April. Centre International de Recherche sur l'Environnement et de Développement (CIRED), Nogent-sur-Marne, France. http://www.centre-cired.fr/spip.php?article1508.

Dorosh, Paul, and Shahidur Rashid. 2013. "Trade Subsidies, Export Bans and Price Stabilization: Lessons of Bangladesh-India Rice Trade in the 2000s." *Food Policy* 41 (C): 103–11.

Drèze, Jean, and Amartya Sen. 1989. *Hunger and Public Action.* Oxford: Clarendon Press.

———. 2013. *An Uncertain Glory: India and Its Contradictions.* London: Allen Lane.

Duesenberry, James S. 1949. *Income, Saving, and the Theory of Consumer Behavior.* Cambridge, Mass.: Harvard University Press.

Easterly, William. 2004. "Can Aid Buy Development?" Address at the Center for Global Development, Washington, D.C.

Economist. 1991. "Survey of Asia's Emerging Economies." November 16: 18.

———. 2013. "Indian Development: Beyond Bootstraps." Review of *An Uncertain Glory: India and Its Contradictions,* by Amartya Sen and Jean Drèze. June 29: 74.

Eggleston, Karen, Jean Oi, Scott Rozelle, Ang Sun, and Xueguang Zhou. 2012. "Aging Population and Poverty Require Stronger Investment in China's Rural Youth." March 14. New Haven, Conn.: YaleGlobal Online.

Eicher, Carl K. 1992. "African Agricultural Development Strategies." In *Alternative Development Strategies in Sub-Saharan Africa,* ed. Frances Stewart, Sanjaya Lall, and Samuel Wangwe, 79–102. London: Macmillan.

Eicher, Carl K., and John M. Staatz, eds. 1984. *Agricultural Development in the Third World*. Baltimore: Johns Hopkins University Press.

———. 1998. *International Agricultural Development*. 3rd ed. Baltimore: Johns Hopkins University Press.

Elliott, Kimberly Ann. 2008. "Biofuels and the Food Crisis: A Survey of the Issues." Working Paper 151. August. Washington, D.C.: Center for Global Development.

Ellis, Frank. 1988. *Peasant Economics: Farm Households and Agrarian Development*. Cambridge: Cambridge University Press.

Fafchamps, Marcel. 2004. *Market Institutions in Sub-Saharan Africa: Theory and Evidence*. Cambridge, Mass.: Massachusetts Institute of Technology Press.

FAO (Food and Agriculture Organization of the United Nations), 2011. *State of Food Insecurity in the World*. Rome: Food and Agriculture Organization of the United Nations.

FAO, WFP, and IFAD (Food and Agriculture Organization of the United Nations, World Food Programme, and International Fund for Agricultural Development). 2012. *The State of Food Insecurity in the World 2012: Economic Growth Is Necessary but Not Sufficient to Accelerate Reduction of Hunger and Malnutrition*. Rome: Food and Agriculture Organization of the United Nations.

Fogel, R. W. 1991. "The Conquest of High Mortality and Hunger in Europe and America: Timing and Mechanisms." In *Favorites of Fortune: Technology, Growth, and Economic Development Since the Industrial Revolution*, ed. Patrice Higonnet, David S. Landes, and Henry Rosovsky, 35–71. Cambridge, Mass.: Harvard University Press.

———. 1994. "Economic Growth, Population Theory, and Physiology: The Bearing of Long-Term Processes on the Making of Economic Policy." Nobel Prize lecture. *American Economic Review* 84 (3): 369–95.

Frankel, Jeffrey. 2006. "The Effect of Monetary Policy on Real Commodity Prices." In *Asset Prices and Monetary Policy*, ed. John Y. Campbell, 291–334, Chicago: University of Chicago Press.

Fuglie, Keith O. 2004. "Productivity Growth in Indonesian Agriculture, 1961–2000." *Bulletin of Indonesian Economic Studies* 40 (2): 209–25.

Gaiha, Raghav, Raghbendra Jha, and Vani S. Kulkarni, eds. 2014. *Diets, Malnutrition, and Disease: The Indian Experience*. Delhi: Oxford University Press.

Galtier, Franck. 2009. "How to Manage Food Price Instability in Developing Countries." Summary of the study concerning instruments devoted to food price instability management, funded by the Agence Française de Développement (AFD) and the French Ministry of Foreign and European Affairs (MAEE). CIRAD and UMR MOISA, France.

Galtier, Franck (with the collaboration of Bruno Vidal). 2013a. "Managing Food Price Instability in Developing Countries: A Critical Analysis of Strategies and Instruments." April. Agence Française de Développement and Centre International de Recherche sur l'Environnement et de Développement (CIRED), Nogent-sur-Marne, France.

———. 2013b. "The Need to Change WTO Rules on Buffer Stocks." July. Centre International de Recherche sur l'Environnement et de Développement (CIRED), Nogent-sur-Marne, France.

Gardner, Bruce L. 2002. *American Agriculture in the Twentieth Century: How It Flourished and What It Cost.* Cambridge, Mass.: Harvard University Press.

Geertz, Clifford. 1966. *Agricultural Involution: The Process of Ecological Change in Indonesia.* Berkeley: University of California Press.

Gelb, Alan, Christian Meyer, and Vijaya Ramachandran. 2013. "Does Poor Mean Cheap? A Comparative Look at Africa's Industrial Labor Costs." Working Paper 325. Revised June. Washington, D.C.: Center for Global Development.

Gilbert, Christopher. 2009. "Understanding Spikes and Speculation in Agricultural Commodity Markets." Paper presented to the Experts' Meeting on "Institutions and Policies to Manage Global Market Risks and Price Spikes in Basic Food Commodities" by the FAO Trade and Markets Division, October 26–27. Food and Agriculture Organization of the United Nations, Rome.

Goldberg, Pinelopi Koujianou, and Nina Pavcnik. 2007. "Distributional Effects of Globalization in Developing Countries." *Journal of Economic Literature* 45 (1): 39–82.

Gready, Jill E. 2013. "Best-Fit Options of Crop Staples for Food Security: Productivity, Nutrition and Sustainability." In *Handbook on Food*, ed. Raghbendra Jha, Raghav Gaiha, and Anil Deolalikar. London: Edward Elgar.

Greenfield, Jim, Maurizio de Nigris, and Panos Konandreas. 1996. "The Uruguay Round Agreement on Agriculture: Food Security Implications for Developing Countries." *Food Policy* 21 (4–5): 365–76.

Grigg, David B. 1974. *The Agricultural Systems of the World: An Evolutionary Approach.* Cambridge: Cambridge University Press.

Grimm, Michael, Stephan Klasen, and Andrew McKay, eds. 2007. *Determinants of Pro-poor Growth: Analytical Issues and Findings from Country Cases.* London: Palgrave Macmillan.

Gross, Adam. 2009. "The Role of Agricultural Commodity Exchanges in Market Price Volatility in Developing Countries." Paper presented to the Experts' Meeting on "Institutions and Policies to Manage Global Market Risks and Price Spikes in Basic Food Commodities" by the FAO Trade and Markets Division. October 26–27. Food and Agriculture Organization of the United Nations, Rome.

Gulati, Ashok, and Shenggen Fan, eds. 2007. *The Dragon and the Elephant: Agricultural and Rural Reforms in China and India.* Baltimore: Johns Hopkins University Press.

Guriev, Sergei, and Ekaterina Zhuravskaya. 2009. "(Un)Happiness in Transition." *Journal of Economic Perspectives* 23 (2): 143–68.

Hardin, Garrett. 1974. "Lifeboat Ethics: The Case Against Helping the Poor." *Psychology Today* 8: 38–43.

Hayami, Yujiro, and Vernon W. Ruttan. 1971. *Agricultural Development: An International Perspective.* Baltimore: Johns Hopkins University Press.

———. 1985. *Agricultural Development: An International Perspective.* Revised and expanded ed. Baltimore: Johns Hopkins University Press.

HLPE (High Level Panel of Experts). 2011. *Price Volatility and Food Security: A Report by the High Level Panel of Experts on Food Security and Nutrition of the Committee on World Food Security.* July. Rome: High Level Panel of Experts.

Hoddinott, J. 2006. "Shocks and Their Consequences Across and Within Households in Rural Zimbabwe." *Journal of Development Studies* 42 (2): 301–321.

Houthakker, Hendrik. 1987. "Futures Trading." In *The New Palgrave Dictionary of Economics*, ed. John Eatwell, Murray Milgate, and Peter Newman, 2: 447–49. London: Macmillan.

Huppi, Monica, and Martin Ravallion. 1991. "The Sectoral Structure of Poverty in Indonesia During an Adjustment Period: Evidence for Indonesia in the Mid-1980s." *World Development* 19 (12): 1653–78.

IFPRI (International Food Policy Research Institute). 2008. "High Food Prices: The What, Who, and How of Proposed Policy Actions." May. Washington, D.C.: International Food Policy Research Institute.

IRAM (group lead), ISSALA, IN VIVO, and CIRAD. 2013. "Food Stocks and Regulating Market Volatility in Africa." Final Report. June. Paris: Agence Française de Développement and FARM, Paris.

Irwin, Scott, Doug R. Sanders, and R. P. Merrin. 2009. "Devil or Angel? The Role of Speculation in the Recent Commodity Price Boom (and Bust)." *Journal of Agricultural and Applied Economics* 41 (2): 377–91.

Islam, Nurul. 1996. "Implementing the Uruguay Round: Increased Food Price Stability by 2020?" 2020 Brief 34. Washington, D.C.: International Food Policy Research Institute.

Jasny, N. 1940. *Competition Among Grains.* Stanford, Calif.: Stanford University Press.

Jayne, Thom. 2009. "Market Failures and Food Price Spikes in Southern Africa." Paper presented to the Experts' Meeting on "Institutions and Policies to Manage Global Market Risks and Price Spikes in Basic Food Commodities" by the FAO Trade and Markets Division, October 26–27. Food and Agriculture Organization of the United Nations, Rome.

———. 2012. "Managing Food Price Instability in East and Southern Africa." *Global Food Security* 1 (2): 143–49.

Johnston, Bruce F. 1958. *The Staple Food Economies of Western Tropical Africa.* Stanford, Calif.: Stanford University Press.

Johnston, Bruce F., and Peter Kilby. 1975. *Agriculture and Structural Transformation: Economic Strategies in Late-Developing Countries.* New York: Oxford University Press.

Johnston, Bruce F., and John W. Mellor. 1961. "The Role of Agriculture in Economic Development." *American Economic Review* 51 (4): 566–93.

Jones, E. L. 1981. *The European Miracle: Environments, Economics, and Geopolitics in the History of Europe and Asia.* Cambridge: Cambridge University Press.

———. 1988. *Growth Recurring: Economic Change in World History.* Oxford: Clarendon Press.

Kahneman, Daniel, and Amos Tversky. 1979. "Prospect Theory: An Analysis of Decision Under Risk." *Econometrica* 47: 269–91.

Kaldor, Nicholas. 1939. "Speculation and Economic Stability." *Review of Economic Studies* 7 (October): 1–27.

Kenny, Charles. 2011. *Getting Better: Why Global Development Is Succeeding—And How We Can Improve the World Even More.* New York: Basic Books.

Keynes, John Maynard. 1936. *The General Theory of Employment, Interest, and Money.* New York: Harcourt, Brace.

Krugman, Paul. 1993. *Geography and Trade.* New York: Norton.

Kuznets, Simon. 1966. *Modern Economic Growth.* New Haven: Yale University Press.

Lagi, Marco, Yavni Bar-Yam, Karla Z. Bertrand, and Yaneer Bar-Yam. 2011. "The Food Crises: A Quantitative Model of Food Prices Including Speculators and Ethanol Conversion." September 21. *arXiv*: 1109.4859.

Leonhardt, David. 2013. "A Cockeyed Optimist." Review of *The Great Escape: Health, Wealth, and the Origins of Inequality*, by Angus Deaton. *New York Times Book Review*, December 22: 13.

Levine, Ross, and David Renelt. 1992. "A Sensitivity Analysis of Cross-Country Growth Regressions." *American Economic Review* 82 (4): 942–63.

Lewis, W. Arthur. 1954. "Economic Development with Unlimited Supplies of Labor." *Manchester School* 22: 3–42.

Lindert, Peter H. 1991. "Historical Patterns of Agricultural Policy." In *Agriculture and the State: Growth, Employment, and Poverty in Developing Countries,* ed. C. Peter Timmer, 29–83. Ithaca, N.Y.: Cornell University Press.

Lipton, Michael. 1977. *Why Poor People Stay Poor: Urban Bias in World Development.* Cambridge, Mass.: Harvard University Press.

———. 1993. "Urban Bias: Of Consequences, Classes and Causality." In *Beyond Urban Bias,* ed. Ashutosh Varshney, 229–58. London: Frank Cass.

———. 2005. "Crop Science, Poverty and the Family Farm in a Globalising World." IFPRI 2020 Discussion Paper 40. June. Washington, D.C.: International Food Policy Research Institute.

Lobell, David, and Marshall Burke, eds. 2010. *Climate Change and Food Security: Adapting Agriculture to a Warmer World.* Advances in Global Change Research 37. New York: Springer.

Lobell, David, Wolfram Schlenker, and Justin Costa-Roberts. 2011. "Climate Trends and Global Crop Production Since 1980." *Science* 333 (May): 616–20.

Losch, Bruno, Sandrine Fréguin-Gresh, and Eric Thomas White. 2012. *Structural Transformation and Rural Change Revisited: Challenges for Late Developing Countries in a Globalizing World.* Paris: Agence Française de Développement; Washington, D.C.: World Bank.

Lucas, Robert F. 1972. "Expectations and the Neutrality of Money." *Journal of Economic Theory* 4: 103–24.

———. 1973. "Some International Evidence on Output-Inflation Tradeoffs." *American Economic Review* 63 (3): 326–34.

———. 1988. "On the Mechanics of Economic Development." *Journal of Monetary Economics* 22 (1): 3–42.

Maccini, Sharon L., and Dean Yang. 2009. "Under the Weather: Health, Schooling, and Economic Consequences of Early-Life Rainfall." *American Economic Review* 99 (3): 1006–26.

Maxwell, Daniel. 1996. "Measuring Food Insecurity: The Frequency and Severity of 'Coping Strategies.'" *Food Policy* 21 (3): 291–304.

Maxwell, Simon, and Rachel Slater, eds. 2003. "Food Policy Old and New." In "Food Policy Old and New." Special issue, *Development Policy Review* 21 (5–6): 531–53.

McCraw, Thomas K. 2007. *Prophet of Innovation: Joseph Schumpeter and Creative Destruction.* Cambridge, Mass.: Belknap Press of Harvard University Press.

McDonald, Robert, and Daniel Siegel. 1986. "The Value of Waiting to Invest." *Quarterly Journal of Economics* 100: 707–27.

Mellor, John W. 1966. *The Economics of Agricultural Development.* Ithaca, N.Y.: Cornell University Press.

———. 1976. *The New Economics of Growth: A Strategy for India and the Developing World.* Ithaca, N.Y.: Cornell University Press.

———, ed. 1995. *Agriculture on the Road to Industrialization.* Baltimore, MD: Johns Hopkins University Press.

———. Forthcoming. "High Rural Population Density Africa: Agricultural Growth, Poverty Reduction, and the Economic Transformation." Draft paper for "Emerging Land Issues in African Agriculture and Their Implications for Rural Development Strategies," ed. T. S. Jayne, Derek Headey, and Jordan Chamberlin. Special issue, *Food Policy.*

Michelson, Hope C. 2013. "Small Farmers, NGOs, and a Walmart World: Welfare Effects of Supermarkets Operating in Nicaragua." *American Journal of Agricultural Economics* 95 (3): 628–49.

Mitchell, Don. 2008. "A Note on Rising Food Prices." Policy Research Working Paper WPS 4682. Washington, D.C.: World Bank.

Morduch, Jonathan. 1995. "Income Smoothing and Consumption Smoothing." *Journal of Economic Perspectives* 9 (3) 103–114.

Mosher, Arthur T. 1957. *Technical Co-operation in Latin-American Agriculture.* Chicago: University of Chicago Press.

———. 1966. *Getting Agriculture Moving: Essentials for Development and Modernization.* New York: Praeger for the Agricultural Development Council.

———. 1978. *An Introduction to Agricultural Extension.* Singapore: Singapore University Press for the Agricultural Development Council.

Munier, Bertrand R. 2008. "An X-Ray of the Risk Module Within the MOMAGRI Model." April. Mouvement pour une Organisation Mondiale de l'Agriculture (MOMAGRI), IAE de Paris (Sorbonne Business School), Paris.

————, ed. 2012. *Global Uncertainty and the Volatility of Agricultural Commodities Prices*. Amsterdam: IOS Press.

Munier, Bertrand, and Anne Briand. 2012. "Modeling Price Volatility on Agricultural Markets: the MOMAGRI Modular Approach." In *Global Uncertainty and the Volatility of Agricultural Commodities Prices*," ed. Bertrand R. Munier, 187–240. Amsterdam: IOS Press.

Naylor, Rosamond. 2012. "Biofuels, Rural Development, and the Changing Nature of Agricultural Demand." Stanford Symposium Series on Global Food Policy and Food Security in the 21st Century, April 11. Stanford University, Stanford, Calif.

Naylor, Rosamond L. and Walter P. Falcon. 2008. "Our Daily Bread: Without Public Investment, the Food Crisis Will Only Get Worse." *Boston Review* (September/October).

Naylor, Rosamond L., Adam J. Liska, Marshall B. Burke, Walter P. Falcon, Joanne C. Gaskell, Scott D. Rozelle, and Kenneth G. Cassman. 2007. "The Ripple Effect: Biofuels, Food Security, and the Environment." *Environment: Science and Policy for Sustainable Development* 49 (9): 30–43.

Neary, J. Peter. 2003. "Competitive Versus Comparative Advantage." *World Economy* 26 (4): 457–70. Wiley Blackwell.

Nerlove, Marc. 1958. *The Dynamics of Supply: Estimation of Farmers' Response to Price*. Baltimore: Johns Hopkins University Press.

Newbery, David M. G., and Joseph E. Stiglitz. 1981. *The Theory of Commodity Price Stabilization: A Study in the Economics of Risk*. New York: Oxford University Press.

North, Douglass C. 1959. "Agriculture in Regional Economic Growth." *Journal of Farm Economics* 51 (December): 943–51.

OECD (Organization for Economic Cooperation and Development). 2008. "The Relative Impact on World Commodity Prices of Temporal and Longer Term Structural Changes in Agricultural Markets: A Note on the Role of Investment Capital in the U.S. Agricultural Futures Markets and the Possible effect on Cash Prices." TAD/CA/APM/CFS/MD (2008) 6. March. Paris: Trade and Agriculture Directorate, Committee for Agriculture, Organization for Economic Cooperation and Development.

Olken, Ben. 2006. "Corruption and the Costs of Redistribution: Micro Evidence from Indonesia." *Journal of Public Economics* 90: 853–70.

Oshima, Harry T. 1987. *Economic Growth in Monsoon Asia: A Comparative Study*. Tokyo: University of Tokyo Press.

Paarlberg, Robert. 2010. *Food Politics: What Everyone Needs to Know*. Oxford: Oxford University Press.

Pardey, Philip. 2011. "African Agricultural Productivity Growth and R&D in a Global Setting." Stanford Symposium Series on Global Food Policy and Food Security in the 21st Century, October 6. Stanford University, Stanford, Calif.

Perkins, Dwight H., and members of the National Academy of Sciences Delegation to the People's Republic of China, 1977. *Rural Small-Scale Industry in the People's Republic of China*. Berkeley: University of California Press.

Peterson, Willis L. 1979. "International Farm Prices and the Social Cost of Cheap Food." *American Journal of Agricultural Economics* 61 (1): 12–21.

Pinckney, Thomas C. 1988. *Storage, Trade, and Price Policy Under Production Instability: Maize in Kenya.* IFPRI Research Report 71. Washington, D.C.: International Food Policy Research Institute.

Pindyck, Robert S. 1988. "Irreversible Investment, Capacity Choice, and the Value of the Firm." *American Economic Review* 78 (5): 969–85.

Pingali, Prabhu L. 2012. "Green Revolution: Impacts, Limits, and the Path Ahead." *Proceedings of the National Academy of Sciences (PNAS)* 109 (31): 12302–8.

Pingali, Prabhu L., and Mark W. Rosegrant. 1995. "Agricultural Commercialization and Diversification: Processes and Policies." *Food Policy* 20 (3): 171–85.

Poleman, Thomas. 1981. "Quantifying the Nutrition Situation in Developing Countries." *Food Research Institute Studies* 28 (1):1–58.

Porter, Michael E. 1990. *The Competitive Advantage of Nations.* New York: Free Press.

Poulton, Colin, Andrew R. Dorward, and Jason G. Kydd. 2005. "The Future of Small Farms: New Directions for Services, Institutions, and Intermediation." Conference on the Future of Small Farms, June, Wye, England.

Radelet, Steven. 2010. *Emerging Africa: How 17 Countries Are Leading the Way.* Washington, D.C.: Center for Global Development.

———. 2013. "Africa's Economic Progress." Letter to the editor, *New York Times*, September 9, A32.

Ramachandran, Vijaya, Alan Gelb, and Manju Kedia Shah. 2009. *Africa's Private Sector: What's Wrong with the Business Environment and What to Do About It.* Baltimore: Johns Hopkins University Press for the Center for Global Development.

Ramey, Garey, and Valerie A. Ramey. 1995. "Cross-Country Evidence on the Link Between Volatility and Growth." *American Economic Review* 85 (5):1138–51.

Rashid, Shahidur, Ashok Gulati, and Ralph Cummings Jr., eds. 2008. *From Parastatals to Private Trade: Lessons from Asian Agriculture.* Baltimore: Johns Hopkins University Press for the International Food Policy Research Institute.

Ravallion, Martin. 1987. *Markets and Famines.* Oxford: Clarendon Press.

———. 1989. "Do Price Increases for Staple Food Help or Hurt the Rural Poor?" Working Paper 167. March 31. Washington, D.C.: World Bank.

———. 1998. "Famines and Economics." *Journal of Economic Literature* 35 (3): 1205–42.

Ravallion, Martin, and Shaohua Chen. 2007. "China's (Uneven) Progress Against Poverty." *Journal of Development Economics* 82 (1): 1–42.

Ravallion, Martin, Shaohua Chen, and Prem Sangraula. 2007. "New Evidence on the Urbanization of Global Poverty." *Population and Development Review* 33 (4): 667–701.

Ravallion, Martin, and G. Datt. 1996. "How Important to India's Poor Is the Sectoral Composition of Economic Growth?" *World Bank Economic Review* 10 (1):1–25.

Ravallion, Martin, and Monika Huppi. 1991. "Measuring Changes in Poverty: A Methodological Case Study of Indonesia During an Adjustment Period." *World Bank Economic Review* 5 (1): 57–82.

Reardon, Thomas. 2010. "Linking Food Market Transformation to Improved Food Security in Asia." Presentation at the Association of Southeast Asian Nations (ASEAN) Food Security Conference, June 17, Singapore. Organized by Nathan Associates, Arlington, Va., with support from the United States Agency for International Development.

Reardon, Thomas, Christopher B. Barrett, Julio A. Berdegué, and Johan F. M. Swinnen. 2009. "Agrifood Industry Transformation and Small Farmers in Developing Countries: Introduction to a Special Issue." *World Development* 37 (11):1717–27.

Reardon, Thomas, Kevin Chen, Bart Minten, and Lourdes Adriano. 2012. *The Quiet Revolution in Staple Food Value Chains: Enter the Dragon, the Elephant, and the Tiger.* Manila: Asian Development Bank, International Food Policy Research Institute.

Reardon, Thomas, and C. Peter Timmer. 2007. "Transformation of Markets for Agricultural Output in Developing Countries Since 1950: How Has Thinking Changed?" In *Handbook of Agricultural Economics*, vol. 3, ed. Robert Evenson and Prabhu Pingali, 2807–55. Amsterdam: Elsevier.

———. 2012. "The Economics of the Food System Revolution." *Annual Review of Resource Economics* 4 (September):14.1–14.40.

———. 2014. "Five Inter-Linked Transformations in the Asian Agrifood Economy: Food Security Implications." *Global Food Security.* http://dx.doi.org/10.1016/j.gfs.2014.02.01.

Reardon, Thomas, C. Peter Timmer, Christopher B. Barrett, and Julio A. Berdegué. 2003. "The Rise of Supermarkets in Africa, Asia, and Latin America." *American Journal of Agricultural Economics* 85 (December): 1140–46.

Reardon, Thomas, David Tschirley, Steve Haggblade, Bart Minten, C. Peter Timmer, and Saweda Liverpool-Tasie. forthcoming. "The Emerging 'Quiet Revolution' in African Agrifood Systems." *Global Food Security.*

Resnick, Danielle, and Regina Birner. 2006. "Does Good Governance Contribute to Pro-poor Growth? A Review of the Evidence from Cross-Country Studies." DSGD Discussion Paper 30. February. Washington, D.C.: International Food Policy Research Institute.

Reutlinger, Shlomo, and Marcelo Selowsky. 1976. *Malnutrition and Poverty: Magnitude and Policy Options.* World Bank Occasional Paper 23. Baltimore: Johns Hopkins University Press for the World Bank.

Robles, Miguel, Maximo Torero, and Joachim von Braun. 2009. *When Speculation Matters.* IFPRI Issue Brief 57. February. Washington, D.C.: International Food Policy Research Institute.

Rodrik, Dani. 1999. *The New Global Economy and Developing Countries: Making Openness Work.* Washington, D.C.: Overseas Development Council.

Rozelle, Scott. 2013. "Lessons from China for Africa." Stanford Symposium Series on Global Food Policy and Food Security in the 21st Century, April 17. Stanford University, Stanford, Calif.

Runge, C. Ford, and Robbin S. Johnson. 2008. *The Browning of Biofuels: Environment and Food Security at Risk*. May. Washington, D.C.: Woodrow Wilson International Center for Scholars.

Ruttan, Vernon W. 1969. "Two Sector Models and Development Policy." In *Subsistence Agriculture and Economic Development*, ed. Clifton R.Wharton Jr., 353–60. Chicago: Aldine Press.

Sah, Raaj K., and Joseph E. Stiglitz. 1992. *Peasants Versus City-Dwellers: Taxation and the Burden of Economic Development*. Oxford: Clarendon Press.

Sanders, Dwight H., and Scott H. Irwin. 2008. "Futures Imperfect." *New York Times*, July 20.

Sarris, Alexander. 1982. "Commodity-Price Theory and Public Stabilization Stocks." In *Food Security: Theory, Policy, and Perspectives from Asia and the Pacific Rim*, ed. Anthony H. Chisholm and Rodney Tyers. Lexington, Mass.: Lexington Books and D.C. Heath.

Sarris, Alexander, Ali Arslan Gurkan, and Ralph W. Cummings Jr. 2009. "Conclusions and the Way Forward." Paper presented to the Experts' Meeting on "Institutions and Policies to Manage Global Market Risks and Price Spikes in Basic Food Commodities" by the FAO Trade and Markets Division, October 26–27. Food and Agriculture Organization of the United Nations, Rome.

Schultz, Theodore W. 1964. *Transforming Traditional Agriculture*. New Haven: Yale University Press.

Sen, Amartya. 1981. *Poverty and Famines: An Essay in Entitlement and Deprivation*. Oxford: Clarendon Press.

Shiller, Robert J. 2003. "From Efficient Markets Theory to Behavioral Finance." *Journal of Economic Perspectives* 17 (1): 83–104.

Singh, Inderjit, Lyn Squire, and John Strauss, eds. 1986. *Agricultural Household Models*. Baltimore: Johns Hopkins University Press.

Slayton, Tom. 2009. "Rice Crisis Forensics: How Asian Governments Carelessly Set the World Rice Market on Fire." Working Paper 163. Washington, D.C.: Center for Global Development.

———. 2010. "The 'Diplomatic Crop' or How the U.S. Provided Critical Leadership in Ending the Rice Crisis." In *Rice Crisis: Markets, Policies and Food Security*, ed. David Dawe, 313–344. London and Washington, D.C.: Food and Agriculture Organization of the United Nations and Earthscan.

Slayton, Tom, and C. Peter Timmer. 2008. "Japan, China and Thailand Can Solve the Rice Crisis—But U.S. Leadership Is Needed." CGD Notes. May. Washington, D.C.: Center for Global Development.

Srinivasan, T. N. 1981. "Malnutrition: Some Measurement and Policy Issues." *Journal of Development Economics* 8: 569–94.

Stewart, Frances, and Ejaz Ghani. 1991. "How Significant Are Externalities for Development?" *World Development* 19 (6): 569–94.

Subervie, J. 2008. "The Variable Response of Agricultural Supply to World Price Instability in Developing Countries." *Journal of Agricultural Economics* 59 (1):-72–92.

Tadesse, Getaw, Bernardina Algiera, Matthias Kalkuhl, and Joachim von Braun. 2013. "Drivers and Triggers of International Food Price Spikes and Volatility." *Food Policy*. http://dx.doi.org/10.1016/j.foodpol.2013.08.014.

Taylor, Alan M. 1998. "On the Costs of Inward-Looking Development: Price Distortions, Growth, and Divergence in Latin America." *Journal of Economic History* 58 (1): 1–28.

Telser, Lester G. 1958. "Futures Trading and the Storage of Cotton and Wheat." *Journal of Political Economy* 66 (3): 233–55.

Thaler, Richard, and Shlomo Benartzi. 2004. "Save More Tomorrow: Using Behavioral Economics to Increase Employee Saving." *Journal of Political Economy* 112 (1): S164–87.

Timmer, C. Peter. 1977. "Access to Food: The Ultimate Determinant of Hunger." In *Food and Nutrition in Health and Disease*, ed. N. Henry Moss and Jean Mayer, 59–68. Annals of the New York Academy of Sciences, vol. 300. New York: New York Academy of Sciences.

———. 1981. "Is There 'Curvature' in the Slutsky Matrix?" *Review of Economics and Statistics* 62 (3): 395–402.

———. 1986. *Getting Prices Right: The Scope and Limits of Agricultural Price Policy.* Ithaca, N.Y.: Cornell University Press.

———, ed. 1987. *The Corn Economy of Indonesia.* Ithaca, N.Y.: Cornell University Press.

———. 1988. "The Agricultural Transformation." In *Handbook of Development Economics*, ed. Hollis Chenery and T. N. Srinivasan, 1: 275–331. Amsterdam: North-Holland.

———. 1989. "Food Price Policy: The Rationale for Government Intervention." *Food Policy* 14 (1): 17–27.

———. 1991a. "What Are the Key Lessons from Asian Development Success Stories?" In *African Development: Lessons from Asia*, 49–103. Proceedings: Strategies for the Future of Africa, sponsored by the Africa Bureau, United States Agency for International Development and Winrock International, June 5–7. Arlington, Va.: Winrock International Institute for Agricultural Development.

———. 1991b. "Food Price Stabilization: Rationale, Design, and Implementation." In *Reforming Economic Systems in Developing Countries*, ed. Dwight H. Perkins and Michael Roemer, 219–48 and 456–59. Cambridge, Mass.: Harvard Institute for International Development. Distributed by Harvard University Press.

———. 1992. "Agriculture and Economic Development Revisited." In "Systems Approaches for Agriculture," ed. Paul Teng and Frits Penning de Vries. Special issue, *Agricultural Systems* 40 (1–3): 21–58.

———. 1993. "Rural Bias in the East and Southeast Asian Rice Economy: Indonesia in Comparative Perspective." *Journal of Development Studies* 29 (4): 149–76.

———. 1994. "The Meaning of Food Self-Sufficiency." *Indonesian Food Journal* 5 (10): 33–43.

———. 1995a. "Getting Agriculture Moving: Do Markets Provide the Right Signals?" *Food Policy* 20 (5): 455–72.

———. 1995b. "The Political Economy of Rapid Growth: Indonesia's New Development Model." In *Research in Domestic and International Agribusiness Management*, ed. Ray A. Goldberg, vol. 32, 117–34. Greenwich, Conn.: JAI Press.

———. 1996. "Does BULOG Stabilize Rice Prices in Indonesia? Should It Try?" *Bulletin of Indonesian Economic Studies* 32: 45–74.

———.1997a. "How Well Do the Poor Connect to the Growth Process?" Consultative Arrangement for Economic Research (CAER) II Discussion Paper 17. December. Cambridge, Mass.: Harvard Institute for International Development.

———. 1997b. "Valuing Social Science Research and Policy Analysis." *American Journal of Agricultural Economics* 79 (5): 1545–50.

———. 2000. "The Macro Dimensions of Food Security: Economic Growth, Equitable Distribution, and Food Price Stability." *Food Policy* 25 (4): 283–95.

———. 2002. "Agriculture and Economic Growth." In *Handbook of Agricultural Economics*, ed. Bruce L. Gardner and Gordon C. Rausser, 2A: 1487–1546. Amsterdam: North-Holland.

———. 2004a. "The Road to Pro-poor Growth: The Indonesian Experience in Regional Perspective." *Bulletin of Indonesian Economic Studies* 40 (2): 177–207.

———. 2004b. "Adding Value Through Policy-Oriented Research: Reflections of a Scholar-Practitioner." In *What's Economics Worth? Valuing Policy Research*, ed. Philip G. Pardey and Vincent H. Smith, 129–52. Baltimore: Johns Hopkins University Press for the International Food Policy Research Institute.

———. 2005a. "Food Security and Economic Growth: An Asian Perspective." *Asian-Pacific Economic Literature* 19: 1–17. H. W. Arndt Memorial Lecture, November 22, Australian National University, Canberra.

———. 2005b. "Agriculture and Pro-poor Growth: An Asian Perspective." Working Paper 63. Washington, D.C.: Center for Global Development.

———. 2008a. "The Causes of High Food Prices." In *Asian Development Outlook Update*, 72–93. Manila: Asian Development Bank.

———. 2008b. "Rural Changes Stimulate Rising Giants." Review of *The Dragon and the Elephant: Agricultural and Rural Reforms in China and India*, ed. Ashok Gulati and Shenggen Fan. *Science* 321 (5889): 642.

———. 2009a. *A World Without Agriculture: The Structural Transformation in Historical Perspective.* Wendt Distinguished Lecture. Washington, D.C.: American Enterprise Institute.

———. 2009b. "Do Supermarkets Change the Food Policy Agenda?" *World Development* 37 (11): 1812–19.

———. 2009c. "Rice Price Formation in the Short Run and the Long Run: The Role of Market Structure in Explaining Volatility." Working Paper 172. May. Washington, D.C.: Center for Global Development.

———. 2009d. "Management of Rice Reserve Stocks in Asia: Analytical Issues and Country Experiences." Paper presented to the Experts' Meeting on "Institutions and Policies to Manage Global Market Risks and Price Spikes in Basic Food Commodities" by the FAO Trade and Markets Division, October 26–27. Food and Agriculture Organization of the United Nations, Rome.

———. 2010a. "Reflections on Food Crises Past." *Food Policy* 35 (1): 1–11.

———. 2010b. "Rice and Structural Transformation." In *Rice in the Global Economy: Strategic Research and Policy Issues for Food Security*, ed. Sushil Pandey, Derek Byerlee, David Dawe, Achim Dobermann, Samarendu Mohanty, Scott Rozelle, and Bill Hardy, 37–60. Los Baños, Philippines: International Rice Research Institute.

———. 2010c. "Did Speculation Affect World Rice Prices?" In *The Rice Crisis: Markets, Policies and Food Security*, ed. David Dawe, 29–60. London and Washington, D.C.: Earthscan.

———. 2012a. "Behavioral Dimensions of Food Security." *Proceedings of the National Academy of Sciences (PNAS)* 109 (31): 12315–20.

———. 2012b. "Feeding the Masses." Review of *One Billion Hungry: Can We Feed the World?* by Gordon Conway. *Wilson Quarterly* (Autumn).

Timmer, C. Peter, and Selvin Akkus. 2008. "The Structural Transformation as a Pathway out of Poverty: Analytics, Empirics and Politics." Working Paper 150. Washington, D.C.: Center for Global Development.

Timmer, C. Peter, Steven Block, and David Dawe. 2010. "Long-Run Dynamics of Rice Consumption, 1960–2050." In *Rice in the Global Economy: Strategic Research and Policy Issues for Food Security*, ed. Sushil Pandey, Derek Byerlee, David Dawe, Achim Dobermann, Samarendu Mohanty, Scott Rozelle, and Bill Hardy, 139–74. Los Baños, Philippines: International Rice Research Institute.

Timmer, C. Peter, and David Dawe. 2007. "Managing Food Price Instability in Asia: A Macro Food Security Perspective." *Asian Economic Journal* 21 (1): 1–18.

Timmer, C. Peter, and Walter P. Falcon. 1975. "The Political Economy of Rice Production and Trade in Asia." In *Agriculture in Development Theory*, ed. Lloyd Reynolds, 373–408. New Haven: Yale University Press.

Timmer, C. Peter, Walter P. Falcon, and Scott R. Pearson. 1983. *Food Policy Analysis*. Baltimore: Johns Hopkins University Press for the World Bank.

Tomich, Thomas P., Peter Kilby, and Bruce F. Johnston. 1995. *Transforming Agrarian Economies: Opportunities Seized, Opportunities Missed*. Ithaca, N.Y.: Cornell University Press.

Torlesse, H., L. Kiess, and M. W. Bloem. 2003. "Association of Household Rice Expenditure with Child Nutritional Status Indicates a Role for Macroeconomic Food Policy in Combating Malnutrition." *Journal of Nutrition* 133 (5): 1320–25.

Trostle, Ronald. 2008. "Global Agricultural Supply and Demand: Factors Contributing to the Recent Increase in Food Commodity Prices." Economic Research Service, WRS-0801. May. Washington, D.C.: United States Department of Agriculture.

Tsakok, Isabelle. 2011. *Success in Agricultural Transformation: What It Means and What Makes It Happen.* Cambridge: Cambridge University Press.

Tversky, Amos, and Daniel Kahneman. 1986. "Rational Choice and the Framing of Decisions." *Journal of Business* 59 (4): 5251–78.

USDA (United States Department of Agriculture). 1996. "The U.S. Contribution to World Food Security." The U.S. Position Paper Prepared for the World Food Summit, United States Department of Agriculture, July 3, Washington, D.C.

van Donge, Jan Kees, David Henley, and Peter Lewis. 2010. "Tracking Development in Southeast Asia and Sub-Saharan Africa: The Primacy of Policy." Tracking Development Project, University of Leiden, Leiden, the Netherlands.

Von Pischke, J. D., Dale W. Adams, and Gordon Donald. 1983. *Rural Financial Markets in Developing Countries: Their Use and Abuse.* Baltimore: Johns Hopkins University Press for the Economic Development Institute of the World Bank.

Vyas, V. S. 2007. "Market Reforms in Indian Agriculture: One Step Forward and Two Steps Back." In *The Dragon and the Elephant: Agricultural and Rural Reforms in China and India*, ed. Ashok Gulati and Shenggen Fan, 264–82. Baltimore: Johns Hopkins University Press.

Warr, Peter. Forthcoming. "The Drivers of Poverty Reduction." In *The Handbook of Southeast Asian Economics*, ed. Ian Coxhead. London: Routledge.

Webb, Patrick, and Steven A. Block. 2004. "Nutrition Information and Formal Schooling as Inputs to Child Nutrition." *Economic Development and Cultural Change* 52 (4): 801–20.

———. 2010. "Support for Agriculture During Economic Transformation: Impact on Poverty and Undernutrition." *Proceedings of the National Academy of Sciences (PNAS)* 109 (31): 12315–20.

Webb, Patrick, and Beatrice Rogers. 2003. "Addressing the 'In' in Food Insecurity." FFP Occasional Paper 1. February. Washington, D.C.: United States Agency for International Development Office of Food for Peace.

Weymar, F. Helmut. 1968. *The Dynamics of the World Cocoa Market.* Cambridge, Mass.: Massachusetts Institute of Technology Press.

Wharton, Clifton R., Jr., ed. 1969. *Subsistence Agriculture and Economic Development.* Chicago: Aldine Press.

Wickizer, V. D., and M. K. Bennett. 1941. *The Rice Economy of Monsoon Asia.* Stanford, Calif.: Food Research Institute, Stanford University. Published in cooperation with the International Secretariat, Institute of Pacific Relations.

Williams, Jeffrey C., and Brian D. Wright. 1991. *Storage and Commodity Markets.* Cambridge: Cambridge University Press.

Williamson, Jeffrey G. 1993. "Human Capital Deepening, Inequality, and Demographic Events along the Asia-Pacific Rim." In *Human Resources in Development along the Asia-Pacific Rim*, ed. Naohiro Ogawa, Gavin W. Jones, and Jeffrey G. Williamson, 129–58. Singapore: Oxford University Press.

Working, Holbrook. 1933. "Price Relations Between July and September Wheat Futures at Chicago Since 1885." *Wheat Studies* 6 (March):187–238.

———. 1948. "Theory of the Inverse Carrying Charge in Futures Markets." *Journal of Farm Economics* 30 (1): 1–28.

———. 1949. "The Theory of the Price of Storage." *American Economic Review* 39 (6): 1254–62.

World Bank. 1986. *Poverty and Hunger: Issues and Options for Food Security in Developing Countries.* Washington, D.C.: International Bank for Reconstruction and Development (World Bank).

———. 1993. *The East Asian Miracle: Economic Growth and Public Policy.* A World Bank Policy Research Report. New York: Oxford University Press for the World Bank.

———. 2004. *Directions in Development: Agriculture and Poverty Reduction.* Agriculture and Rural Development Department, World Bank. September. Washington, D.C.: World Bank.

———. 2005. *Managing Food Price Risks and Instability in an Environment of Market Liberalization.* Agriculture and Rural Development Department Report 32727-GLB, Washington, D.C.: World Bank.

———. 2007. *World Development Report 2008: Agriculture for Development.* London: Oxford University Press.

Wright, Brian. 2011. "The Economics of Grain Price Volatility." *Applied Economic Perspectives and Policy* 33 (1): 35–58.

INDEX

ACKNOWLEDGMENTS

This book would not exist if it were not for Peter Agree's wise, and persistent, counsel. I first met Peter, now the Editor in Chief at the University of Pennsylvania Press, in my office at the Harvard Business School, in 1984. *Food Policy Analysis* had just been published for the World Bank by Johns Hopkins University Press. At the time, Peter was an editor at Cornell University Press, and he wondered whether I might be interested in publishing something there. I was. The result was *Getting Prices Right* and the start of a long and very productive relationship.

As the food crisis was unfolding in 2007–8, Peter asked again if I might want to publish something with him. We talked often over the next five years, usually with him picking up the lunch tab. I submitted several different outlines for books, none of which actually materialized. Finally, early in 2013 at our favorite Thai restaurant on the Upper West Side in New York City, Peter insisted that I simply had to "write the book you've already written." I took him up on that advice, and the present book is the result. Thank you, Peter, for not giving up on me. And thank you for the excellent editorial assistance provided by your staff.

In the course of writing a book, especially one that reflects on a very long career, many debts are incurred, some personal, some institutional. The Center for Global Development agreed to "commission" this book as part of my continuing relationship with the Center as a Nonresident Fellow, using funds from a grant from the Bill and Melinda Gates Foundation for work on food security. Vijaya Ramachandran, a Senior Fellow at the Center, guided the process of writing this (and several other things) over the past two years. In particular, Vij was a source of enthusiasm and optimism at times when both were badly needed at my end. Writing a book can be quite depressing at times, and Vij made sure I got through those times.

Excellent research assistance was provided by the Center's Katriel Friedman, who helped put the tables, figures, and index together. Katriel also read through each of the various drafts of the book and provided very insightful comments about what was working and what was not.

As part of its normal review process for commissioned books, the Center asks an external and an internal reviewer each to provide substantive comments on recommended changes before publication. Fortuitously, Professor Rob Paarlberg, an influential political scientist at Wellesley and Harvard who writes on the politics of food and agriculture, served as the external reviewer. Rob and I have worked with each other for over three decades, and his extensive comments turned out to be extremely helpful in turning draft 1.0 into draft 2.0.

The internal reviewer for the Center was Charles Kenny, author of *Getting Better: Why Global Development Is Succeeding*. His comments also turned out to be very helpful, especially in bringing a somewhat more optimistic tone to parts of the manuscript that he found unduly negative. Some of Charles's optimism was felt as I went from draft 2.0 to 3.0 and is reflected especially in the final chapter of the book.

At a review meeting held at the Center in December 2013, a number of colleagues came together to offer suggestions on how to improve the early draft that they had read. I was not able to follow all of their advice, but I hope they each see a serious effort in this published version to deal with their suggestions.

As I look back over an academic career spanning more than four decades, I am struck by how influential my students have been. In a broad sense, that influence is seen in their highly successful careers in the development field, but I mean it in a narrower sense. My students have influenced how I think about agriculture and food policy. What do students need to know in order to become successful food policy analysts? To answer that question, much of my teaching and writing has been directed at their learning process. I still remember an anonymous comment on the course evaluation from a student in my Harvard class on the world food economy in the late 1980s: "When I started this course I did not know that rice price policy even existed. Now I know it is the most important thing in the world." The connection between a good lecture and a successful student is not always direct, but when it happens, it can be quite inspiring. *Food Policy Analysis* was written because we felt that students needed something better to read than the standard texts on agricultural economics and development. Its success provides deep motivation to follow with a volume that I hope will have similar influence and longevity.

Finally, my debt to my longtime editor, collaborator, partner, and wife will be obvious to all readers familiar with my writings. Carol thought she had managed to retire a decade ago, when I retired from academia in 2003. She would be done with converting the brilliant ways I *wanted* to say things into prose that *actually* said what I meant. This was a tedious and sometimes contentious role. Retirement from that process was welcome, especially because we had been at it since we were juniors in rival high schools in 1958, competing in the Ohio State Scholarship tests (she beat me every year in math).

So it was somewhat reluctantly, but recognizing the potential stakes, that Carol picked up her red pen in November and transformed draft 3.0 into its current publishable form. We had many long conversations about how to fix all the problems with the initial drafts. Those conversations have vastly improved both the substance and readability of the book. My colleagues and students will recognize immediately the deep imprint of The Supreme Editor Herself.

My love and thanks to Carol.

Milton Keynes UK
Ingram Content Group UK Ltd.
UKHW011419250823
427470UK00001B/78